Devo
Within Living Memory

This Book Belongs to

Margaret Buckle

1997

WITHIN LIVING MEMORY SERIES

Other Counties in this series include:

Bedfordshire
Buckinghamshire
Herefordshire
Hertfordshire
East Kent
Northamptonshire
Shropshire

Somerset
Staffordshire
Surrey
West Sussex
Warwickshire
Wiltshire

Devon
Within Living
Memory

Compiled by the Devon Federation
of Women's Institutes from notes
sent by Institutes in the County

Published jointly by
Countryside Books, Newbury
and the DFWI, Exeter

COUNTRYSIDE BOOKS
3 Catherine Road
Newbury, Berkshire

ISBN 1 85306 250 2

Designed by Mon Mohan
Produced through MRM Associates Ltd, Reading
Printed in England

Foreword

Devon is the third largest county in England and is unique in having two separate coastlines, each with its own focus of trade and communications. This has led to recognisable differences in temperament, vocabulary and dialect in the local people. It is a county of great beauty – of cliffs and long sandy beaches, of moors and bubbling rivers and of gentle green pastures.

The last 70 years have seen great changes in the county. Mechanisation on the farms has been followed by an exodus of young people from the villages. Properties are often bought as holiday homes or by retired people from outside the county. The improved road network has made hitherto remote areas much more accessible and the summer months now are dominated by the tourist trade.

There are still among us folk who remember life in our villages before the coming of the motor car, electricity and television. It is thanks to members of the Devon Federation of Women's Institutes, who have collected the material, and Pat Macdonald our co-ordinator, that we are all able to enjoy the reminiscences of those for whom a very different way of life is Within Living Memory.

Joyce Vale
County Chairman

Acknowledgements

Devon Federation of Women's Institutes would like to thank all the members and friends who supplied material for this book through their local WIs.

All the contributions were of value in deciding the shape and content of the finished book, and we are grateful for them. Sadly we were not able to include extracts from every submission. To do so would have meant duplication and account had to be taken of space available.

We are particularly grateful to Judy Barber who did the attractive pen-and-ink sketches throughout the book, to the Kingston History Society and to Cotleigh WI for providing the cover photograph.

Pat Macdonald
Co-ordinator

Contents

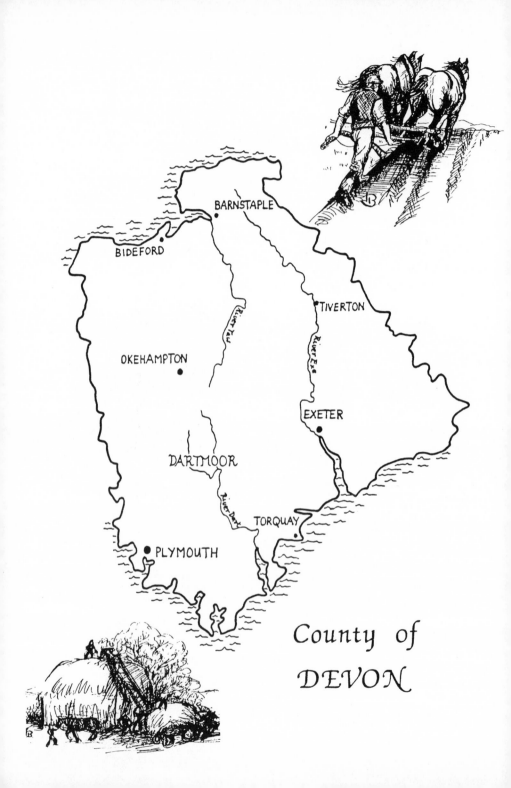

BARNSTAPLE

BIDEFORD

TIVERTON

River Taw

OKEHAMPTON

River Exe

EXETER

DARTMOOR

River Dart

TORQUAY

PLYMOUTH

County of
DEVON

TOWN & COUNTRY LIFE

SOME TOWNS AND VILLAGES REMEMBERED

Life in our towns and villages has changed so much over the past few decades that it is sometimes hard to believe we are talking of the same century, let alone within living memory! Here are just a very few 'snapshots' of life as it used to be.

BRENTOR

'I can recall Brentor 60 years ago, so I will endeavour to record village life as I remember it then.

Come with me to the school then, where there were between 40 and 50 pupils and two teachers – a headmistress and an infants teacher. When I was between five and six years I remember vividly being told to instruct the little girl who shared my desk in the art of knitting. We had thick wooden needles and thick wool and my instructions were "In, out, through, off."

Being a Church of England school the vicar was a regular visitor. I recall one such gentleman being at our annual Christmas party when a question and answers game was in progress. To the question "How old am I?" a pupil had written 92! Not complimentary to the vicar – I don't suppose he was more than 50 years of age!

What a lovely aroma comes from the bakery as we skip along on our way home from school. There saffron cake and bread in vast quantities were baked, not only for our village but delivered to many villages around. This was a family business run by Mr Alf Brimacombe and sons. On a summer's day large sieves of sultanas, raisins and currants were to be seen drying on the walls of the approach to the shop. Occasionally we'd run in for a pennyworth of sweets. What a decision we'd have to make! Shall it be lambs tails, those gaily coloured sugar-coated sweets, raspberry or lemon drops, green gobstoppers or shining yellow sweets with sherbet in the middle? With a deft twist of the fingers a piece of paper is miraculously turned into a cone-shaped bag and is safely tucked into the pocket of one's apron – or "pinny".

A dozen or so turkeys were kept by the postmistress's mother, a Mrs Minhinnick, at the smallholding adjoining the post office. These gave much pleasure to the children as they trotted from the

10

Sandford village street in the 1930s. Little changed in villages across Devon until after the Second World War.

yard across the road into the field opposite. The chant of "Turkey, turkey, show your pride" often resulted in these creatures fanning their beautiful tails.

The Southern Railway was of course our transport, fare to Tavistock then being sevenpence ha'penny return and about two shillings return to Plymouth – a great adventure this, to spend a day at Plymouth. If trains coming from the Tavistock direction could be heard more clearly than when they were coming from the direction of Lydford, we knew rain was on the way, the wind was "back". But the sound from trains being more pronounced on the upward track meant the wind was "up" and colder, drier weather was imminent.

Mail for the post office arrived and was despatched by train and carried to and fro by various people over the years. I well remember a character of sterling worth, a Mrs Polly Medland, carrying the mail bags over her shoulder. All letters were sorted here and outgoing mail was franked at the post office. The only public telephone was in the corner of the post office and was probably only used in cases of extreme urgency. One postman, a Mr Daniel Cooke, was also the village cobbler. What a collection of footwear on his bench in his tiny shop near the Methodist chapel. Boots of all sizes lay there and a few ladies' shoes, maybe some leggings which needed a new strap or a buckle stitched on. Even with a mouthful of tacks the cobbler could

11

carry on a conversation with anyone who cared to call, a childish mind wondered what disaster would befall if he sneezed and tacks slid into his throat instead of outwards! Mr Cooke had a fine voice and sang many a solo at Christian Endeavour meetings held next door. A connection between soles and souls perhaps? Many years before he proudly led the village band in a procession around the village – before my time alas!

The blacksmith's shop was a popular meeting place for farmers, here children would revel in seeing sparks fly from the fire as iron for horseshoes was heated in it and the ringing sound of the iron being hammered into shape on the anvil could be heard in our homes. The butcher's shop always seemed a busy place, housewives as ever purchasing meat to cook wholesome meals for families. No doubt some went into pasties, with swede, turnip, onion and potato for the men of the household to carry for their sustenance during their long working day. Many men were farm labourers, some worked on the railway and others at the stone quarries between Mary Tavy and Tavistock. Milk was not delivered, it could be bought from the numerous smallholdings. Families employed by Mr Frank Ward of Burnville had free milk. In fine weather one walked through the path fields and along the drive to Burnville House where a cheery housemaid, kitchen maid or cook would fill the enamel or aluminium can with scald milk. Nothing ever tasted so good on a hot summer's day as a long drink of this from the lid of the can on the return journey! Butter was also supplied. It really was the golden hue of buttercups and shaped into a round and always a print on the top, one being of thistle flowers and another of St Michael's church on Brent Tor.

With the strong winds of March shouts of delight rang across the moors as youngsters gathered there for "swaling" – the burning of gorse. Oh, the fun to be had running from bush to bush with strips of flaming newspaper. It was a grand sight from the village, this red inferno which crept across the moors. Little regard was given to the ugly black patches which remained until Mother Nature took a hand and covered it in green as the year went on.

Cottages were occupied in some instances by the same families for generations and a great sense of neighbourliness abounded. Sorrows and joys were shared and in an emergency of any kind help was readily given. How fortunate we were to live in such an atmosphere of peace and contentment. This is particularly remembered by recalling Sunday summer evenings when people stood or sat outside their homes and listened to the peal of bells from St Michael's ringing across the countryside before and after the evening service. May they ring for future generations and our little village remain secure guarded by the sentinel of Brent Tor on one side and Gibbett Hill and the majestic Tors on the other.'

BIGBURY ON SEA

'I intend to talk about Bigbury on Sea, some of the things I've heard about and have known for the last 80 years. We will start about the roads. Before 1906 it was a metalled road down to Folly and from there down to Bigbury on Sea it was a cart track. There was another cart track which led from the top of Folly Hill facing the sea to the right coming down what we now know as Parker Drive. These were the two access methods, both only cart tracks and they were used mostly for taking stuff off the beach. Ships used to call on the beach at one time, unload coal and take away corn and other things the farmers used to produce. In 1906 when the Duchy of Cleveland sold off, a syndicate bought Bigbury on Sea and the road down from Folly was developed. The syndicate consisted of about six people, mostly from Plymouth, and they started to build, the place developing ever since.

Before this time there were only two houses down there, one being on the Island and the other Warren Cottage which is now the Bay Cafe. There was accommodation down at the fish cellars which people working in the pilchard business used to live in and they eventually became dwelling houses but not for long. The fish cellar was the big business of the area. It was a joint concern and the pilchards used to be put into barrels and sent away, much to the European countries, Portugal and even Italy. One thing on the Island concerned with the fish industry was the building on top of the hill. People will tell you it was a chapel, but it never was, that was the "huer's" hut and previous to 1930, all it consisted of was four walls with four windows and a roof. The chapel, I've been given to understand, was possibly down where the hotel is now, but no one ever knew for sure, at least not in my lifetime.

I got a lot of my information from the Bardens family, old Minnie Bardens who lived at Warren Cottage was a source of information and having married into the Bardens family I know quite a lot about it. Now the pub on the Island was to my certain knowledge owned by the Bardens family in 1558. I got that out of the church registry. On the bottom of the first page of the registry in 1558 was the funeral of a Bardens of Bourgh Island and on the top of the same page is a Woodmason, so I am on the top of the page and on the bottom is my wife.

There have been a lot of stories about the Island, the most notable one being about Tom Crocker. Tom Crocker became a pirate when

13

Whit Cunliffe, who ran the hotel, started making up a few stories to popularise the Island. He even "found" his flag in the pub on the island, although I'm sure the Bardens who owned the pub for all those years would have found it a long time before he did, but he had to make his story good, so Tom Crocker became quite a person. Now I can tell you how the Crocker story started.

I got this from Minnie Bardens, who was the daughter of the publican at the start of this story. Farm labourers from Bigbury Court used to go down to the Island and cut seaweed for agricultural purposes. They would load the carts and then adjourn to the pub for a drink. The pub had some new cider in at this time. Now, new cider can be a little bit fatal in one respect and Tom Crocker was taken short as the saying goes. Ever since, the spot he had to nip away and find has been known as Tom Crocker's hole. I have a book of 1846 with a Crocker's name in it as having lived in the village. My aunt couldn't quite go back to that time, but the Crocker family were living in Bigbury Court tied cottages around this time.

When the Bardens family left the pub it was taken over by a minstrel/comedian named Chirgwin, who used to "black up" for his show. One night he rubbed a sore eye smearing the makeup into a diamond shape and ever after he was known as the "white eyed kaffir". I liked and knew him well and he once gave me a very nice model yacht. He died about 1925/6, his wife continuing until Nettlefold built a hotel there, mainly for his influential friends, the fish cellar being the garage for the many Rolls Royces that used to come down with the guests.

On Park Road there was a school, locally known as the Crapper, run by a Dr Whittaker. This was a summer school for Empire children and there were sometimes as many as 60 there for the summer. When the school left it became the Bay Hotel, later getting a licence when it was the only pub in Bigbury on Sea and very popular it was. It was a very nice building with verandahs all around it and a dance floor where you could go for a very fine dinner. It later changed its name to the Chichester and not so many years ago closed due to the deterioration of the building, woodworm I believe, anyway it's all gone now.'

SUMMER ON PLYMOUTH HOE

'I was born in Plymouth in 1930 and my home was within a short walking distance of Plymouth Hoe. My mother and I spent many summers alone as my father was a Royal Marine who spent months at sea.

Summer days were happy days. With other service families we

14

would visit the sea front for swimming and then play games in the West Hoe park or on the slopes of Plymouth Hoe. On summer evenings large numbers of local people would walk the promenade as family groups and listen to the military band concerts from the bandstand. There was also the coming and going of the Sunderland flying boats to watch as they took off and landed in the Sound. On special occasions, such as the 1937 Coronation, we all enjoyed the fireworks and bonfires. We also admired the gardens on the Hoe which were always well kept and at night the avenues of trees were lit by Chinese lanterns.

For those of us with fathers serving on board Royal Navy ships, the happiest days were when we watched our father's ship return home; it was wonderful to see these very large ships sailing into port, their decks lined with the crew and the Royal Marines Band playing such stirring music. I was always treated to a new dress and sunbonnet for those occasions!

During the war years the Hoe was much quieter; we didn't know when the ships were returning home and sometimes they never did.

Somehow the hot balmy days of the 1930s never returned after the war; but when I stand on Plymouth Hoe I can still in my mind's eye see the ships and often imagine the bands proudly playing on the bandstand. It seems sad that this happy and contented time has been lost for ever.'

HOLCOMBE ROGUS

'The only commodity not available in the village was coal, which came up from Westleigh, otherwise everything was available. Mr Kingdom, the tailor, came from Sampford – he would measure my father for mohair waistcoats. Jimmy Bliss at Durleymoor made gates and hurdles and did thatching and shoe repairs. Peat was dug near Durleymoor Cross. Russells Stores kept literally everything. Bread was baked by Mr Parsons at the end of the present Waterloo Stores – pasties were baked once a week which the schoolchildren would eat for their lunch. There were also the travelling vans with paraffin, food, fruit etc being sold out of the back of the same vehicle with no worries about "food hygiene".

The "Holcombe" chairs made in the village were taken by horse and cart to Burlescombe station and sent to High Wycombe, then the centre of the furniture trade. It was not unknown for furniture made in the village to be convincingly "antiqued", when it would be taken after dark to Taunton for sale.

Mail came by train from Wellington to Burlescombe from where it was collected by the postman, Mr Holley. He travelled on foot as far as Hockworthy where he spent the rest of the day in a little hut until it was time to return with all the outgoing mail for the train at Burlescombe. He died at 90.

Living in the village was like living on an island – we were self sufficient in necessities and entertainment. The two main points were the school and the church, and people would go to the vicar rather than the local policeman to sort out a problem. There was the church boiler to be stoked on a Saturday night, the organ to be blown for two services on a Sunday, Sunday school in the afternoon taken by the vicar and his wife, and the choir. There was a football team which played up Black Lane, a cricket team, tennis courts in the field by Thatches. Fete Day was an all day event with sports, tug of war, skittles all week. There was also Sampford Fair and Lamb Fair (by Lamb Inn).

Water was much more plentiful. The village was supplied by the Court system, but there were also ponds everywhere and pumps were common. The streams were quite clear and home-cured hams were soaked in them.

Gipsies frequently parked on Chimney Down and came round selling clothespegs, lace, brushes, elastic and similar items – a trade wiped out by the arrival of Woolworths. On one occasion as a child

The mail coach was a familiar sight on the road between Plymouth and Exeter in the early years of the century. Mr James Northway is the driver in this photograph.

16

I had a badly gashed knee which had failed to respond to any treatment by the local doctor. When the gipsy woman came round she offered to treat it if my mother bought something. She rubbed powdered brimstone into two white handkerchiefs and tied them round my knee promising it would be healed in a fortnight – which it was.'

HONITON

'Honiton people drew their water from natural springs at the turn of the century – the one from Holy Spring was considered specially pure and was used for bathing eyes.

As Honiton High Street was so wide, the cattle market took place there. Horses were sold at one end and cattle and sheep at the other. Everyone kept their doors shut on market day to keep out the animals, as many a cow got wedged in a passage and required several men to pull it or push it out backwards. The farmers came to pay their bills on market day and my father, who had an ironmonger's in New Street, used to give them a free meal after they had paid.

A fair took place in July which was opened by the Town Crier. The funfair was started on the Wednesday and was held in a field in Streamers Meadows – the horses and cattle grazed in the field opposite. On market days there used to be an ox roast on the corner opposite Marwood House.

In my early youth cartridges were made in the town to be sold to local farmers. One day there was an explosion which blew the roof right off but only one man was injured.

No traveller could get into or out of Honiton without paying a toll, the amount depending on the number of wheels on the vehicle. It was threepence for a two-wheeler. The tolls were abolished in 1911 and bonfires were lit on the surrounding hills in celebration.'

WESTLEIGH

'Westleigh of yesteryear was a far cry from the village we know today. Muriel and Daphne have lived in Westleigh all their lives. Their parents had a small farm which supplied the villagers with their milk, whilst the butter and cream was taken to Tiverton market by their mother. She cycled the ten miles there with a large wooden container tied onto the carrier. Sometimes she would bring back a quantity of boots from Lennards shoe shop, and these were purchased by the villagers who paid for them weekly. There was a lot of poverty and it was only by paying for them in this way that they avoided going barefooted.

Going to school at Burlescombe, Muriel and Daphne walked across the fields. On their way they passed an old woman who sat outside her cottage mending the quarrymen's trousers. Her fingers were always very sore and were wrapped in bandages. This was because the corduroy was so very stiff – and she repaired the trousers for threepence a pair! Farther along the road by Canonsleigh Abbey they passed the stone-breaker sitting at the roadside. He had a leather pad over his left hand, whilst in his right hand he held the hammer tapping away the stone to make road chippings.

Everyone in the family helped on the farm as their father was also the local postman. He walked 19 miles daily delivering the post. Later he had a bicycle, but as the area was very hilly it meant he still walked a great deal – but this time having to push the cycle!

Westleigh was an active village with the quarries. There were five inns (quarrymen needed to quench their thirst), a baker, a butcher, post office, a lace repair shop and, of course, the village blacksmith. He was kept very busy with the quarry ponies as well as the farmers' horses and the ponies owned by locals who might have a trap or carriage.

One of the highlights of the year was the Bazaar. This was a large van bringing all sorts of household goods. The outside of the van was strung with pots and pans of all types *and* chamber pots. How these items were never broken was a source of amazement considering the bumpy roads the van travelled along.

Once a year Whitelegs Travelling Fair came to the village. This was set up in a field close to Canonsleigh Abbey. The children were very excited, particularly with the helter-skelter and roundabouts.

Another special occasion was the Sunday school treat. This was held at Muriel and Daphne's farm. There was a big swing and see-saw built for the occasion in one of their fields. Their mother provided all sorts of goodies and sweets. Sports were held and there were prizes for the winners of the many races before everyone sat down to eat an enormous tea.'

STREET TRADERS IN KINGSTEIGNTON

'The Step Lady came early one morning each week with her pail and hearthstone, was supplied with water, then cleaned two flights of eight steps for threepence. The rag and bone man, pushing his barrow, would give a balloon or paper windmill on a stick for two empty jars. The cats-meat man would supply you daily with pieces of horsemeat skewered on a stick for the cat for a halfpenny each. If you were out it was put through the letterbox unwrapped. The cat always found it.

The milkman delivered in fixed-lid metal cans from a small churn brought from his horse-drawn float to your door. The knife grinder came with his drum to stick the knives in, then he turned the handle to sharpen them. The lamplighter with his long cane lit the street lamps at dusk and again at dawn to extinguish them.

The Lavender "Girls" in season, sang along the road "Who'll buy my sweet lavender?" while knocking at the doors. The haberdashery man called with his fibre case containing cottons, elastic, buttons, etc. The coalman calling "Coal" in a hoarse rasping voice, with his horse, a great creature, pulling the coal cart, scared me as a little girl. The newspaper boys would call "Extra, extra" after special events, like the Boat Race result. Price a halfpenny a copy.

The baker's cart carried bread in baskets covered in green baize. Gipsies selling pegs always had a young baby in arms and would ask for old clothes. The ice cart would be on its way to the fishmonger's with large blocks of ice like bales and small boys trying to collect the ice chippings from the back.

Then on Sundays came the muffin man with his tray on his head ringing his hand bell, and the shrimp and winkle man calling his wares from his small barrow.'

THE PUB AT BROADHEMBURY

'In the early years of the century the village pub was used as a meeting place for locals, where the men would drink beer at twopence a pint and cider at threepence. Meals were provided (mainly bread and cheese) as in 1911 the pub was managed on behalf of the People's Refreshment House Association – this obliged them to provide food and this was done mainly by using produce from the garden. When this was disbanded the manager took over the running of the pub as a tenant of the estate. The landlord cooked as he had been a Sergeant Major in the Marines in charge of catering for officers. They also let out their spare room, mainly to reps who would stay for just one night. Cider was the biggest seller, bought mainly from Whiteways. Beer was supplied by the brewers in Burton on Trent and sent to Sidmouth Junction by train, from where Mr Jenkins would collect it on his waggon.'

ESTATE LIFE

Many villages were still part of large estates, owned by the local lord or lady of the manor. It could be a secure and peaceful life, but it was always necessary to remember one's station in life.

THE LADY OF THE MANOR

'The lady of the manor who owned most of Dunkeswell village in the early 1900s would give a Christmas party every year to all the schoolchildren. A huge decorated tree contained a present for each child. Also, in the summer, the children used to be driven in three decorated waggons drawn by horses with their best harness and brass bells and given tea on the lovely lawns of Wolford House. They played games and had sports, and on leaving were given a large currant bun and a bag of sweets.

Mrs Simcoe, the lady of the manor, used to arrive at church in a carriage and pair with a footman to open and close her carriage. If we were driving to church in our trap and we saw the Wolford carriage already in the village, Mother would whip the pony and hurry him on, afraid of being late. The church was full every Sunday and Mrs Simcoe would see that all her servants were there and all her tenants, their wives and families, and you had to have a reasonable excuse if you wanted to stay away. I remember the two pews full of her indoor servants. She used to provide their hats, or rather black bonnets tied with black ribbon. I thought they were nuns for years. Mrs Simcoe gave a family bible to all who were married chaste, and if she was not sure she would keep the bible for nine months.'

'People dressed according to their station in life. My mother told me that my great-aunt, a farmer's only daughter, lived at Upottery. They were tenant farmers of Lord Sidmouth. There was a village function to which everybody was invited. My great-aunt was having a dress made for this by the village dressmaker. The same lady was making a dress for Lady Sidmouth. When Lady Sidmouth was having a fitting she happened to see my great-aunt's dress, which was as good as the one she was having made. Lady Sidmouth forbade my great-aunt to wear the new dress to the function.'

LIVING ON THE ESTATE

'When I was small my family lived on an estate at Buckland Filleigh, under Squire Scott Browne. My Dad was head cowman, with a Kerry herd. My Mum did the dairywork. She had to scald two large pans of cream each day, and one pan was left for raw cream which went to the big house. Mum had five shillings a week and Dad's wage was around £2 10s 0d a week. I learnt to milk when I was about ten years old, as the squire bought three Jersey cows and the one I learnt on was very quiet. I had to milk her each side as her udder was too wide.

We would love to listen to our Dad telling about his younger days. One comes to mind about how he and his friend went to Newton St Petrock church to get jackdaw's eggs. On their way home they met the vicar and they had put the eggs in their caps. Boys always had to raise their caps in those days, so you can guess what happened!

Each Christmas we had a lovely party at the big house. Each child in the school had a gift valued at five shillings. We could choose what we would like. I can remember having a doll's pushchair and a teddy bear and many other things.

Also at Christmas there was a bullock killed at the farm for the squire's staff. I can remember watching the butcher cleaning the tripe with lime and water. My Dad, and all the men that worked for the squire, would go to the big house just before Christmas and would come home with a lovely piece of beef, suet, dried fruit, tea, etc.'

'Almost all the land and buildings in Holbeton parish were owned by the Flete estate. Most of the villagers were tenants, the only people to live on or farm their own property were in the hamlet of Battisborough Cross which had belonged to a neighbouring landowner whose estate had broken up.

Besides the magnificent church which dates back to Norman times, and a chapel, there were two public houses, three general stores, a butcher, baker, post office, blacksmith and carrier all to serve a population of just under 1,000.

The tenant farmers employed some of the men, but most people worked on the Flete estate. There was an indoor staff of 22 at Flete House, plus the gardeners, foresters, grooms, carpenters and all the others needed to maintain a large estate.

The tenant farmers were the wealthy of the village, but for them too it was a life of hard work and modest returns. The estate kept a firm (and usually benevolent) eye on them. They could only sell their produce to approved customers and were not free to offer grazing for out-parish animals unless estate approval was given. They were not allowed to take in lucrative summer visitors, or use barbed wire on the land.'

'Netherton, which included Lower Netherton, belonged to Squire Pack of Netherton House. He also owned the lovely woods, the area of which is now near the Centrax factory.

In the 1920s, at Easter the children of the tenants of the estate would be invited to hunt for Easter eggs carefully hidden away on the lawns of Netherton House, and on Christmas Eve the coachman would deliver a present for each child in the village.'

'In 1930 Axmouth consisted of 53 cottages and houses, eight farms, two public houses, a post office and grocer's shop, a golf course and a coastguard station, and all this, plus the fishing rights on the rivers, was owned by the lord of the manor at Stedcombe House. The children attended the village school, which was also owned and run by the estate.

In those days the village was very quiet. The men were employed on the estate and a few women were employed as housemaids up at the manor house. Some people cycled to Seaton to work in the shops or boarding houses. Everyone living in estate property had to be careful not to offend. For example, two men poached pheasants and were caught. They were given a day's notice to get out of their homes. They quickly went to the manor to apologise and promised not to do it again, and they were allowed to stay.'

FIRE AND DISASTER

It isn't so very long since the fire engine was pulled through our streets by horses, and the pump was laboriously hand-operated. There must have been many a time when the fire was out before the brigade got there! The sound of the maroon might signal another type of disaster for someone, and there were also floods to be prepared for.

'NEPTUNE'

'Neptune was an old horse-drawn fire engine which needed a minimum of eight men to pump the water up. It had been in North Tawton for as long as anyone remembered. The horses had to be brought to the engine when there was a fire and it is said that they had the habit of stopping at The Globe (now The Copper Key) on their way. They didn't rush quite so much if the property alight was insured. The most important thing to do on the way to the fire was to fill their cider bottles. This engine was used to block Essington Road when invasion was expected. It was in use during the Second World War and was sold after the war for £1.

The factory hooter was originally used to call out the brigade, one hoot for town, two for a country fire. Later a maroon was used and also at one time the church bells. Of course the two horses used to pull the fire engine might be anywhere working when the maroon went off and had promptly to down-shafts and rush to the engine. A load of anything at all might therefore be found abandoned in the road at such times. The firemen were paid four shillings per quarter.

Charlie Knott was the man in charge of the two horses at one time. When needed for a fire he went to the field and harnessed the first horse. Whilst Mr Knott was harnessing the second horse, the first one quietly and obediently made its way up the street and always stopped at the door where the fire engine was kept. Mr Knott rode up on the second horse. It seems that the leader of the brigade was known as The Chief Engineer! Many stories are told about Neptune and its firemen.

The brigade, for instance, attended a fire and the head of the brigade, Harry Squires (paper shop), could not find the key of the engine shed. He asked who could remember the last fire and one

23

of the firemen said, "My word," (or similar) "I remember the last fire was at Jimmy Stentiford's behind The Globe and I put the key down Bessie Stentiford's back to stop her nose bleeding."

Our postman, Harry Tiller, was in charge of the fire brigade at another time. One day, Mum saw a crowd of men go up the hill, with "something" drawn by two horses. The men were pushing as if to help the horses with their burden. Then the postman came and Mum asked him what it was. "Oh, that's the fire brigade and I'm in charge so I must hurry and finish my round. It's a rick fire a few miles on. I've got my bike, so expect I'll be there before them."

The Gostwyck Hotel burned down in 1917 and it was necessary to call out an extra engine from Exeter. This arrived with the firemen wearing helmets, the first ever seen in North Tawton. The sight of the helmets frightened Sid Bennett and Phineas Knapton into thinking that the Germans had arrived.'

GETTING TO THE FIRE

'When there was a fire in Crediton 70 years ago, a man would cycle round blowing a bugle to summon the firemen. Then they would go to the railway station and get the cab horses. These would be taken to where the fire engine was kept. They used four horses to pull the engine. In and around the countryside there were plenty of streams to provide the water needed for fire fighting. The pump was fitted on an adjustable plank across the engine and two men either side of the engine pumped the water. In Kenton, however, the engine was not pulled by horses but by men.'

'Sandford's fire engine was kept in the lean-to in Fanny's Lane. It was last used around the turn of the century for a hayrick blaze at Long Barn. Pulled by two horses and pumped by two men each side of the machine, the hoses were so badly perished they had to use their handkerchiefs to try to stop the leak. By the time the firemen were mustered and the horses caught and tackled up, harnessed to the engine and galloped to the fire, there was every chance the fire would already have burned out.'

THE CHURCH FIRE

'The fire at St Michael's church, Honiton, broke out on Sunday 26th March 1911. The sexton discovered it when he went into the church at 9 am to prepare for the morning service. He heard a noise like rushing water and looked up to see a sheet of flame roaring between the ceiling and the roof. After telling his wife to

24

save what she could, he ran down Church Hill to inform the church officials, the police and the fire brigade. Mr Cox, the captain of the fire brigade, had to pass the message verbally to each fireman individually so that it was 10.30 am by the time the brigade with its ancient but powerful hand engine arrived. Many local people went and carried out movable articles including the communion plate, altar ornaments, processional crosses, candlesticks and some large oil lamps used to light the church. They also dismantled some of the fixtures too.

The rector had telephoned Exeter for the city brigade with its steam engine to come and help. The brigade chief collected 15 men, the steam engine and four horses and dashed to (what is now) Central Station where a special train awaited them. The horses were soon boxed up and the fire engine loaded and "The Fire Fighter Special" was on its way to Honiton just after 11 am and arrived within 30 minutes.

Water supply was the main problem. The nearest hydrant was 300 yards away from the church and of limited pressure. Until the arrival of the fire brigade from Exeter, the local fire fighters used water from a ditch which had been hastily dammed, passing it along two lines of men between the ditch and the church. Two local businessmen had provided extinguishers.

The Exeter brigade drove their engine along (what is now) Marlpits Lane to the mill stream on the corner of Honiton Bottom Road and the water was pumped from there into a canvas tank erected on the church path. This involved pumping water through 1,900 ft of hose rising to a distance of 200 ft.

Much of the church was destroyed including a magnificent carved oak screen considered to be one of the most perfect of its kind in England.

Walls and pillars, though damaged, remained standing and the tower built in 1480 of stone from a Buckerall quarry was untouched. The only casualty was a young man who received a cut from falling masonry.

The estimated cost of the damage was put at about £8,000. It was believed to have been insured for between £3,000–£4,000. The building was restored at a cost of £2,900 and rededicated on 30th August 1912 by the Bishop of Exeter.'

FLOOD

'After Sidmouth was flooded in the 1920s, folks living at the bottom end got into the way of studying the phases of the moon, time of high tide, direction and force of wind. If the wind was a strong

25

southerly, with a full or new moon and high tides during the night, it was a case of up on to the table with floor coverings, chairs, and buckets of drinking water in case the worst happened. Also dry kindling and coal so as to be able to get a fire going!'

COUNTING THE MAROONS

'Living in Trefusis Terrace in Exmouth, I remember a coastguard calling in 1938 to ask my mother to undo all the windows facing the sea, as rocks in the channel were going to be dynamited as they were a danger to shipping. It was very exciting to see the tremendous fountains of water and hear the explosions rattling the windows. Also we would count the maroons – two for the lifeboat and three for the fire engine. If it was two, my brother would race to get the car out and drive down to the lifeboat station, often picking up a lifeboatman running down the hill still pulling on his oilskin jacket, and he would help to pull the lifeboat across the road with heavy ropes.'

CHARACTERS AND CUSTOMS

Country life would not be complete without tales of the doings of local characters – somehow people seemed to be so much larger than life in the old days, perhaps because we got much of our entertainment from watching the antics of others before television came along.

VILLAGE CHARACTERS

'Several years ago there used to be a man called Dicky who lived in a cottage some miles from South Molton. He used to call on people and they would give him a meal and as soon as he finished it he said, "Well, I have had all I am going to get here, so I'll piggy me way home." He used to dress up to go to church and attended Harvest Teas. One day he went to Molland Cross church tea, and as he was eating Farmer Huxtable said, "Don't worry about paying, I'll do that." After a while another farmer said the same, to which

Dicky replied, "That's all right mister, Farmer Huxtable is paying for this, but next week I be going to Heasley Mill tea, so you can pay for that."'

'An elderly gentleman was in the habit of driving to church in his pony and trap and tying the pony to a field gate near the rear entrance to the church. One Sunday after service he came out to find the pony had been taken out of the trap, the shafts of the trap pushed through the field gate and the pony hitched back in the shafts the other side of the gate.

One way of earning some money in the years between the wars was to catch moles for their skins. A Cotleigh boy had some mole traps set in a field close to the river. When he visited his traps after school he found he had caught a trout – caught and put in the trap by a nearby local.'

'Tommy was a farmer in Dalwood's neighbouring parish of Shute. He was a cheerful, quiet sort of a man, and he owned a rather large docile horse. One day Tommy went out to the field with a halter in his hand to catch the horse, or rather to put the halter on, as the horse was so docile that he seemed asleep on his feet half the time, but on this occasion there were young men watching behind the hedge with a catapult. When Tommy ambled up to the horse one of the chaps let fly with a tiny pebble which caught the horse a stinger on the rump, upon which he did an impression of the Lloyds Bank stallion, up on his hind legs with his front legs waving in the air. Poor Tommy was so taken aback, he turned tail and ran for home. I don't think he did much ploughing that day, and when at a future time he was walking behind Dobbin, he must have wondered whatever had got into him, as they slowly plodded on.

The roads of Dalwood were kept tidy, the verges cut and the ditches cleared by a team of roadmen. Though they all seemed to have individual sections to do, it was said that you could tell where they lived as the section nearest to their homes was kept immaculately, as the opportunity arose of slipping home for breakfast. Nelson was a road man who lived with his spinster sisters in a cottage on the slope of Danes Hill. They were makers of home-made wine and Nelson would have his daily ration along with his 'levenses beside the road he was working on. Most of them took an inordinate pride in seeing that their length was kept to a standard.

George lived in a small cottage behind the telephone kiosk in the village. Rabbit trapper by profession he looked like Jimmy Edwards with a handlebar moustache. He was an habitué of The Tuckers

Arms in the days of Len Westcott and his wife, a regular inhabitant of the chair next to "chimley corner", where during the summer he would sit with his cronies with a sack containing a squishy article and a pint of scrumpy. He would cautiously drink halfway down the glass with one eye on Len's missus, who if he was incautious enough to drain the glass would whisk it away, but George was too fly for that. Having drunk half the contents he would await the first of the summer visitors who, spying a real life country character in George, would invariably offer to replenish his glass. It was estimated that most summer evenings he would only buy the first pint but would go home replete. One of his sayings that would mystify and intrigue the visitors was his announcement that he was going home by "rail" and to those who didn't know they assumed he meant British Rail and wondered where the station was situated. Of course, what the old reprobate meant was going hand over hand by the rail attached to the river bridge.

One of the great characters at Hawley Farm had the nickname "Mister". He had several fields in the Larkshayes area and he never went anywhere without his gun, apart from his trapping activities. Now and again he would catch a rat in his trap which he invariably flung over the hedge into the driveway to the house at Larkshayes and the owner would duly fling it back. This would go on for several days till either the cat intervened or the smell got too much. One day he was chatting away in one of the fields overlooking the road going up to his farm when he spied one of his sons leading the horses back from ploughing. Hastily excusing himself, he dashed off home muttering that he had left some poisoned bait in the horses' crib with enough poison to kill half Dalwood. Another occasion with perilous overtones was when he left a box of cartridges in the oven, as he said "just to air like". Luckily they were found in time, but one of his devastating acts was when one evening the boys were quietly at home sitting around the table near to the open fire. They were all practically asleep after a substantial supper, the room was silent, when suddenly the shotgun which had been left loaded went off with a tremendous explosion up the chimney, frightening everyone to death. Mister's claim to fame came when he found some gold sovereigns in one of his fields. Of course he told a few people and eventually it came to the notice of the Coroner and an Inquest was duly called for. Mister said he had lost several of the coins and his voluminous trousers complete with the hole in the pocket were duly produced in court and held up as evidence, but as far as is known the Klondyke at Hawley Vale petered out.

Another George lived at Dickens Marsh. He owned a filling station on the main Honiton road, the site of which has been taken up by subsequent road widening, near Andrewshayes. He had the honour of serving the late Lawrence of Arabia with petrol when he rode his big Harley Davidson motorbike to and from Clouds Hill; of course he was then known as Private Shaw. It was quite a ritual buying petrol as George operated the swing arm to facilitate putting the nozzle in the tank and then operated the handle which pumped back and forth to pump the petrol up, first making sure that the little inspection glass was primed full. He sold sweets and chocolates and cigarettes and tobacco, but if you arrived after 8 pm he would refuse to serve you cigarettes as his licence was only valid until that time. He mended bicycles, and although he had hundreds of little tobacco tins lined along the wall filled with bits and bobs of cycle parts George knew what was in each tin. He would take enormous pains to mend a bicycle, spending probably all day and his charge would be only a shilling or two. Another sideline was wireless sets. The only snag was being short of 'baccy when it was football night. The committee filled his shed to overflowing, and while the intricate task of team selection was in progress, I am afraid even Lawrence of Arabia would have had to make do with camel's dung if he was short of a fag.

Cecil owned the village petrol pump situated just opposite The Tuckers Arms. As a sideline he also charged accumulators. These were square glass jars with terminals on the top and filled with an acid mixture, which required charging at intervals in order to supply the current for the wireless sets then in use. The main thing to guard against when carrying an accumulator was to see that the contents didn't trickle down the front of your clothing; it would burn practically anything and was extremely corrosive. Cecil was short in stature and short sighted, and one of the thrills in those days was sitting in Cecil's car on a trip to Axminster, with Cecil peering through the spokes of the steering wheel and trying to make out the approaching traffic. On one occasion he was turning onto the main road from the old road. You had practically a blind entrance on this road and, after safely negotiating the turning and reaching the highway, he said to his passengers, "Is the road clear?" They replied, "Yes, except for the bus," to which Cecil replied, "What bus?" The journey continued with the passengers on the edge of their seats.'

MY GRANDFATHER

'It was late April 1935. I arrived at my grandparents' home, not far from my own home, to be greeted on the doorstep by my Grandma, a stern but kindly lady who had brought up ten sons and a daughter. "I suppose you've come to see your grandfather," she said. I almost felt like saying, "Can Grandad come out to play?" The object of the exercise for the pair of us was to go bird's-nesting. He was a man full of nature lore and could find rare nests that I would have missed and was well known in his younger days as a very skilled poacher.

"We'll go down to the river Axe and do a bit of moorhen's nesting today," were his first words. Off we set for Abbey Gate along the river bank when suddenly he pushed me quickly away from the edge. "There's a girt big salmon under the bank and we'll have him," said Grandad and promptly stripped down to his vest and longjohns. It was quite a bitter day and knowing Grandad must have been about 75 years old, I feared for his health.

He dropped stealthily into the river four or five yards below the salmon, up to his chest and warily made his way upstream and then, a huge flurry of water and a 15 pound salmon was thrashing on the bank. A shout of, "Don't let the b...... get back in," brought me back to reality and I grabbed it and shoved it further back in the field.

Grandfather crawled out of the water, picked up the salmon by the tail, and with a quick karate chop at the back of the head killed it. He calmly dressed and stated, "I think we'd better go on home now," the salmon strung around his waist under his jacket.

Grandad was only caught poaching once, wheeled up before the local JP, Mr Cornish of The Cedars, now the Cedars Hotel. He was fined seven shillings and sixpence, with a month to pay. Times were hard with a large family, so he poached a salmon, took it to the rear door of The Cedars and sold it to the housekeeper for – yes, you've guessed it – seven shillings and sixpence!

Many, many, happy hours I spent in the company of my grandfather, listening agog to his tales and absorbing most of his knowledge of wild life. I can even catch a rabbit with a flat hat – but that's another story. He passed away at the ripe young age of 93.'

LADY ASTOR

'My schooldays were spent at the Palace Court School in the poorest part of Plymouth. Jobs were scarce in those days and the children were ill fed and clothed. The MP for the area was Lady Astor, who spoke her mind with great force both inside and out of the Commons, and she greatly incensed the mothers of the local children by saying they looked like monkeys and needed feeding up. When it became known that she was going to visit the school, the mothers attempted to invade the premises in force and, although more amused than frightened, Lady Astor allowed herself to be smuggled out of a window at the rear into her waiting limousine. It is not known for certain whether there was any connection between the two events, but soon afterwards a creche was opened nearby for babies of the poor.'

SUPERSTITIONS

'Devonians aren't quite as superstitious as the Cornish but there isn't a lot between them. We weren't allowed to wash clothes on the family's birthdays or on New Year's Day; we didn't buy brushes in May; we had to spit when we saw a white horse; and if we saw a magpie on its own, we had to say, "Good morning, Mr Magpie". When someone was taking an examination or going for a job, they had to walk out of the door and you threw a shoe or slipper after them, to wish them luck. They mustn't look back and you mustn't say anything.'

'There were many superstitions and habits which had their place in custom and folklore. Men would make a point of shaving on a Saturday night and boys also made a show of being able to shave then as well, as a sign of their manhood; carving knives were always sharpened then, too; finger and toenails had to be cut before Sunday and at Sunday lunch saying grace was never to be missed. New clothing was always worn for Whit Sunday, though it was usually only the firstborn who had new clothing for most of its life as a child, later children having hand-me-downs; the hair and nails of a baby were never to be cut during its first year of life lest the clippings were used to obtain an evil influence over it.

If a pregnant woman stretched up to hang washing on a line above her head she risked the baby being born with the umbilical cord around its neck. When curing bacon or ham a woman must take great care never to touch the meat during her period because this would make the meat go off, and she must never wash her hair during this time either.

The drainage hole in the base of the old stone font was not so much for ease of emptying the vessel as to ensure that every drop of water that a child had been christened with was fully drained away so that no evil person would use it to exert control over the child. This precaution was always done before the family left the font.'

CHURCH AND CHAPEL

Church and chapel were at the heart of every community, Sunday being kept as a special day and most families attending services at least once and usually more often. The church year was a calendar of the seasons themselves and Easter particularly evokes nostalgic memories. Children were expected to go to Sunday school – whether church or chapel often depending on the quality of the outings to be expected!

SUNDAY BEST

'We went regularly to church on Sundays, although it always meant an early start to get the milking and feeding up done in time. Only the essential work was done on Sundays, so there was a rush to get in and put on our best clothes. These were only put on for going out. I never knew my father to go anywhere without changing into his good clothes, whether it was to church, on market day or visiting, and my mother always took pride in putting everything ready for him. He had a great pride in appearances, as did my mother and all my relations were the same. When he came home from anywhere, he would change back into his working "togs" and get on with his work. Town dwellers would say they had never seen a poor farmer, not realising what pride the farmers had. When my mother took paying guests to help with the family finances, my father was very embarrassed to meet them in his working clothes, especially if they tried to take a photograph of him.'

'We went to chapel three times on Sundays – twice to service and in the afternoon to Sunday school. No other activities were allowed on Sunday and we had to remember the text of the sermon and tell my grandfather what it was about. As we boys grew up we all had a new suit each year from the sale at Cornishes in Exeter, costing ten shillings each. We did not have any choice in the matter. The one given to us was for Sunday best, while last year's suit was taken for second best or passed on to the next one in line down in size, until they became working clothes. I recall my mother in law saying she put 36 patches on Grandpa's shirt and she spent every evening darning socks for the next day.'

NOT ON A SUNDAY

'The daughters of the squire at Denbury Manor used to play tennis on Sunday afternoon. The rector could see this from his house and told the squire that it should not be allowed. To prevent the rector from seeing what went on in his garden, the squire proceeded to build the Manor walls higher by approximately five feet.'

THE SEXTON

'The sexton of Tipton St John church of 40 years ago tells me he was paid £3 a week and had the cottage rent free. His duties consisted of lighting the fires in the school and the church and also looking after the churchyard. As he was grave digging one day, on virgin ground as he thought, someone came along and said, "That's my grave you're digging!" This individual had bought that particular site some time previously – no doubt the only man to look into his own grave!'

'Looking after the churchyard at Broadhembury was a major job and the village sexton spent a great deal of time on it. He would walk to church carrying a faggot on his back to heat the church for services, and he would climb the tower each day to wind the clock. (The day after he retired the clock hand fell off and they had it converted to electricity.) He would also dig the graves, charging £3 to decorate a dug grave with ferns and flowers in the netting. He cut the grass with a Tarpin, an early form of lawnmower, and the schoolchildren were employed to cut the grass on the graves and were paid a farthing each. They could also earn a penny for blowing the organ. Before the church was lit with electricity, part of the sexton's job was to light the gas lamps that hung from great chains from the ceiling.'

THE CHURCH AND THE PUB

'There were two pubs in Clayhanger in the distant past, and apparently the last remaining one was bought up by a teetotal Methodist, who promptly closed it down. Evening church services then dwindled, as folk liked to go into the pub and socialise after the service.'

EASTER TIME

'Although not a very religious family, most of our friends and our activities seemed to be connected with the church. We did not mix with the Nonconformist chapel folk and certainly not with the Roman Catholics – I think this was very general in small towns at that time! One of the favourite festivals we looked forward to was Easter – after the rigours of Lent when we had the lighter evenings in store, school holidays and the promise of "outings", again usually connected with the church. Sunday schools had to be very careful to weed out the opportunists who would attend several schools in different churches in order to get on the list of as many "outings" as possible!

We really kept the Lenten period in those days; Pancake Tuesday, then fish on Ash Wednesday with church services or study groups during the week, "toe rag" or dried fish on Good Friday with a lovely egg sauce, lamb and then rhubarb on Easter Sunday. I well remember the Hot Cross Bun man coming in the streets early on Good Friday morning, crying his wares, when my father would rush out and buy some of his buns for breakfast. We children gave up sweets for Lent, in fact I once made myself quite ill by eating cough sweets (having a sweet tooth) which weren't supposed to count! During this period no dances were held, or parish socials or any jollification. Hence Easter was greeted with relief and we all sallied forth to pick primroses to decorate the church. Another reason for our joy was the Easter egg presents. We always had huge ones sent from relations in London and they always arrived in perfect order. Everyone enjoyed the Easter services, with the well known Easter hymns, and after that the promise of the holiday from school, just over a week as I recall.'

'Sunday school played a very important part in our lives in those days. The week before Easter each year saw groups of children setting out from Beer to the fields at Woodhuish where primroses grew in yellow carpets. We took picnic lunches with us – we were usually unaccompanied but our mothers never worried about us, they knew where we were and what we were doing, perfectly safe in those days. We would sit happily for hours picking primroses for the church decorations. Gran would give us a ball of sock wool to tie the delicate flowers into bunches of 15 flowers and two leaves, as required by the church. These small bunches would eventually be studded into a chicken-wire arch which extended over the main church aisle at St Mary's parish church in Higher Brixham. Any bunches over would decorate the drip trays of the umbrella stands at the end of each pew. All the Sunday school pupils would work away to see who would win the book prize for the pupil picking the most bunches. I can remember my little brother and I one year picked over 500 bunches and my mother and grandmother filling baths, buckets

34

and bowls to accommodate the flowers overnight before we could take them to the church. The church at Easter was always beautiful and of course the children attending the Easter services gazed with pride at their floral effort and waited expectantly to hear whether he or she had won the coveted book!'

CHAPEL

'Sunday was Chapel. From the time one stretched in bed in the morning it made its impression. On the wall opposite the bed was the text "My times are in Thy hands" – this surrounded by roses.

Roses were repeated on the hat (bought for Anniversary). All little girls on Sunday were framed in straw and tied under the chin with satin ribbons. Perhaps it was the rosy hat that made Sundays so summery, or maybe it was Alleluia, the pony, harnessed to the trap and ready for off. (Alleluia had a dual purpose – he took the second son on his back to the grammar school every day but Sunday). We would bump our way to the tiny chapel – Wesleyan naturally – pulling at the vetch and stitchwort as we passed.

Outside the chapel the men removed their caps and revealed shiny lilywhite foreheads and there would be an orgy of smiling and hand-shaking before we entered the little varnished place.

Two oil lamps hung from the roof, and apart from the tortoise stove in the corner there was little else except the harmonium.

The harmonium was pumped hard with the feet, so that the player seemed to be practising for a race. It knocked and bumped through the melody, but nevertheless we sang happily and lustily without a choir. There was no resident reverend, just a series of lay preachers from the community. One in particular wheeled his bicycle up the aisle, propped it against the far wall, removed his cycle clips and climbed to the rostrum. "Praise the Lord," he would say, and we bent our heads.

Then followed a lot of "Praise the Lords" and "Alleluias" and nodding of heads; and then we were out in the sunshine, having delivered one ha'penny into the collection plate and secreted the other in a knicker pocket, to be used for a Nestlé chocolate bar another day.'

'Our chapel in the village of Longdown was built just after the First World War, a Wesleyan Methodist faith, which brought help and consolation to several generations of villagers. The building was made of corrugated iron and wood and was quite snug, with about 35 wooden chairs. The Anniversary was held on August Bank Holiday and was well attended. People looked forward to this very much, walking out from Exeter or coming out on the Devon General bus. It was something that everyone enjoyed – the lovely views which were so different from the city streets and the lovely teas, farthing buns with cream and jam, fancy cakes and sandwiches and gallons of tea; the water for this was boiled in an old copper furnace and it was my job to feed in sticks under it and keep the water boiling. After tea and before the evening service, people used to walk up the hill to the woods, though I could not understand their great pleasure at the views and the things in the hedgerows, it meant little to me, I'd seen it all before.'

THE GOSPEL HALL

'Every Sunday morning, without fail, my sister and I had to attend the 11 am service at the Gospel Hall with our parents. No organ was allowed at morning service. One sat in complete silence waiting for one of the Brethren to be moved, either in the form of a hymn, a prayer, or a passage of scripture. Women were allowed no part but sometimes, when a different tune had been tried without success, my mother would start them off on the right track. At twelve noon, there was an awful strangulated gurgling from the clock as the timing mechanism had been partly removed to prevent the twelve chimes from disrupting the proceedings. We hoped that we were on the threshold of release but, without fail, at 12.10 precisely every Sunday the same Brother would get to his feet announcing that he had been moved to a portion of the Scriptures. It was always from 1 or 2 Samuel or 1 or 2 Kings and lasted until 12.30 at least.

There were two Bible classes in Woodbury which met at 2.30 each Sunday. The church one was run by two maiden ladies, and the chapel one was run by my uncle. Numbers fluctuated violently between the two, depending on where the summer outing was going that year. As a result, the outings got better and better.'

SUNDAY SCHOOL TREATS

'I was in the choir at St Giles', Weare Giffard. You could earn a penny ha'penny a week, a penny for being at church and a ha'penny for choir practice. I was also in the church Sunday school. We thought the chapel children had better outings – they went to Exmouth or Bude. We usually went to Westward Ho! but we once went to Woolacombe.'

'One year, the chapel Sunday school outing was to Exmoor. The charabanc was full and it ground slowly and smokily up Porlock

Hill. On passing an old roadman cracking stones beside the road, my uncle called to him, "We are on the way to Heaven, my man." Taking his pipe from his mouth the old man replied, "The sooner you get there the better, else you'll boil!"'

'The highlight of the year was the Sunday school outing. This was a united affair at Okehampton, schools of all denominations going off together in a specially chartered train. The schools closed for the day. Parents and friends all went on the outing, and Okehampton was a dead town until our return. When the train pulled into the station at night when we returned, there was the town band ready to welcome us and we all marched down Station Road following the band – tired and often sunburnt. It was a marvellous sight to see, 300 people being welcomed home in such a way. Sadly, this died out in 1939 on the outbreak of war.'

'Attendance at Sunday school had to be very good to qualify members to go on the annual outing. During the Second World War years this annual outing was eagerly anticipated and it brought much happiness to all who participated. I remember one wonderful day when the charabanc arrived at the door to the church and like a Giles cartoon 50-plus children of assorted ages piled into the vehicle, together with some grown ups. It was so exciting for me because I had never been on a charabanc before and it seemed we travelled many miles before we arrived at the "party-field" on Dartmoor.

We were soon sorted into teams and various races were organised. Oh what bliss when we won! The prize was a 'joey' – an octagonal threepenny bit. Then there was twopence for the second prize and one penny for the third. Some of the children went home much richer than when they had started out for the day. A picnic tea was provided by the local farmer's wife and not a crumb was left uneaten. Plenty of home-made lemonade accompanied the food. I thought I was in heaven. Then there was the magical journey homeward and so much to tell my parents about a truly wonderful day. This "party-field" became a very special place to me when I had my own children and my thoughts often go back to the first time I went there on the Sunday school outing in 1942 when I was twelve years old.'

GETTING ABOUT

At the beginning of the century people had very little choice – they walked or they used real horse power. The bicycle brought more freedom to the country dweller, and then the country buses began to replace the old carrier's cart and opened up a new world of travel to ordinary people. Cars were still rare until after the Second World War, but most people travelled by bus or by train (if they weren't still using the horse and trap!). 'Do you remember steam trains?' asks one Devonian. Don't we just – nothing has ever quite taken their place.

COUNTRY ROADS

'Before tarmacadam, country roads were made of stones pressed into more stones and earth/mud by a steamroller. The stones were brought from local quarries as quite big rocks and dumped in what we now call lay-bys. I clearly remember the stone breaker who came to Kingston when I was a small child in the 1920s. He rode a tricycle and came each day from I know not where, probably a neighbouring village or hamlet. He must have set out very early as his pace on his tricycle was slow, even stately, as he sat bolt upright on it.

On arrival at the pile of stones he would remove his jacket and work in shirt and waistcoat, corduroy trousers tied below the knee, and hob-nailed boots. He put on "glasses", only instead of any lens there were crossed wires designed to keep the flying chips of stone out of his eyes. The eye pieces were quite small and, as I was a timid child, I found them rather frightening because I could not see his eyes.

He would work for days on end cracking the rocks into stones suitable for road mending. Some time later the steamroller would arrive with its attendant caravan. This was not like the sleek bright caravans we see today, but more like a big box on wheels with a stove pipe sticking through the roof. The steamroller driver lived in it whilst going around the area.

A gang of roadmen with picks and shovels would lay the stones for the roller to go over and over until they were well pressed in and level. When it was done we would be set up for another year, or until the rains washed the mud and stones away leaving potholes and ruts.

In spite of the rather rough roads, these were the days when tradesmen called at the house. A baker came from Ermington, about six miles away, with his horse-drawn cart, another baker, the butcher and a grocer came from Modbury, five miles away, and the coal was delivered on a traction engine which often got stuck as the driver overshot our lane on the corner and went into the stream.

In wet weather we were splattered with mud from any passing traffic and in summer we were enveloped in clouds of dust. But in winter, when it was freezing, it was fun to crack the ice in the ruts and puddles on the way to school.'

THE STAGE COACH

'My mother told me of the agitation and excitement in Hatherleigh in the early part of the century when the horse-drawn coach approached. To get up the steep hill the coach had to take a fast run. The coachman blew his horn continuously and all the mothers rushed out to grab their little children who were playing in the street. This was an exciting event!'

THERE WERE FEW CARS

'Our first car (about 1927) was a Coventry Premier. It had a hood and a dicky seat. My sister and I would be strapped in the dicky. It never seemed to rain but we always had to get out and walk up steep hills and sometimes the car would only go up in reverse gear!'

'There were few cars at Ashprington during the 1920s and early 1930s. The doctor had one and the mill owner. There were steam lorries that made deliveries and took paper to the station from Tuckenhay paper mill.

Most of the farmers had horses and a pony and trap. The baker in the village had a horse van, as did those in Harbertonford and Cornworthy. The butcher at Bow Bridge had two horses, a van and a trap. The majority of people had to walk to Totnes for the market.

The local coal merchant had three large carthorses and a pony. He delivered coal to all the villages for miles around. His coal came up the river to Tuckenhay Quay – barges being another form of travel. Most of the boats were Dutch or German, sometimes French, and wonderfully clean considering the cargo. Most spring tides saw a boat up the river bringing coal for Mr Manning or the mill. Local stevedores unloaded the boats with wheelbarrows along a nine inch wide plank. They drank rough cider all day long but I never heard of anyone falling off that plank.

I can't remember the date of the road being tarred, but as it was done by teams of Welsh miners it must have been in the late 1920s. The road to Bowden Pillars was widened. Then the buses started up and we could go to the cinema in Totnes.

The horse was still used by many farmers, and the pony for market. One Cornworthy farmer drank rather a lot and was often loaded into the trap; usually at the Kingsbridge Inn, Totnes. Peter the pony would be told to go home. He would stop at the Waterman's and the Maltster's Arms where the innkeepers would repeat the order to go home. Peter then continued up Corkscrew Hill to the farmhouse. Nobody ever got a car to do that!'

LIGHTING UP TIME

'Most important of all was Lighting Up time. The law was very strict on this. The village policeman hadn't many criminals to catch so riding without lights even a couple of minutes adrift was grist to his mill. Bicycles had gas lamps. A large glass front to light the way and a small red and green glass on the side, red on the right side and green on the left. The bottom of the lamp unscrewed and carbide was put in it. Then water in another container was allowed to drip on the carbide thereby making gas. The gas went up a little funnel, you struck a match, applied it to the funnel and if you were lucky you got a light going. If you allowed water to reach the carbide too quickly it got saturated and so no light. At the other end of the scale the thing would catch fire and the smell had to be experienced to be believed.'

THE CARRIER AND THE COUNTRY BUS

'There was a carrier in South Milton, his father and grandfather had been carriers before him. He would go every day with his horse and cart to the market town, taking boxes of anemones, primroses and daffodils to the train (all to go to Covent Garden in London), day old chicks, rabbits in crates, and trunks and bicycles for visitors returning after their holidays. Whilst in Kingsbridge he would do any shopping, or fetching goods on approval – even collecting large objects like wardrobes from the sale room. He would sit on the top of a wardrobe and plod home after stopping for a pasty and a pint in a village nearby. He would then deliver all the goods to village folk for sixpence per item. He would leave his horse untended outside the cottages whilst he collected his money – and chatted – and the horse would wander along grazing until the carrier caught up with him again.

40

The 14-seater bus often could not make the steep hill out of the village, so the men would be asked to get out and push. On market days the farmers and wives filled the bus so all the school children (me included) were told by the driver to stand in the middle aisle so the ladies could sit. This gave us a great opportunity to knock off the hats of the passengers as we lurched around the winding lanes. Everyone wore hats.'

'When my father, Edward Frank Watts, retired in May 1975 a chapter in Budleigh Salterton's history came to a close. Changing trends and three daughters (instead of sons) had finally seen the demise of the local carrier business which had been serving the town and East Devon for almost 90 years.

Philip Watts started the business with a horse and cart in 1889 and this method of transport was still in use at 1903 when, on Whit Monday that year, he handed over the reins to his nephew Ernest Frank, who had just come of age. The days were very long, starting well before eight in the morning and sometimes not finishing until eleven at night. The four-hour journey to Exeter terminated at the White Hart Hotel in South Street where a number of country carriers made connections and obtained adequate refreshments! This was a

Frank Watts' new Foden steam wagon modernised the family carrier's business in 1910. The Watts served Budleigh Salterton for almost 90 years.

41

welcomed break in days when road surfaces were terrible. In winter they usually had to wade through deep mud covering ruts and in summer the horses churned up clouds of white, choking dust. My grandfather, Ernest Frank Watts, had been used to hard work, starting school when only two years old and leaving at the age of twelve to work on a farm. Sometimes he rode on a donkey behind his uncle's cart, learning the routes and regular customers.

In 1910 Frank, as he was known, quickened the pace by purchasing a new Foden steam wagon. With Tommy Loman at the wheel, the vehicle carried the goods noisily over Devon's hills on steel tyres which were treacherous in wet weather. The rattling and bumping got him down so rubber tyres were later fitted, enabling him to safely reach speeds in excess of 5 mph! Tighter legislation and increased taxes from about £1 a week to £4 10s 0d caused steam wagons to become less popular so Frank bowed to the inevitable and bought a Chevrolet covered truck. The new petrol vehicle cost only £200, compared to the £510 paid for the Foden which was sent to the scrapyard for 30 shillings. An important agency was held with Sutton & Co, an overnight parcel carrier from London.

In 1907 Frank had married Anne Norton at Temple Methodist church Budleigh Salterton, being the second couple to be wedded there following its recent construction. Frank knew every brick in the church for he had hauled them there on his wagon.'

THE TOAST RACK

'The first bus from the village to Exmouth, a five mile journey, was a huge red charabanc with beautiful brass door handles. Each row of seats stretched from one side of the vehicle to the other, and there was a door at each end of the row. It was open but there was a huge rolled up hood at the rear which took a long time to be unrolled so you were usually drenched before it reached you. The return fare was fivepence. A few years later it was replaced by a covered vehicle with open sides and slatted wooden seats. It was very uncomfortable and we called it the Toast Rack.

There was always a queue waiting for the bus. An old lady who took in washing used it frequently. With her washing basket under her arm, and swinging both basket and free elbow energetically, she always managed to get to the front of the queue. She was known as Mrs Push-Shovey.'

THE BLUE ENSIGN

In 1920 my grandfather, Ernest B Hocking, bought a first model

Ford car with a canvas hood that folded back to an open car. He used this as a hire car to take people to various outlandish villages to visit relatives, namely over Exmoor and South Devon. Previous to this he owned a gravel barge named *The Thistle* and a coasting vessel named *The Susannah*.

In 1922 he changed the Ford for a Sunbeam car and also a charabanc which used to hold about 20 people. He named his garage and bus "The Blue Ensign" being of a nautical background. They were painted blue with a yellow band around the sides.

His son, my father David Hocking, left the sea to help run the business. They ran a regular timetable bus service from Appledore–Bideford.

There was also another firm of buses named "The Brown Bear"; these buses were painted brown.

The local organisations used to hire the Blue Ensign buses to take them on their annual outings during the summer months, namely the church, the chapels, the bellringers, the laundry girls, etc. The buses had little doors each side to let each row of passengers in because the seats were the full width of the bus, with a running board both sides to use as a step up into the bus.

As the business grew he bought two more buses and Walter Cook used to drive one and an uncle, William Evans, used to drive the other. These trips were sometimes quite hair-raising with the steep hills of Devon and bumpy roads. It was in the days of canvas tyres, when it was nothing to have to mend about six punctures on the way to Exeter.

I recall my father telling us of the day he took the Territorials to Lympstone. The previous few weeks there had been torrential rain, and the day in question it started blowing a gale on the homeward journey. That night dozens of trees had fallen across the road so they could neither go forward or backward. At Newton St Cyres they all had to abandon the charabanc, and sleep in the church until the roads were cleared the next day by the county council. They knocked up the baker's shop because they were all pretty hungry by this time and the villagers loaned them blankets because the church was freezing cold. One old gentleman, a Mr Jewel of Northam whom I delivered milk to years after, used to say to me, "Ask your father if he remembers the trip to Lympstone." My father's reply was, "As if I could forget!"

When the cars were used for weddings they were bedecked with white ribbons tied on the bonnet. I remember my mother washing and ironing them and my sisters used to roll them up ready for the next wedding.

After the weddings my father would drive the couples in to

43

In the 1950s, new-look filling stations began to appear on Devon's roads, as pictured here at Welland. The roads themselves were still quiet and motoring a pleasure.

Bideford station to catch a train to their honeymoon destinations, and some couples would hire the car to drive them to Torquay and he would then fetch them back the following week.'

ON THE TRAMS

'We had trams in Plymouth for many years between the wars. They ran along iron rails in the middle of the road, two sets, one in each direction. They had two decks, the upper one not covered, and on a fine day it could be very pleasant riding up there, and rather fun.'

REMEMBER STEAM TRAINS?

'Do you remember steam railways? Does the name Waterloo recall smells and sounds through clouds of steam? "Will passengers for Sidmouth and Exmouth please travel in the rear two coaches?" The something-past-ten train always had through carriages attached so that they could be slipped off at Sidmouth Junction.

The journey took a bit longer then, but the last part when the local train with its somewhat long-funnelled engine stopped every few minutes, made it all worth while. The village and station names were a delight: Ottery St Mary, Tipton St John, Newton Poppleford strung along beside the water meadows of the river Otter, where children

44

waved and the occasional fisherman checked his watch as the train passed. A little away from the river was East Budleigh station (which every child knew was really at Otterton) where there was always a camping coach at the end of a siding, with other families on holiday. Next came Budleigh Salterton with the station name in round white pebbles on the steep bank of the cutting; there always seemed to be plenty of porters and a rather grand stationmaster on hand.

Then the line crossed a magnificent brick arch which had a splendid echo if you were in the lane underneath. In a moment, after the great height of the bridge the line dived into a deep cutting, grassed and primrosed then, but now filled with trees, before emerging into fields again round the village of Littleham. The station, just past the village, was close to Grandad's house. Luggage was left with the porter who brought it round on a handcart after tea for the princely sum of sixpence. At the back of Grandad's garden the line dived down a steep incline to Exmouth and how those stout little engines had to chuff and puff in clouds of steam to get up it on their return trip.

Although it was sometimes referred to as "the flyer" this was no express; returning in wartime, my father would judge the state of the Otter in the hope of a day's fishing before his leave was up, and then spot mushrooms in the fields, so that a foraging party could be sent out in the evening. Alas, Dr Beeching . . .'

EXCITING LIVING THINGS

'When I was old enough to understand, my mother told me how the rocking chair in the ground floor bedroom of 4 San Remo Terrace, Dawlish, was gently rocking during my birth. It was a very high tide and very stormy that October night. The waves were high and crashing over the sea wall and over the railway line which runs between the beach and those houses.

Those trains were steam, lovely exciting, living things. If it was raining we could watch the trains from the "sitting room" window. If there was no time to get to the bridge we stood on the balcony. But sometimes, we could see the train coming from Dawlish Warren. My father would say, "Quick, train," and holding my hand we would dash out of the house, over to the bridge and stand in the middle to "feel the train" and be enveloped in the steam as it thundered under the bridge on the way to Dawlish station. It did not always stop there – the express was more exciting. That footbridge has gone now but the base of it can still be seen on the sea wall.

In those far-off days the mail was picked up by the Mail Train without stopping. At the side of the line was a post and arm, on

45

which was hung a large mail-bag, containing letters destined for all over England. As the train rushed past, it swung out a metal arm and hooked the mail-bag off and so into the train, where the mail was sorted during the journey. One memorable day, the hook missed and tore open the bag – it was full! – and the contents scattered over the beach. Fortunately the tide was out and I remember gathering up the flying letters in all colours and giving them to my mother, who in turn gave them to the very worried railway staff. Being a fine day there were many little girls and boys enjoying this extraordinary entertainment during their afternoon walk.'

THE PRIDE OF THE STATIONMASTER

'The railway came to North Tawton in 1858. It was a very busy goods station and was important to the wool factory, Taveners flour mill at Newlands, the local gasworks, and the agricultural community in general. In the 1920s there were at least ten passenger trains daily in each direction and about two goods trains. Taxis charged sixpence per passenger to collect people from their house or deliver them to their door and there were at least four of them engaged in this work.

All the goods waggons were shunted around the station by the station horse. This was a heavy shire horse which walked beside the rails and pulled the waggons into the goods shed for loading and unloading. Cattle trucks were also handled like this.

The station was the pride of the stationmaster, who made sure there was a welcoming fire in the waiting room and courtesy extended from the ticket office. The platform was swept daily and the flower beds kept free from weeds. The gold braid round his peaked cap would be shining and his buttonhole would display the flower of the day.'

THE PORTER AND THE GUARD

'When I was a child I went to Exeter for my holidays to stay with my aunt. My uncle kept an umbrella and tobacconist's shop in Bath Road. My mother would take me to Tavistock station and put me on the train and ask the guard if he would look after me and see that I got off at Exeter. I was about eight years old at the time.'

'During the late 1940s my brother and his wife made the journey from Honiton to Exmouth by train, changing trains at Tipton St John. The porter was asked how long a wait there would be and his reply was, "About ten minutes, sir."

"In that case," asked my brother, "have I time to get a drink at The Golden Lion?"

"Yes, sir," replied the porter, "I will come and let you know when the train is coming." He did just that!

The same porter played for the local football team, and the game would often be held up while he saw to any passengers that came in during the Saturday match.'

WE ALWAYS USED THE TRAIN

'As small children we watched the Territorials marching down to the railway station to entrain their horses and gear after summer camp at Willsworthy on Dartmoor. They left from either Brentor or Mary Tavy station. The GWR Mary Tavy station was fully manned, the stationmaster with gold braid on his peaked cap (the SR stationmaster only had a plain cap). At Bickleigh the staff always trained the rambling roses along the fence – very pretty. We always used the train.'

'In 1936 the train fare from Crediton to Exmouth was sixpence, so it was known as the Woolworth train.'

WHEN I STARTED

'When I started on the railway in 1936 at Axminster station it was quite a busy place. There were connections to Lyme Regis with a through coach to London on weekdays so that passengers did not have to change. In the summer season six coaches were detached from the London train for Lyme Regis and another six went on to Seaton. On the return journey both sets of coaches were connected up again at about 3 pm for London. On the route to Lyme Regis was Combpyne, advertised as "Combpyne for Rousdon and walks to the landslip." There was also a camping coach for holiday people.

There were about 30 staff at Axminster station: the Traffic Dept, Carriage and Waggon Dept and the Engineers Dept. I worked as an oiler at 15 and then as a waggon repairer and then as a train examiner.

We worked three shifts. During "nights" we often had ten to twelve freight trains to examine, with about 50 to 70 waggons on each train. It entailed quite a bit of walking. The paper train used to unload the papers at about 4 am. W H Smith came up from Exeter, sorted the papers and delivered to towns and villages on the way back. The freight service was also very good. Trains used to leave Nine Elms, London, at 8.50 pm and arrive at Axminster at 5 am.

47

All stations had their own goods waggons. Goods were delivered to shops in Axminster by 9 am. Goods were returned to London five days a week on the 5 pm from Axminster.

We had a siding for repairs to waggons. I have helped to change hundreds of waggon wheels and done other repairs. We also maintained milk tanks at Express Dairies, Seaton Junction, and United Dairies at Chard. About 20 tanks were sent to London every night, each containing 3,000 gallons of milk.

Before the war, we had the Devon County Show at Millwey Rise. All the machinery came by rail: extra staff were employed. On market days, the railway loaded as many as 20 to 25 cattle waggons and sent them to all parts.

When the Americans built the hospital at Millwey Rise during the war, the Red Cross trains used to bring the wounded GIs from France to the station and the army ambulances took them to the hospital.

It was in 1966 that the main line was altered to single line and the Lyme Regis branch closed. For one day before the closure the railway went on strike for the public to try to save the branch lines. It was the only time I was on strike in 50 years. You know what happened – Dr Beeching had his way.'

HOUSE & HOME

THE WAY WE LIVED THEN

Whether our home was an ancient rambling farmhouse or a tiny terraced cottage, we all shared a way of life which had not changed in many respects from that of our ancestors. They may seem picturesque and romantic, but often our houses were cold, dark and damp – and there were far too many rats and mice about for comfort! The kitchen was usually the heart of the house, warm and cosy and filled with the aroma of baking day.

THE FARMHOUSE

'The farmhouse where I was born in 1935 was long, divided into four large rooms upstairs and down. The only heating was from a small grate in the sitting room and a large open fire in the front kitchen/living/dining room. Much of the cooking was done over the open fire or in the cloam oven in the wall beside it.

During the 1940s we had an oil cooker in the back kitchen, this cooked fine if it was a calm day, but the least bit of draught made it "smitch", and all the food tasted oily and was covered in a black film. With three doors opening into this room, none of them fitting very well, calm days were few and far between.

The pump and pump trough were in the back kitchen along with the milk separator, the furnace for boiling clothes, faggots of wood and "back sticks" for the open fire in the front kitchen, a large work table and a cupboard in which shoes and best boots and leggings were kept.

Working boots and leggings were kept either just inside the back door or in the back porch beside the mangle. The walls were whitewashed and the floor was of stone. The fourth room downstairs was the dairy, cold on the warmest summer's day, an ideal place for the pans of milk to stand for 24 hours prior to being scalded and to cool after. The salters and trennells containing salted pork stood on the floor under the table, barrels of apples in straw against the wall, beside a tall cupboard encased in perforated zinc. All perishable foods were kept in this safe away from mice and cockroaches.

Flour was bought by the sack and kept in the flour hutch in the dairy. I am not certain of the weight of a sack of flour – probably 56lbs, but with our sized household that did not last long. We were my grandparents, their four sons (the eldest being my father), my mother and myself, then three evacuees were billeted at our house, making a household of eleven. Just as well the bedrooms were large! The biggest had two double beds and one single – this was the boys' room.

There was no roof space, all the bedroom ceilings were on the underside of the gable roof. Condensation was no problem, but frost was. My grandfather had a large moustache which froze to the bedclothes on more than one occasion, and this was not the only thing to freeze in the bedroom! A mat either side of the bed was the only floor covering. The walls were colour washed, over generations of lime wash, visible once more as soon as the colour flaked off.'

'Our farmhouse in the 1930s was built in Elizabethan times for a Merchant Adventurer. It had all the grace of that period, constructed of Devon stone with a courtyard and gardens enclosed in walls ten ft high. The garden was mostly put down to vegetables but there was a small knot garden with trim box hedges. The courtyard was paved with yellow stable bricks, scrubbed down daily, and up the walls grew climbing roses.

The yard had a meal store and a covered part where there was a stone trough, the pump for the water, and the copper and mangle. There was also a grindstone for sharpening the farm tools. The farm dogs slept in the yard at night or, if it was cold, in the meal store. Another room off the yard, called the back kitchen, had the separator for the milk and a shelf where the oil lamps were kept. These were filled and trimmed every morning and the glasses cleaned with newspaper. Stairs went up from that room. Here were to be found a stack of faggots, two immensely long clothes lines, and the ricks of corn awaiting the threshing machine. The winter store vegetables were kept in the cellar – apples, potatoes, carrots, and the seed corn for the following spring.

The kitchen was a wonderful room, paved in slate, with a huge hearth-fire which rarely went out. A large log called a back stick was put in and this smouldered away waiting for the faggot in the morning to start it off again. A very large Ledstone range was on the back wall, with a tank at the end for hot water, filled each morning. The range was blackleaded with brass handles and shone like jet. There was a scrubbed table with forms either side, and a huge brass oil lamp with an opaque glass shade hanging over it. During the winter, friends would visit in the evening, the women going into the parlour and the men playing solo at the kitchen table.'

'Our home was a farmhouse, mid-way between the two villages

of Loddiswell and Aveton Gifford and over one mile from each. The house was in two distinct parts, the front part gabled, and obviously built on and added in the Victorian era when farming was in a prosperous spell. It was large and cold and bare by today's standards; there were five bedrooms, drawing room, dining room, front kitchen, back kitchen, dairy, pump house and outside lean-to washhouse. A new bathroom had just been put in under the front stairs and part of the hall comprising bath, basin and toilet with water laid on from a rainwater tank outside, so plenty of water (only cold of course) when it rained! Hot water always had to be carried, so baths were usually still had in the tin bath in front of the open hearth fire, with the big three-fold screen (which was covered in pictures cut from calendars and magazines).

There was a large front hall and dark stained stairs up to the two best bedrooms, which were used for visitors, furnished with brass beds and dark oak furniture with barley-twist legs, a square of congoleum on the floor, dark varnished surrounds and two hooked wool rugs. A very smart black and gold set of toilet china adorned the wash-stand; jug and large bowl, soap dish and tooth mug and two matching chamber pots to put under the bed. The other front room had similar furniture, but the china set was yellow and white pastoral scenes. The other three bedrooms were reached by the back stairs, simply furnished, but all beds had lovely thick feather ties on top of the horsehair under-mattresses. They all had their wash-stands and china sets, for the ladies always expected to wash in the privacy of their bedrooms; the men usually preferred to sluice themselves down under the pump, as well as their taking the last turn of the Saturday night bath.

The drawing room had a carpet square (the only one in the house), a three-piece suite in grey and black moquette, a very large mahogany sideboard with mirror, and the piano, our only source of musical entertainment, used for Sunday evening hymn singing. (We all loved the lively Sankey hymns.) All the ladies in the family were good pianists and my aunt and my mother had a special duet they used to play called "Glittering Dewdrops". I loved to hear them all play, but although I had piano lessons for many years, never reached their standards.

The dining room was more used, very thick walls and a much more cosy room, with old leather chairs. Only lino on the floor, but a large thick woollen rug by the fire, made by Mum and Dad in their courting days, which lasted until I was grown up. Once furnished then, there was no thought of making changes.'

'A local farmer had a cobblestone floor in his sitting room and when it was suggested the floor should be replaced, he said it had been all right for his father before him and it was all right for him.'

COTTAGE HOMES

'Core Hill Cottage was a four bedroomed, one storey house built in the early 1800s, of stone collected in the vicinity and lime mortar, which was liable to disintegrate if it got wet. There were no damp courses, so in winter it was chilly and damp. There was no electricity and the water supply was an open well in the covered lean-to at the back. It never dried and at normal times was full of clear soft water, but in very heavy rain the surface water got in and it became like brown soup. We then had to fetch buckets of water from elsewhere. Cooking and heating was by a small blackleaded stove built into the bottom of a large chimney with a small oven attached which turned out excellent meals if the wind was in a certain quarter. Sometimes the fire would not draw and then meals would be late or undercooked. The doors of the cottage were not the best of fits and feet were liable to get very cold in the draught, so it was most comfortable to draw up a chair and put one's feet in the oven to get them really warm. My father's wages were £1 10s 0d a week, but the cottage went with the job so there was no rent to pay.'

'Our little cottage in Okehampton is now part of the museum. We had no electric and no indoor toilet, we had to go quite a distance for that. We had no back door. When it was a dull day we had to keep the front door open for the light.'

'In the 1920s our house was made of cob and roofed with corrugated iron, with concrete floors covered with rush mats. These could easily be removed whenever we were flooded, which was quite often. It was a tied cottage in the woods on Lord Clinton's estate at Weare Giffard and had no labour saving devices, but our cottage was always spotlessly clean. All our water came from a well in which a lump of lime was kept to keep the water pure. We had an open fire for cooking and heating and a large saw-like contraption hung in the centre from which a kettle and stewpot were suspended. Our baking was done in a cloam oven. Bundles of twiggy sticks had to be collected, put in the oven and lit. When this was burnt away all the ash had to be raked out and the oven would remain hot for the day's baking. Our table was white wood which was constantly being scrubbed to keep it clean.

In 1934 we moved to Vine Cottage, which was literally a vine cottage where grapes were planted outside, trained up the walls

Before even the most basic of mod cons, cottage homes like this terrace of houses at Weare Giffard were often cold and damp, despite the roses round the door!

through doors at the top of the house and grown under the glass roof which our cottage had.'

'The cottages at Huntsham were, to modern standards, very primitive. Practically all the rooms had cold floors of lime and sand, with no practical damp proofing.

Cooking was by paraffin or on the open fire, which was about six ft wide. This had a bar across the chimney, with crooks hanging down to hang crocks or kettles on. The kettles had an extension called a handy-maid. A three-legged iron stand called a brandis was at the side to stand the saucepan on. If you were not careful when you lifted the lid off the crock a lump of soot would fall in.

Furnishings were bare necessities. Tea chests and sugar boxes made good storage chests for bedding and spare clothes. Children often sat on logs, with a cushion. Few could afford armchairs for comfort. An old saying was "Go to bed and save fuel" – hence the large families I suppose.'

54

'Home for me in Ivybridge with my parents, three brothers and three sisters, between the years 1925 and 1939, was a one down and two up terraced cottage in a row of three. The front door opened onto a passage which housed my father's bicycle, a large pram, hoops and sticks, and boots and shoes. This passage led to a high-walled yard in which there was a washhouse and lavatory. In the washhouse was an iron copper, which was lit with sticks and coal on Mondays for washing clothes, and on Saturdays for bath night. The yard was crisscrossed with lines for hanging out the washing, with a large wooden prop which leaned against the wall when not in use.

The downstairs room had a coal-fired range, and the flues had to be cleaned every week and the range cleaned with blacklead, applied with a round brush, left to dry and then polished until it shone. After the cooking the range doors would be opened and a guard put around to protect us. All water was drawn from a tap in the yard, and had to be heated on the stove. Washing up was done in a bowl on a well scrubbed table and the dishes placed on a tray to dry. Mother did all her baking on the table, on which we also ate our meals. At the end of the day a large chenille cloth was spread and we all sat around to read or play games, or Mother would have her sewing machine out to make or mend clothes. On the opposite wall to the stove there was a dresser with a bottle of cod liver oil and malt on the lower shelf, and we all had a spoonful before setting off to school.

Two steps up from the living room a latched door opened into a landing large enough for a bed, which two of my brothers shared. My parents and the youngest baby had the larger room, and we girls had a double bed in the second room. There was only gas lighting in the two main rooms, so we children went to bed with a lighted candle, and had lots of fun making hand pictures on the walls.

In 1939 we moved to a large house that Father bought with a deposit of £100 saved from sixpenny pieces.'

MORE LEISURED TIMES?

'"In more leisured times"? Yes, probably today's young Mums think that we oldies had more leisure as we seldom had a job outside the house. But imagine an existence where the power cut goes on forever because there are no lines to bring electricity, no pipes to bring water into the house, no cooker that can be turned on or off as needed, no vacuum cleaner, no washing machine, no electric iron, none of those gadgets that speed up cooking and cleaning today.

Nowadays when most of the great open hearths in old Devon houses have been closed in, the young dream of how pleasant it must have been to sit beside the huge log fire. But we had scant leisure for sitting. To housewives, it was "that dratted fire", labour intensive and unpredictable, the only source in the whole dwelling of warmth, heat for cooking, boiling a kettle, even warming the milk for the baby's bottle. And every drop of water for whatever purpose had to be carried in from an outside pump. Worse, all dirty water had to be carried out again. Worst of all, plodding through rain or snow to an icy outside loo at the bottom of the garden!

Young and green, I came to West Devon from a northern county with coal ranges and the kettle singing on the hob. These dark, cavernous Devon fireplaces were completely alien to me. They demanded skills I never fully mastered, in spite of all the help from kindly neighbours who took pity on my ignorance. At first light I padded across the chill slate floor, put a handful of tinder against the still warm back-log, and prayed the match would catch and start the fire. Then I filled the kettle by dipping water from a pail brought in the evening before, and set it to boil for a morning cup of tea by swinging the crook along the stout iron bar that spanned the hearth at head height. One crook was for the kettle, another for a heavy iron pot of water for washing, and the others for cooking pots. An iron frying pan could be set over the embers on a trivet, or on a clever gadget with a ratchet to adjust the slope.

One summer afternoon I was given a lesson on how to make strawberry jam in a pan on the trivet, blowing up a small fire just enough to bring the jam up in a frothing boil, but not too much flame or the jam would taste of smoke. And I learnt how the potatoes must be boiled first and set by the fire to keep warm, and then the greens cooked quickly, because it took too much fire to keep two pots going at once.

Very soon I realised why the bare slate floors were so suitable. Not only were they easily cleaned of the dust and twigs from the firewood, but also the chill from them eased the heat where the cook was labouring, and hard labour it was. Getting the right amount of heat at the right moment required great expertise. I was a novice with that dratted fire. For me, it either blazed or smoked, no glowing embers, and too often I ended up with a soot-streaked face and a sorry apology for dinner.'

RIGHT UP TO THE STARS

'I was born in 1902 in a very old fashioned farmhouse with a thatched roof. In the corner of the kitchen we had a fire on the hearth with seats on either side. When we sat on these at night we could look right up the chimney and see the stars.'

A MIDDLE CLASS FAMILY

'My mother, father and I lived in Belstone in the 1930s, in a three storeyed house set in its own grounds on Skaigh Lane. I left boarding school in 1935 and lived at home with my parents whose eldest son, an army officer, had died in India. The younger son lived in Filton, working his way through the Bristol Aeroplane Works there, coming home for weekends on a large, noisy and powerful motorbike.

At that time we had a girl from the village living in who acted as cook/housemaid and a gardener who lived in Sticklepath but walked up every morning. A true countryman, he knew all the signs of weather, the moor and its inhabitants. When the weather prevented him from going on the garden he would chop sticks, clean out the sheds or rake the paths. These paths he had made, along with the drive and tennis court, by hiring a horse and cart and hand-loading it with slack from Ramsey Mine in South Zeal. This has arsenic in it so never grows weeds. In summer he would go out into the "high moor" and dig turves and set them up to dry for peat, which he later brought home in the cart for using on our open fires.

We had an Esse for cooking and a boiler in the back-kitchen to heat the water. Here the gardener had his lunch, cleaned the shoes and did other odd jobs for the maid.

My mother always had a cup of tea at eight o'clock, the signal for my father to go and have his cold bath, which he had every day before breakfast at nine o'clock. By then I would have been out and fed my horse. My morning was taken up in cleaning out the stable, grooming and exercising. Meanwhile my father would be cutting flowers for my mother to arrange in the house; there were always masses, he had wide herbaceous borders all down the kitchen garden as well as in the front of the house, and a wild garden of flowering shrubs, trees and bulbs with rhododendron and azalea flanking the drive and a greenhouse for winter plants.

Lunch would be at 1 pm, after which my mother would rest for an hour, changing into an "afternoon dress" and preparing the drawing room ready for her friends to come and play bridge. My father might write letters in his "den" or go up to the Belstone Men's Club and play billiards. I played tennis in summer and badminton in winter when I was not out hunting. There was tack to see to and bedding down and feeding; a horse takes a lot of time. About 6.30 I would have a bath – good and hot and necessary! Both of us ladies put on long evening dresses and my father a dinner jacket whether we were having company or not. Dinner was at 7.30, sherry before and coffee afterwards served on a salver in the drawing room. We would listen to the wireless, my father reading, my mother and I knitting, sometimes we played card games but the "work" of the day was the crossword in the London paper – it had to be completed before we went to bed at about 11 pm.'

HEAT, LIGHT AND WATER

'Mod cons' were few and far between in the good old days – though perhaps the soft glow of lamplight and the sparkling water from the well were compensations. Lack of running water made bath night and, especially, washday times of hard labour. Washday came round with monotonous regularity and really did take all day when soap powder and spin driers were unknown. The 'little house' at the bottom of the garden is another well-remembered tribulation, though sometimes running water was 'laid on'!

SPRINGS AND TAPS

'The source of our water supply on the farm at High Bickington when I was young was a spring way up the valley in the woods. It came into the farmstead by way of a filter, an area approximately six ft by four ft, enclosed with brick walls, about 30 inches deep and divided into three compartments. In the first were fairly large pebbles, in the second smaller ones, and in the third gravel, the whole being covered. My sister and I used to lift the cover up sometimes to have a look. We found it quite fascinating.

The water supply never failed but in very hot weather we found it was not cool enough to make the butter, so we had to fetch water from another spring some way from the dairy and this was always ice cold.'

'Before we got a generator in 1948, hand-pumping the water at Manaton had taken a half hour each day. When I was a child it was much more fun fetching the drinking water from the spring in the field. Tap water came from a shallow tank, so we collected the drinking water in jugs from a spring which ran along an old piece of moss-covered piping on its way down to join the stream in the woods and tasted wonderful.'

'In about 1910 I remember an old lady at Bittaford fetching her water in two large buckets, using a hoop round her waist, from a public tap about ten minutes away. She did this once or twice a day in all weathers.'

COMING ON MAINS

'When Sir Francis Drake was Mayor of Plymouth he was asked by the housewives of the town whether fresh water from the moors could be brought to them, as they had none in their homes. He took up the matter and leats were made from the area of Burrator, winding down across the moors to the town carrying water for their needs, and until after the First World War this water was still flowing locally in Yelverton although by then it had also been piped here and down to the town. In the misty winter nights the leats could be a source of danger for people coming by the last train at night from Plymouth, for public lighting had still not reached Yelverton in the early 1920s – only a very limited supply of electricity had been started by a Mr Heath from a small hut near Willowby Park for the terrace of houses there and the rest of Yelverton was dependent on oil lamps.

When Drake took the water down to Plymouth the leats did not go round by his home at Buckland Abbey or by Crapstone and Buckland Monachorum, and it was not until 1920 after the war that I was asked to get on the Yelverton Parish Council and see what I could do about it. I had come from Edinburgh with my young family and had settled at Willowby Park – but I was very dubious whether first a woman Councillor would ever be considered, and secondly about the opposition of the farmers on the Council, who all had good wells on their farms, to any possibility of paying a Water Rate to Plymouth if it was piped to the villages. In spite of their extreme need none of the villagers had a tap in their homes, and three families had to share an earth closet at the end of a garden. Their only way to get water was by pails from a small brook, or any little spouts of rain water.

However, to my surprise, I did manage to get on the Parish Council, and although the Clerk wished me to go on the Buckland Cemetery Committee I informed him that I had come to work for the living, not for those who had died. He assured me that the graves there were longer, and wider, than in other cemeteries – I asked if that was due to the phrase "to turn in one's grave" if one was not satisfied over some matter. Having come on the Council for getting water piped over, I felt the other members might interest themselves in the graves.

It took me three years, as the water question was always turned down – but I found that my one hope lay in the Women's Institutes which had just started. I went round to them speaking on the need for good fresh water in homes for the children, many of whom died from throat troubles due to impure sources – surely each week any small amount put in a box from their weekly housekeeping money would soon get the Water Rate, which at that time in Yelverton was very cheap, rather than taking flowers to the cemetery on Sundays for children whose lives might have been saved. This aroused interest among mothers and grandmothers, and the village hall at the end of the three years was packed for the last parish meeting.

During the meeting the well-to-do local bachelor farmer who was Chairman (and who had gone through the First World War on his nearby farm with no rationing and well looked after) got up and said it was good exercise for the women to carry pails of water up the steep Buckland Hill – there were no school meals at that time and in hot summer it was difficult enough to get water for their dinners. He was a very stout man, and to hear him saying that it was good exercise for pregnant women to carry pails when he could not have carried even half a pail of water up even half the hill, made me so indignant that I told him what I thought of him. The meeting then became very enthusiastic and carried the water question through.

I was able to go right into Plymouth and see the Town Clerk, Mr Ellis, and begged him to get Mr Howarth, the Water Engineer, who lived at Yelverton, on to the job at once! Burrator Lake had to be made deeper, but eventually the water was piped over to Crapstone and Buckland, and later on to Milton Coombe, and the cottages gradually got indoor sanitation and baths.

The following year there was a very severe drought and both locally and in Plymouth water had to be rationed for a spell. The villagers asked if I had foreseen this! Having been in India during droughts out there and seen the suffering of the natives, and the damage to crops, I was glad that our villagers and others over here had been spared that suffering.'

'Electricity came to Brampford Speke in 1933 but another more precious commodity did not go on line until 1950 – water.

Several of the larger houses had their own wells, the rest had to use the nearest pump and these were strategically situated around the village. Each household had to pay the Water Board £5 for the stopcock and one resident pleaded that he didn't want water laid on – but he still had to pay.'

BATH NIGHT

'The bath was in the scullery covered with a wooden lid. This had

60

linoleum on and during the day was used as the table. Bath nights meant the boiler in the outhouse had to be filled with buckets of water from the house, which were heated and then taken back to the house again, so at least three people had to bath in the same water.'

'Every Friday night my brother and I would have our weekly bath. My mother or father would put a tin bath in front of the range or stove, on which were placed two big iron saucepans of water to boil. Cold water was put into the bath first from a galvanised bucket which was fetched from a pump about 500 yards from our house at Newton Poppleford. Lots of other homes used the same pump. After our bath we were given brimstone and treacle or Beecham's Pills in a spoonful of jam – I suppose this was to clean our insides as well as our outsides.'

WASHDAY

'Washing day almost always started on Sunday evening after chapel in our house.

First, the fire was laid in the fire-basket under the copper; the copper was usually in the corner of the kitchen, built of brick with the copper itself made of cast iron. In some cases it was a purpose-built washhouse at the back of the house or across a yard, perhaps with a coalhouse and woodhouse as well.

Next, the water would have to be pumped up from the well (always remembering to have a cup of water ready to prime the pump or else there would be no water) and carried in buckets to fill the copper (about five gallons). Then all the galvanized iron baths (large to small) would be put out on long forms. One bath was used for soaking; hot water for this was obtained by heating up the iron kettles on the kitchen range on Sunday afternoon and evening so that heavily soiled clothes could be soaked overnight. One bath was used for washing and one or more for rinsing (or streaming through) and one for blue. This was a cube of Reckitts Blue tied up in a piece of cotton sheet or hanky. It was placed in the water until the right colour of blue was obtained, then removed and hung up to dry ready for use on the next washing day. The blue was used to keep the whites white. One bath was placed under the mangle for the last rinse or stream. A big bowl of Robin starch was made last thing at night and was thinned down with more water depending on how stiff the clothes had to be.

There was an early start on Monday morning. The first job was to get the fire going and this was done by taking out some hot embers from the kitchen range which was kept going all night. When the water was hot enough, the whites were washed and then placed in the copper and pushed down with the copper stick which was usually a clean broom handle about three feet long and never used for anything else. Then the soap powder was added, this being Persil, Rinso or Oxydol or even grated yellow soap, and a handful of washing soda. While this was boiling, the coloureds would be washed and if the colours did not run they would also go into the copper, but only staying in the boiling water for a few minutes.

By this time the kitchen or washhouse was full of steam, but smelling lovely especially on a frosty morning in winter. The coloureds would be taken out first with the aid of a copper stick, streamed or rinsed through and then starched – tablecloths first, then pillow slips and aprons and hankies last – then put out on the line.

The heavily soiled clothes that had been soaking all night would then be washed. While the whites continued to boil the rest of the household jobs would be done, such as making beds, cleaning out the sitting room grate and all the rooms would be tidied and dusted.

The starched clothes would be brought in damp and rolled up tightly and put in a flasket (a Devonian word meaning clothes basket). Next the whites would come out of the copper and would be rinsed or streamed through and then blued and put through the mangle. Usually these mangles were fairly large and made of cast iron and wood. Some folded down to make a table. The rollers were made of wood with a big screw on top to tighten the rollers or lift them. The clothes would come out nearly dry and then would be hung out on the line. If the line was too low a wooden prop was used. This was a long stick cut from the woods or hedgerow like a long Y.

Any thick and heavy clothes – overalls, trousers or skirts – would be placed on a board and scrubbed and then rinsed and hung out to dry last. The baths would have to be emptied and wiped dry and hung up in the outhouse. Any fire that was left would be put into the kitchen range. Any hot water left in the copper was tipped out and used to scrub the kitchen floor, the back toilet floor, the porch and the steps.

Towels, sheets, tea towels and any thick clothes when dry would be brought in, shaken and folded straight and put through the mangle again and then aired off. The starched things would be ironed that day and the rest were left folded down in the flasket until Tuesday which made it easier to iron them.

On Mondays most people had an easy evening meal about six o'clock of cold meat, pickle and bubble and squeak, with any

62

left-over sweet from tea on Sunday – apple tart and cream or suet pudding with raisins (spotted dick) or, if there was time, a rice pudding was put in the range in the early morning and left to cook slowly all day. The cold meat was left over from Sunday's roast and the bubble and squeak was cooked in an iron frying pan – there was nothing to beat it.

What a difference today, any day can be washday. Just press a button and it's done and hardly any ironing and yet I miss the lovely smell of the clothes boiling away in the copper.'

'On washday the three older boys in our family were told to fetch the water. This was brought from a spring running in the village square or from a tap in a tank along the top road about a quarter of a mile in the opposite direction. Then the fun and games would start. First we boys would fight over the buckets. After some argy bargy we would set off carrying two buckets each. One of us would get to the tap first and start filling his buckets. They were almost too heavy for us. As one was filled it would be put aside, then someone would tip it over and we would start all over again. Eventually the buckets would be filled for the journey back to the house. They were heavy, but we would start to roll and bump each other, spilling water all the way back. We would arrive at the house with buckets half full. This went on until the copper and baths were filled with enough water for the washing. We were wet and the road was like a river. Someone was sure to come in and tell Gran, "I zee they dratted byes been at it again."'

'The cottages at Plymtree were terraced, two down and two or three up. Many of the terraces had backs opening together, and shared lavatories and coppers for washing clothes. These communal coppers caused more neighbourly bad feeling than anything, each hidebound housewife wanting to do her washing early on Mondays. The brick built furnaces with a copper inside for boiling clothes had to be lit from underneath, very useful for burning up all the household rubbish.'

'My washday job, when towels had been put into the tin bath with pure soap flakes to soak, was to jump up and down barefooted on them!'

AT THE BOTTOM OF THE GARDEN

'We lived on a farm to the north of Dartmoor in the 1940s. Our loo was a three-holer over a rushing stream in a deep ravine. Owls roosted in the roof, making eerie noises. A visit after dark was hazardous, as the geese always awoke and wished to join us, so we had to arm ourselves with a lantern and a stout stick. This trip was quite an adventure, especially for guests.'

'There were tied estate cottages at Sandford where it was necessary, when the river flooded and one was using the toilet, to sit and hold one's feet up as the water rushed past!

Our toilet was a shed at the bottom of the garden (the closet), a bucket with a scrubbed wooden seat. A pan of ashes was kept in the corner for sprinkling on the bucket after use. Our toilet paper was squares of newspaper tied together with string, attached to a nail within easy reach. It was surprising what news you missed the first time round.'

'Our outside toilet at Denbury was at the end of the garden in the summer and moved closer to the house in the winter. I remember sitting on the wooden slats and, as I got up, losing my Sunday hat in the bucket!'

HEAT AND FUEL

'Before the First World War there were no roads into Kingston, only cart tracks, so the only way to get coal to the village was by barge from Wales and it came to Wonwell beach.

The farmers of the village gathered together to fetch the coal with their horses and waggons. It was stored by local people, one store being at the top of the village behind the Britannia Inn.

The barge came in once a year and there would be enough coal collected and stored to last the village a twelve month period. The barge would come into the river on the tide and anchor. The tide turned the barge astern seaward. The first waggon would then come off the slipway and get loaded up, sometimes the horses being in three or four ft of water. The process of loading up would take only two or three minutes and then the waggon would be away and the next come in line. I was a boy, twelve years old, when I went to collect half a ton of coal in my cart; most carts would take over one ton.

There was always a spare horse at the foot of the slipway which was harnessed to help up the steepest part of the lane to Blackpost. The barge would stay at the river until it was completely empty, perhaps two or three days.'

'Coal was brought to Noss Mayo and Newton Ferrers by sea. The

Mashford brothers used long poles to propel their coal barge from Plymouth to the quay at Bridgend, not too difficult as the sea is so shallow, and then it was unloaded into big baskets and delivered by horse and cart at the price of two shillings and sixpence.'

'In the early years of the century, mothers and children would spend all day in late summer collecting cones from the pines and fir trees on East Budleigh common. This was for fuel.'

'We used to buy a small stretch of woodland from the Poltimore Estate, usually in Long Wood, to cut down for firewood. This was called coppicing. After cutting down the small trees we used to rip off the bark with a special tool, to be dried and sold to the tanyard. We hired a horse and cart for the day, usually a Saturday, to bring the firewood home, where we sawed it up in the required lengths for our fireplace.'

LIGHT AND ELECTRICITY

'Thinking of years ago, what a difference electricity has made to life. For years I have been so thankful on coming home in the dark to just switch on the light instead of having to find matches and lamps or candles. I had to fill the lamps with paraffin and clean the wicks. They did not give a very good light. They had a shade to throw the light down and were placed on a table, so we sat around the table to see for sewing. There were small lamps as well as candles which we carried to go to bed, or anywhere else. I would shield the light with one hand to go through a doorway as often the draught would blow it out. A lantern was used for outside work. I can't think how we managed to see. The Tilley lamp came later, It had a mantle that lit up when air was pumped into it. It gave a really bright light but could be temperamental. I can also remember using a lantern lit by a candle. It gave a dim light and winter nights seemed very dark with muddy roads to walk along.'

'Our house at Lydford was lit by carbide gas (acetylene). It came out from Coxside, Plymouth in drums, a white stone which was placed in two troughs under a miniature gasometer in the brick-built gas house. Water dripped onto the stone to make gas. The sludgy residue was used to fill in the potholes in the drive and farm lane, and most effective it was, hardening nicely.
   The rooms all had numerous gas mantles, even the conservatory. The sitting room had a chandelier with six jets. Far too hot to light them all, and rather dangerous we felt. Electricity came later, when

the Army requisitioned the Manor Hotel and ran the electricity down across the moor.'

'When I was very young there were no street lights in Sidbury. At night people carried around little iron lanterns with glass sides and each containing a short candle. Our houses were lit with oil lamps and flickering candles.'

'When we moved from Newton Abbot to Dalwood in 1951 we had been used to all main services, but here we had none of them. Electricity was supplied by a huge engine, with a large table covered with 48 batteries which had to be topped up with distilled water every day. When the engine was running the sound was thunderous and made the whole house vibrate so that it felt rather like being on board a large ship. After some years we replaced this engine with a neat little Start-o-Matic, which came on as soon as you turned a switch. We eventually got mains electricity in the late 1950s.'

'Electricity was started in Lynton and Lynmouth on the same day that the Cliff Railway was opened – Easter Monday 1890. It was the second hydro-electric plant in Britain. It was not until 1921 that the water power was supplemented by an oil engine. Lynton and Lynmouth had street lighting before London.

The hydro-electric works were built on the side of the East Lyn river beneath the row of cottages on the left hand side of Watersmeet Road going towards Watersmeet, just before the entrance to the old school building. These were the old electricity cottages built for the electricity workers. Water was pumped up to the top of Summerhouse Hill by a ram which was fed down a leat from about a quarter of a mile up the river. The water was stored at the top of the hill and fed down a three inch pipe to drive the hydro-electric generator. This supply was in operation until 15th August 1952 when it was put out of action by the flood.

It has been questioned why it could not have been brought back into use after the flood, but this would not have been a viable proposition. The demand for electricity had already outstripped the supply in the late 1940s. No further cookers or other high load appliances were allowed to be connected, and all the cookers had to be a special low wattage storage type with a heat retaining cover over the hot plate similar to a Rayburn or Aga cooker. What really sealed the fate of the old plant quite apart from the flood damage, was the fact that like many of the electric supplies in England before they were nationalised, it was a non standard supply. It was 110 volts 100 cycles. There was the odd transformer to boost it to 220

66

volts, but being 100 cycles made it very inefficient. For example, electric motors had to be especially made and they lacked power. A quarter horse-power 100 cycle motor had to be about the size of a two horse-power standard 240 volt 50 cycle motor to do the same work. At the time of the flood the old water turbines were nearly worn out. I remember watching the attendants. One had to be on duty at all times, and he was continuously adjusting the control valve because the governors were so badly worn and the speed of the turbine was constantly fluctuating.

These days of course, one man alone would not be allowed to be left in charge under those conditions, so even if some of the old gear could have been salvaged it was not an economic proposition.'

FOOD AND DRINK

Home-made butter and clotted cream, home-cured bacon and hams, home-made cider – food may have been plainer in the past but we thrived on it. Some old dishes may not have a wide appeal today – such as rook pie or lambs' tails – but nothing was allowed to go to waste when we were almost self sufficient. Of the pig, nothing was left but the squeal!

HAND-MADE BUTTER

'At my home in South Devon in the 1930s we had lots of hens and chickens, an assortment of horses, dogs and cats, and two Guernsey cows, who provided us with wonderful creamy milk.

Some of the milk from each day's milking was put straight into jugs for tea, porridge and the children's mugs but most of it was poured into enamel pans which were left overnight on the cold slate dairy floor. In the morning the pans were placed on top of huge double boilers and gently heated on the kitchen range. The cream rose slowly to the surface, forming a thick yellow crust. Next day this crust would be firm enough to skim off with a perforated metal skimmer, some being put into a dish for eating at once and the rest into a bowl for butter making.

The skim milk left in the enamel pans was used not only for

cooking – we had lots of rice puddings! – but also for making a wet mash for the young chickens. The cats got their share too.

We made butter every three or four days. This was done literally by hand. A big wooden tub was scrubbed, scalded with boiling water and then chilled under the cold tap in the scullery. The butter-maker's hands were also scrubbed, soaked in the hottest possible water and then held under the cold tap. Icy cold it was in winter, as I found out when mother decided I was old enough to be entrusted with butter making.

First I tipped the cream into the tub and stirred it round and round with my hand. It was essential to have the correct speed; too slow and the butter would not "come"; too fast and there was the risk of getting whipped cream which no amount of coaxing would turn into butter.

When the butter started to "come", it was safe to go faster to encourage the buttermilk to separate. This was poured into a bowl to be used later for making scones. Then I ran cold water over the new butter several times to remove any surplus liquid. Some salt was rubbed in and the butter was ready for patting up.

Patting up was done with wooden butter pats. The pats were oblong with fine grooves on the inside to prevent the butter sticking to them. Patting up was fun; one could make square lumps for breakfast, little balls for eating with cheese and biscuits, fancy rolls and whirls for tea parties. I looked on my handiwork with pride.

Nowadays you can buy golden yellow Devon butter in superior dairy shops but I am sure it is not made by hand in a wooden tub with unpasteurised milk. The EEC food safety experts would have conniptions!'

CLOTTED CREAM

'Our cooking was done on a large kitchen range, fuelled by coal. On top of the range stood large pans of milk. The cream, having been allowed to come to the surface overnight, gradually turned into a layer of golden, thick scalded cream – Devonshire cream, now known as clotted cream. When cold, this was skimmed from the surface with a special flat skimmer and piled into large bowls, to be sold to a number of appreciative people.'

'In Devon cream teas, scones seem to have replaced "tuft" cakes. These were made with a bun dough and shaped into rounds the size of a scone. When baked they were split open and filled with cream and jam.'

BUTTER AND MAZARDS

'My mother used to get up at 5.30 am each day and, from a wooden tub, make the butter by hand, patting it into squares. My mother used to enter her butter in the Devon County Show and she also had a stall selling farm produce in the Pannier Market, Barnstaple, for 25 years. During the war she used to make up all the separate butter rations and take them into the Pannier Market, driven by my father in his Chevrolet car, for all her registered customers, who were waiting in queues. We also grew raspberries and strawberries which were taken into Barnstaple shops, and during the war people queued for fruit.

My father used also to buy mazard greens. These were orchards of delicious black cherries, unlike any to be had today. The mazards were taken to Chulmleigh for the fair, with me as a small child sitting in the back of the car and, by the time we reached Chulmleigh, my face was completely black from the juice of the mazards I had eaten on the way. The greens were guarded from dawn every day by men shooting the birds, otherwise they would have eaten the lot!'

ROOK PIE AND LAMBS' TAILS

'Once a year at Sandford there was a rook shoot and my mother would make rook pie. I remember the jelly-like mixture of rook meat with hard boiled eggs under a pastry crust, thick and tasty. Many rooks were boiled first to tenderise their flesh.'

'It was an old custom at Buckland Filleigh on Good Friday to cut off the lambs' tails. This is when my mother in law taught me how to make lambs' tail pie. I made my last one in 1961. We laid the tails on the dairy floor. When ripe we plucked off the wool, then singed them and soaked them overnight in salt and water. We then cut them in small pieces, added bacon and onion, and put them in a pie dish covered in a pastry lid.'

FAVOURITE FOODS

'On Sunday a big joint of beef or leg of lamb was cooked (blade bone of beef was about a penny ha'penny a pound). The dripping was collected and used all the week on toast. Bones were boiled down and the stock used. A big marrow bone was cut up and the marrow taken out and used for suet puddings, the rest boiled and skimmed and the stock used for soup.

Often a big meat pudding was tied up in a cloth and boiled for hours until the men came home, and when it was opened in the centre the juices ran out. Pigs' heads were made into pork pies with hot water crust and slices taken out to the workers in the fields. Brawn was also made from pigs' heads and brains were tied up and boiled in a muslin bag and served on thick wedges of toast. Tongues and trotters made good stews with carrots, potatoes and onions and home-made pease pudding.'

'Kettle broth was made by breaking up bread into small pieces and putting them in a basin with a lump of butter, salt and pepper. Boiling water was poured on and it was left for a minute, then stirred and some milk added. This was always our breakfast in winter.

Lambs' fries were a tasty dish when the lambs were castrated. Toe rag was salted cod, soaked under the running water of the chute all Saturday night and boiled on Sunday morning, and made into a delicious breakfast with a lump of butter. Teddy and Point was roast potatoes with only a small portion of beef in the middle. Our traditional way of cooking beef was to cook it in water, with the potatoes, with flour added at the start (in cold water) to make the gravy.

Saffron cakes and buns were prepared on a Saturday night, then the dough was allowed to rise beside the fire's embers and they were cooked on Sunday morning. Enough pasties were baked on Sundays to last the week. The pastry must not be too short, as they had to withstand being thrown down a mine shaft to the men below in olden times in Mary Tavy. Lickey pie or pasty was leeks and bacon cooked in pastry.'

'As a child, I did not like swede. One day my grandfather said, "You must eat it, it is underground beef." From that day to this, that is what I think of it as.

My grandfather always had a basin of broth for his breakfast made with bread and dripping from the fried bacon plus hot water and seasoning. In his pasty he took to work there was fat bacon and potatoes – that was his choice. He lived to the age of 93.'

'Laver was a chief source of food at Mortehoe and another staple was limpets. When the foundations were dug for the new post office in the late 1920s, thousands of limpet shells were found. Rabbits were trapped and roast rabbit was a treat – a rabbit cost sixpence to buy and the pelt could be sold to the gipsies for threepence.'

'Lots of the women used to take their Sunday dinners to Attwells the bakers in North Tawton to be cooked in their big ovens. We would see them carrying home their white cloth-covered trays and the

aroma was very tempting. The charge was one penny per dinner.
It was also common practice for people to take their fat, fruit and
sugar to the baker. He would supply the necessary dough and make
it into cakes. They were known locally as Cauley Cakes. Each one
was identified by putting a piece of named paper with the fruit etc.
The baker then put this on top of the cake before baking it. One local
lady now in her seventies says she collected her Cauley Cakes from
the baker at five o'clock one night and had her baby at eight o'clock.
We don't know if this was the result of the cakes.'

'During August we would pick blackberries to be made into jam
or wine. My Gran made wine from almost any fruit or vegetable
– potatoes, parsnips, beetroot, oranges, sloes, mangolds, rhubarb,
elder and gooseberry. Her dandelion wine recipe called for four
quarts yellow petals and one gallon of warm water previously boiled.
Stir well and cover with a blanket. Leave the mixture standing for
three days but stir it frequently. Strain off petals and boil the liquor
for half an hour with the addition of the rinds of one lemon and one
orange plus a little ginger. Add three and a half lbs lump sugar to
each gallon plus the flesh of the lemon. When cool ferment with
yeast on toast. Leave it standing a day or two then put into a cask
and in two months bottle it.

In October we would pick sloes, which are best after a frost, and
nuts were gathered and kept for Christmas and acorns for Pig. He
was very fond of those. Hens like dandelion leaves.

In the spring when the fowls were laying well, Gran pickled some
eggs for winter use. About six dozen would be put into a large
earthenware pot. Waterglass was poured in, a saucer put on the top
and they kept perfectly, and were used for cooking during the winter
months for cakes and puddings, when the hens stopped laying.'

GINGER BEER

'Charlie Wylie at Ellacombe, Torquay, made ginger beer for his sweet
shop, as well as nearly all the sweets he sold both in the shop and
from market stalls in Torquay and Dartmouth. The ginger and a
substance called barm, which I sometimes fetched for him from a
nearby brewery, was added to the water in wooden tubs, and slices
of lemon were then floated on top. When the liquid was ready it
was bottled in stoneware bottles. The bottles were stoppered with
corks which were tied down with string. After the ginger beer had
been kept like this for some weeks and the string was cut, the cork
shot out like a bullet from a gun, propelled by the gases which had
generated.'

KILLING THE PIG

'Most families raised a pig that was fed upon scraps of vegetables and small potatoes mixed with meal and "swills", which was often the washing up water, but there was no washing up liquid in those days. Pig-killing day was an event, the poor creature was killed early in the morning and the skin was scraped clean with gallons of boiling water from the boiler that was over the open fire. When the skin was clean the pig was opened and the innards taken out and the carcase was hung up to set overnight.

Nothing was wasted. The meat was cut into joint-size pieces and put into an earthenware round or oval container and covered with a pickling brine and left to cure. For the first week of the curing each piece of the meat was turned daily and when it was ready each piece was wrapped individually in a clean cloth, usually a washed and boiled flour bag, then it was wrapped in newspaper and hung in the chimney to finish drying out and to be smoked. The intestines were taken to the village pump or a stream if there was one nearby and washed until they were clean, then they were left to soak overnight in salted water. They were then washed again and filled with the pig's offal that had been cooked with groats to make hog's puddings. The small intestines were usually strung together to make chitterlings. The hog's puddings were boiled in salted water for approximately 15 minutes and had to be pricked with a large needle to stop the skins from bursting. The pig's bladder was washed and dried then blown up with a bicycle pump to make a football; it was a very strong ball too. The fat belly bacon was often fried or roasted and was much favoured by the hungry family.'

'A couple of pigs were killed each year (at different times) and the ham and bacon was salted in a large salter. A salter could be a large wooden thing big enough to put a whole pig in – made the same way as a barrel, but oval shaped. Smaller salters were made of clay pottery and glazed inside. These had pottery lids. Salting was done with pure salt bought in 28lb blocks from the local coal merchant. A layer of meat, then a layer of salt filled the salters, finishing off with salt. Meat was turned every few days, adding more salt if necessary. Saltpetre was put in around the bone. Another way was to make a brine of salt, brown sugar, saltpetre and sal prunella and water, boiled up together then cooled. The salter was filled with meat, covered with the brine, leaving for a few days. The meat was removed from the brine and the brine then brought to a boil. The meat was then replaced.

After about six to eight weeks hams and bacon were dried off and put into ham bags (large bags made of sturdy cotton). They were hung up on a wooden rack attached to the kitchen ceiling. Pigs were very fat then, so a layer of fat was taken off the side of pork and used as bacon. To get fresh pork all year round neighbours would kill their pigs at different times of year and gave each other a piece of fresh pork.'

HUNGRY DAYS

'School days were hungry days. We would go off having had a plate of boiled rice or a spoonful of fried potato on a slice of bread. School lunch was two sandwiches of beef dripping, bread and jam, syrup or brown sugar mixed with the margarine, and tea. Stew or some other hotpot or soup when we got home, having picked sticks for the fire on our way. We often ate flowers and leaves from the hedgerows, nuts and berries, apples from orchards or a swede from a farmer's field, which we'd hack the skin off with any sharp flint stone we could find, if we were hungry or thirsty.'

CIDER MAKING

'When we made cider at Kingston years ago we used to knock the apples down from the trees and make a heap in the orchard, about four cartloads to the heap. Then we'd take them down in four cartloads and tip them up the top of the pounders. There used to be a horse going round in under, driving the crusher and a man on top would push the apples into the crusher and then they would fall down into the big container, a vat as we used to call it, and would stay there till next day.

The next day we would go down early in the morning, somewhere about three o'clock, and one man would throw out the muck (crushed apples) and Mr King, he used to spread it around, and then he had handfuls of reed to spread on the muck to keep it in place, until you'd emptied the container. Then he used to go round and pull with chains, pulling down the press to press out the cider. He went round turning the press as much as you could do with your hand at first, and then he used to put on a big handle the size of a telegraph pole and that one would really press it down, and went around times and times and times. When he got the muck down really flat the cider would all run out in the big container, and he would have a dipper, a big dipper, and small barrels with a funnel on the top and put it in the barrels. Then someone would come in the morning, whoever's cider it was, and take it away and empty it into casks, they'd be about 50 gallon casks, and he'd bring back the empty ones. Mr King had already screwed down the muck again and taken some more cider and we would gather that and take it back. By that time the next person was coming down in and he'd bring his four cartloads and put them up top, and they would be crushed down ready for next day. It went on like that for about a fortnight – longer than that, from the end of October to nearly Christmas.

Almost every farmer round here had orchards and they were all doing pounding, they were all making their own cider. You reckoned there was about twelve or 14 farmers here, starting off from Torr Down, Clying Mill, Langs, Langston, Palmers', Tom Rogers', Vicarage, and then there was Okenbury, Scobbiscombe and Wonwell and they all used to come round, and Wonwell used to have two or three lots.

The horse used to go round the pounder and we used to go round in a circle with the big wheel up top with notches in it that used to drive the crusher. We had to shovel the apples into the crusher and the crusher would mash them all up. There was only one horse, the poor thing used to come out sweating streams because he was very nervous in the dark. He couldn't go anywhere he could only go round as he had the wall all the way round him. He just had to go in and walk around and round and round until the whole load of apples was put down through the crusher. Sometimes it used to run empty and old Farmer King would shout out "Apples!". That's how cider was made.

They used one horse to break the apples down but they would come with a pair of horses to take the cider away to the farms and for emptying the casks.

We used to nip in and see if we could pinch some of the apples and we used to go in with a hollow wheat reed and suck up the cider through the straw and drink it. We were in there one day, three or four of us, I was lucky, I was out on the end. Farmer King caught two by the scruff of their pants and another between his knees and stuck their heads in the cider. I was lucky being on the outside and ran out of the door.

In 1933 I remember they were pounding the apples and I went in to Farmer King and asked him if I could buy a barrel. That was about 32 gallons and I got it for eleven shillings. I'd been down the Barbican in Plymouth and bought a barrel that had had whisky or something in it and the cider would take the spirits out of the wood. Only thing was, I used to get too many visitors on a Sunday morning! Fresh from the pounder it was very sweet but by the time they'd stored it, it was quite palatable. We used to pour it out in a glass and it was like champagne – sparks used to come up from the bottom of the glass and it was really lovely.'

'Twice each week the local haulier would arrive at the cider cellars in Woodbury and load his barrels from the hogsheads of cider. The barrels were then delivered to a pub four miles away. Sometimes a barrel would be sent back by the landlord with a complaint that it was "ropey". I asked the cellar man if he was going to throw this cider away. "Can't afford to do that," he said, "Come down after tea and I'll show you what we do." So I did.

First he emptied the cider into another barrel. Then he took a long strip of brown paper which had been soaked in sulphur, lit it, put it into the barrel and closed the bung tightly. In about 15 minutes the bung was opened, the paper removed and about a gallon of liquid molasses was poured into the barrel. The cider was then replaced. This barrel was despatched with the other in the next load. When the haulier returned next week, he was asked if the last load had met with the landlord's approval. "Oh yes. The best lot of cider he'd ever had," was the reply.'

SHOPPING AND CALLERS TO THE DOOR

Going to the shops was not such a regular occurrence as it is today, in the times when local traders such as the butcher, the baker and the grocer took orders and delivered to the door. It was a treat to enter the doors of the bigger stores, such as the Co-op, with its well remembered aromas and its concern for the customer's comfort. There were other callers to the door, too, and who did not at some time respond to the Wall's ice cream man's invitation to 'Stop me and buy one'!

GOING TO THE SHOPS

'Mother always bought her groceries at the Co-op in the 1930s, because then she got her "divi". In those days the shop had polished mahogany counters and a marble counter for the dairy produce. Huge blocks of butter were kept on the marble slab and customers were served individually, by dividing off pounds, or quarters, with two butter pats. Sugar, raisins, currants, rice and biscuits were all kept in large tubs and things were scooped and weighed to suit the customer and double wrapped in coloured paper. The biscuit tins were lined up in front of the counter and were tilted with glass tops, so that customers could see the different varieties.'

'Shopping was so different in the 1920s. On Saturdays my mother and I went to Plymouth town. It was about three miles but we usually walked because underneath the station railway bridge there was a "hole in the wall" shop and my mother sometimes bought me a marshmallow bar with the tram fare we saved by walking. We came home by tram with the ordinary less-heavy shopping. The weekly order was always left at Underwoods and a boy with a basket on his bicycle would deliver it later. The first item on the order was always the same – three bags of flour (21 lbs). One bag was made into bread, one into cakes and one into pastry. I made my first pasty when I was about four years old and had to stand on a stool to reach the table. Mother made me crimp and uncrimp the pasty until she was satisfied with the result.'

'To help my mother make ends meet, twice a week in the early 1930s I would take a big basket and wait in a queue with the other boys and girls outside Daw's bread and cake shop in Dartmouth for twopennyworth of stale bread and cakes. Once a week I went to the fruit and vegetable shop for twopennyworth of mixed vegetables. Another day it was to the butcher's for sixpennyworth of meat pieces. My Mum was short of money most of the time. I used to go with her to Dartmouth Guildhall to collect a five shilling voucher to be exchanged for food at a grocery shop. Before you were entitled to a voucher an Inspector would visit your house to see if you had any non-essential items that might be sold to buy food.'

'Because Newtown was a village within the city of Exeter, the shops provided everything for day to day living. The "selling out shop" supplied all manner of groceries and beer and local pensioners also remember three bakers, five hairdressers, two fried fish shops, five grocers, five pubs, a newsagent, a confectioner, a bootmaker, two builders, a house furnisher, a motor engineer, a wireless engineer, dairyman, post office and stationer, a butcher and a painter – and this was just Clifton Road.

Street traders sold watercress, cockles and mussels and wet fish, milk that came in churns that you took your jugs to for filling, etc. One gentleman of note was Taffy Thomas, who sold clothes pegs, saucepans, kettles, candles, matches and penny whistles. He collected jamjars from the children in exchange for sticky sweets. His wooden cart was a familiar sight. When Taffy died his stable was found to be packed solid with the jamjars.'

MARKET DAY

'Each stallholder at Bideford Pannier Market had a permanent position on long back-railed benches, and the large wicker hamper was also a permanent fixture. It was padlocked, and scales and a trestle were kept inside. On arrival with your goods, the trestle was taken out, the hamper lid opened back on to it, and all covered in a snowy white cloth on which the goods were displayed – poultry, vegetables, eggs, cream, butter, bunches of flowers etc. The women wore white waist aprons on top of thick coats, scarves, boots etc as it was always cold and draughty. All the stalls had their regular customers and these "specials" would be privy to a mysterious greaseproof paper-wrapped parcel occasionally. I later discovered this was hog's pudding, much prized by everyone.'

'My father drove the horse and trap to the local market, held every Saturday at Honiton. Mr Muller, a fisherman from Beer, used to walk pushing his loaded hand-cart to Honiton each week. My father always gave him a shilling and he would wrap and send a whopping selection of fish to the Black Lion Hotel to be taken care of by the ostery woman until my father set off for home. He also bought a week's supply of meat from a local butcher, who ran a stall in the main street.'

THE OLD BAKERY

'The family at Lustleigh's Brookfield Bakery didn't quite make the century. In the late 1800s bread was baked in the old faggot oven. Bundles of wood or faggots were put into the oven and burnt to heat it. The bread dough was made by hand, and when it was ready for baking the oven was swept and washed and the dough in 2lb and 4lb sizes was placed on the bottom of the oven, no tins were used. It was delivered by horse and cart.

Life went on the same for years until after the First World War. Things were changed. The old oven was turned into a flour loft, and Russian and Canadian wheatflour was bought to mix with the soft English kind. The new loaf was made and baked in a double-deck coke-fired oven. Double-deck means two doors. Proof loaves went into the top, and squares or under tins in the bottom. Baking with coke gave the bread a unique flavour – folks will tell you that even today. Delivery was now made by a bull nose Morris van.

After the Second World War, I came, married to the son, and we set up home at the bakery and carried on much the same.

A Lister water-cooled petrol engine was used to make the dough. It started at 5 am and if the baker was late so was the postman and a few clayworkers. The exhaust pipe was taken up and out through the roof. When in action it echoed through the valley. It was time to get up or turn over for 20 minutes until it was silent.

The 1950s and 1960s were easier as you could get things to sell. Lyons, Brooke Bond and Twinings all called with tea, St Ivel with cheese, Danish Bacon and Gibbons the wholesale grocers of Newton Abbot. Biscuits were popular; Wrights sold 37 different varieties. Each manufacturer had its own salesman or travellers. Most of them wore black bowler hats, dark suits and carried a rolled black umbrella (proper gentry looking). They went the American way to sell, "Morning Madam, I am here to sell you . . ." Usually by this time I had a customer to serve. Then they would start all over again, parrot fashion. After a few times you got fed up and said, "what be 'e selling, Bye?"

The Brookfield Bakery at Lustleigh in about 1900, soon after the family took over the business. The bakery and general store survived almost a century until competition from supermarkets forced closure.

One thing I do remember well and it was very popular, it was toe rag, dried salted cod. You soaked it overnight, had it next day boiled with vegetables and a few boiled teddies and a drop of brown sauce on it.

Then came the 1970s and 1980s and things got harder. Super-markets came and the little shops went to the wall. Sliced bread came into being and we bought a slicer. The early types were large and heavy. It took both hands to pull up the weights, but by the end of the year I could do it with one hand, I developed muscles in my shoulders and back I never knew I had.

As the saying goes, if you cannot fight them join them. We did and bought the sliced bread from the factory, but we still made our own until 1986 when my husband died. My son, the last of the line, and myself decided to close the business side and live in the house.

Now it is up for sale after 98 years, a great lifetime, and smells of hot crusty bread.'

FOOD TO THE DOOR

'There was little need to go to town from Peters Marland as grocers from Torrington used to send someone out every fortnight to take your order and deliver the following week – dealing with both grocers meant you had delivery each week. Three bakers from adjoining villages came twice every week, which meant you could have one call six days a week if you dealt with them all (one used to get to us quite late on Saturdays, often when it was bathtime for our three evacuees and myself in front of the open kitchen fire!), and three different butchers used to travel round, mainly on a Friday.'

'Branscombe potatoes were brought to Sidford by horse and cart, always very early in the season and a great treat. The fish man would cry "Fish alive-o!" and we would go out with a plate to be filled for sixpence.'

'The baker came round three times a week to West Down. That would be Barnstaple Bakeries and a Mr Howard from Braunton. Butchers came from Braunton and Ilfracombe and groceries were brought to the village by International Stores and India-China, in spite of having a couple of shops in the village.

My father, Jim Brown, would travel round with his horse and waggon with ironmongery, things such as oil (paraffin), soaps, mats, buckets, candles, saucepans, china etc. It would be Lee on Monday, Marwood on Tuesday, West Down on Wednesday, Georgeham and Croyde on Thursday.'

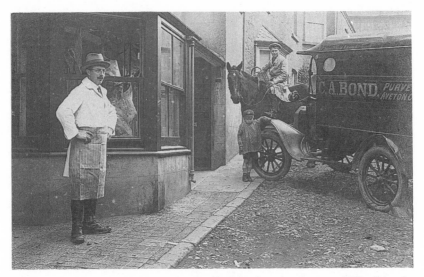

Butcher Bond's new motor van outside his shop in Aveton Gifford in the 1920s. Motorised transport would gradually supersede the delivery boy on horseback, seen here with his basket over his arm.

'Life in our small riverside town in the 1920s was slow and rather sedate. Everyone from the dustman (with his horse and open cart) was addressed as "Mr". Milk was delivered from churns into enamel cans with domed lids, or jugs covered with saucers, and then kept, along with other perishable goods, in a wooden safe with a perforated zinc front. This stood in a shady spot outside the scullery door.

Other dairy products were delivered by donkey and cart by two sisters who "came in" from a neighbouring village. They wore voluminous dark skirts and button boots – rather old fashioned for the post-war era. There was great excitement when they suddenly arrived in an Austin Seven car, which they manhandled to turn round at the end of the road, because the sister who drove had, to quote her words, "not had time to learn to go backwards".

Fish were landed at the slipway by local fishermen and sold at the door in a very fresh state, often jumping from the plate to the floor.

Very few people shut their outer front door, and the glass inner door was opened by turning the handle, so anybody could step inside and announce their arrival. If the outer door was shut, this was taken as a sign that the occupants had "gone to Exeter".'

'In 1939, war broke out and I came to live in Bishops Nympton when I married Wilfred Chanter. Wilfred's dad had decided to part up the bakery business between him and his brother, one in South Molton and one in Bishops Nympton. The bakehouse wasn't a shop – when people wanted bread or cakes, they went right into the bakehouse to buy it. On Sunday they'd cook people's dinners.

Before the war there were two delivery vans taking bread, buns, doughcakes, doughnuts and so on round. There was only one van – or any old car that would go – in the war. When Wilfred was in the army, on Monday and Thursday mornings I went to Eastacott, Mariansleigh, Alswear and on to Meshaw and Middle Ash Moor. I didn't do Rose Ash – that was in the afternoon and Mr Pester did that. On Tuesday and Friday I did the run, through Bish Mill to Abbott's Cross and on to Yeo Mill and back along the main road. On Wednesday and Saturday it was Newtown, Reach, Mornacott, Three Horse Shoes and Aller. We always carried chains for the snow, and there were always two of us. We walked to some farms, or they would sometimes leave a note of what they wanted in a milk churn on the stand at their gate.

I used to do cream by post from here – the dairy was across in next door and the cows had the fields at the top of the village, with a shed up in front of Mr Bramley's house. We'd carry the milk down to the dairy and made clotted here in the kitchen. I sent some for years to Wales. We sold cream and milk only – though my mother had made butter for years on the farm and sold it in South Molton. The milk was sold by the can, no bottles, people came and collected it.'

'I lived in the centre of Bovey Tracey. The man who worked at the Co-op would collect my mother's order. He had a smiling red face and he would sit, his pencil poised and say, "Tea toffo soap starch boo". My sister and I would wait for him to say it, fascinated that he could say it so quickly.'

OTHER CALLERS

'We had a weekly visit at Alverdiscott from a man called George Lewis who got his living by selling small goods from a basket, walking his rounds from Bideford, up and down lanes for many miles. He sold things such as cottons, combs, shoelaces etc in the country, but on his rounds in the town he would sell vegetables and flowers that he had collected from the farms.'

'One of the highlights of the year for Plymtree was the Sixpenny Bazaar – a lorry with slatted sides and top hung with everything you

81

could need; milk cans, enamel jugs, pails, pans, funnels, saucepans, bowls, frying pans, kettles, galvanised iron buckets, bowls, baths, dipping bowls. One could hear it coming along the rough roads from Langford. The scissor/knife grinder came too on a tricycle sort of apparatus, pedalling away to sharpen knives, scissors, shears etc. My grandfather had a hand-operated grinding stone he used to sharpen hooks and knives, shears and sheep shears for villagers, and guess whose "hand" had to do the "operating".

The paper-man on Friday delivered the *Western Times* and the *Devon-Exeter Gazette*. One could hear him coming along too – he used to ring a handbell. He would get a bus to Hele Cross from Exeter and walk to Plymtree and I think Clyst Hydon, delivering papers on the way, working his way round Plymtree back to Cullompton and then back to Exeter by bus. My grandfather was unable to read so each Friday evening my grandmother read the *Western Times* to him – local people being fined for riding bicycles without lights – allowing pigs/dogs/cattle to stray on the roads. These things were big crimes in those days. A column written by Jan Stewer in the Devon dialect was read, also an account of the previous week's hunting by the East Devon Foxhounds.'

'Papers daily were delivered by men on bicycles and Sunday papers by two young men on bicycles from Ottery St Mary. Papers cost about a penny each. All these people sold *The Old Moores Almanack* which no home must be without. This wasn't in book form as it is now, but a real almanack (not a calendar) that was a long continuous piece of paper which opened out from being folded.'

'In the 1920s at Huntsham, Clocky Baker would call round mending clocks. Another man came grinding hooks, shears, knives and scissors etc. Charlie Hutchings the chimney sweep came on a tricycle with his tackle; he liked a drop of paraffin to rinse his mouth afterwards, and he enjoyed his cider, a piece of bread and a ham bone to pick for dinner. Fishy Gillard of Bampton sold fish from his pony and trap as well as newspapers.'

THE CHIP VENDOR

'There was a chip vendor at Torquay in the 1920s, with his hand-propelled vehicle, who was stationed on the slipway of the inner harbour on the Strand most weekend evenings in the summer. He sold very thick chips, sprinkled with coarse salt and vinegar, that had been cooked on a coal-fired heater in a large pan filled with dripping.'

*The 'stop me and buy one' Wall's ice cream man of the 20s and 30s –
his bicycle bell called the faithful to buy his Snofrutes and vanilla bricks!
(Reproduced by kind permission of Wall's Ice Cream.)*

WALL'S ICE CREAM

'Nowadays, if you heard a bicycle bell being rung incessantly in the
road outside, you might think it was just a child being irritating. Not
so in the 1920s and 1930s. Then, it would probably have been the
Wall's "ice cream man" trying to attract custom.

The sound of that bell to me as a child was exciting and wonderful.
Whenever my brothers and I heard it we would stop whatever we
were doing, hurry out of the gate and dash along the road. Out of
breath, we'd reach the friendly, uniformed salesman as he sat on his
tricycle – a big, navy blue affair – and gabble off our orders. Usually
we chose a Snofrute for a penny or a twopenny Brickette. The man
often served you as he sat on the saddle, reaching down into the
big box.

The Wall's trike supported at axle level a big cold box, also navy
blue. This was about two ft six inches long and was not a refrigerator
but contained enough dry ice to keep all the ice cream at the right
temperature.

The Snofrute water-ice was my favourite. And it was cheap. It was
about four inches long and the taste and texture of it were like those

83

of an iced lolly. But it was the shape of a small Toblerone and fitted with an open-ended cardboard cover. You pushed it through with your finger at one end, gradually, and sucked it at the other! There were about half a dozen other types of ice cream you could buy, all more conventional. The largest of these was a large brick which cost one shilling and sixpence.

It must have been the rationing of fats and sugar for about a dozen years during and after the war that caused the trikes to disappear; very sad. But when you think of today's traffic, maybe it's just as well.'

FROM THE CRADLE TO THE GRAVE

We were much more likely to be born, to suffer our illnesses and to die in our own homes in the past. Calling the doctor was for emergencies only in the days when his visits had to be paid for, and most families relied on tried and trusted home remedies to ward off sickness – some of them more appealing than others!

WEDDINGS

'It was quite rare for anyone except the gentry to marry outside the village of Woodbury until the First World War. Some were daring enough to wed someone from a neighbouring village, especially if the girl had been in service here or if there was another branch of the family in the village. After the war we became more mobile and things changed, with quite a lot of new blood coming in. The expansion of the Royal Marine camp at Lympstone meant that Woodbury girls had a bigger choice and often left the village with their new husband. The Second World War again brought great changes, with men bringing "foreign" wives home, and evacuees and land girls marrying into the village.'

'There was a lady in Upottery who made and embroidered many dresses for village weddings. The bride's dress was long and made of silk or velvet and quite often hand embroidered with a tight fitting veil. Bridesmaids wore coloured dresses and hats and carried little posies. The men wore ordinary or dark suits and bowler hats. Rose petals or rice were thrown. There was usually no honeymoon, the couple going straight to their new home or to Mum and Dad's.'

'At Bridestowe a kettle band was played under the window when the couple returned from their honeymoon. This consisted of all kinds of metal objects, tin trays, pans, kettles etc.'

A wedding at Aveton Gifford in 1925. The bridegroom's bowler hat was essential wear at weddings and funerals!

BIRTH AND CHURCHING

'My mother in law had already brought up five children before she herself got married. Her older brother's children were left motherless when the youngest was four months, and the oldest six. She had promised to look after them and did so until the girls left school and were able to keep house for their father. Then and only then did she marry.

My husband was the youngest of three boys and when the youngest child was born – a girl – the men had gone off to work early that morning. His mother was alone with two small boys aged two and a half and four. During the morning she was in pain and knew the baby was on the way. She tried to persuade the little boys to walk to the next farm, but they were too frightened to go. When the men came home for dinner they helped her up to bed and almost at once the baby was born. Then Grandfather had to catch the horse, harness it to the trap and drive about a mile and a half for the District Nurse and bring her back. It was a wonder the baby survived!'

'There was always a spinster lady who would come and stay at the birth and then for two weeks after – she would receive her keep and a pittance.'

'The District Nurse at Woodbury was a godsend. She was a motherly woman with a wonderful calming influence. She went everywhere on a bicycle in all weathers, and we trusted her more than the doctor. Often, girls having their first babies only had old wives tales to go by but the nurse helped a lot. She also delivered the babies at home and came regularly afterwards to see that feeding was going on all right. She lived in the village so was always available in an emergency and would always come. She could "make do" in the humblest home with very little equipment. But she was very strict and insisted on cleanliness and the children were quite in awe of her.'

'Most mothers were churched after the birth of a child and before the christening. This was a community event, as were weddings and funerals. If not invited guests, we would watch from the school lane overlooking the church.'

HOME CURES

'A great remedy, supposed to clear the blood, was brimstone and black treacle (awful stuff). Also, my mother would cut the middle out of a swede, fill the case with brown sugar and leave it to soak – good for colds.'

'Hair was washed in rainwater with coal tar soap and rinsed with vinegar "to help keep the lice away". If you developed a cough your chest was rubbed with goose grease and a sore throat was treated with a "smelly sock" wound round your neck. A stye on the eye was treated by having a gold wedding ring rubbed across it. Boils were very common and treatment very painful. A bottle was filled with hot water. After a while it was emptied and the bottle neck placed over the boil "to draw out the core". Painful but it worked.'

'I remember finding coltsfoot growing in a ditch near our home at Lydford; my grandmother used to make a "magic" soothing ointment, with a lard base, from this plant.'

'The blue bag for bee stings, lemon juice in hot water for a cold, Friar's Balsam breathed in for chesty coughs. The steaming washhouse was considered good for this too. And I remember the tarred fishing nets hanging up to dry on the quayside being considered a good remedy for wheezy chests too.'

'For whooping cough, place the child in a shed with a flock of sheep so that their breath can be inhaled. To stop a wound bleeding, find a large cobweb and wrap it round the wound.'

'My mother used to make elderflower tea for us to drink when we had colds; elderflowers and blackcurrant leaves were picked in the summer and dried on newspaper in the sun. Then they were packed in paper bags and hung in the chimney corner until needed, when a handful was put into a teapot and boiling water added. When it was ready, a spoonful of golden syrup was added and we had to drink it hot and go to bed. We also had blackcurrant tea, which was made with a spoonful of home-made blackcurrant jam and boiling water; this is very good to drink in the night for a sore throat.

One of our neighbours used to make a mixture from dandelion roots for the relief of indigestion. She suffered from ulcers on her legs and to heal them she made an ointment from pennywort leaves and wild violets; I used to help her daughter gather them from the hedges.'

'Mum's cure for sunburn was bathing with new milk, very soothing.'

'My mother sliced raw onions with brown sugar, covered them for a while until the sugar dissolved and gave us this syrup for colds and chesty coughs. Hot farm cider with added ground ginger and sugar taken before going to bed would sweat out a cold.'

'Warts were cured by castor oil or rubbing with the inside of a broad bean pod.'

'Plain flour was used to stop bleeding. It was used on animals too, for instance if a cow knocked its horn off, a bag of plain flour was spread on the wound to stop the bleeding.'

'Soot from the chimney back was used to clean and whiten teeth, or they were brushed with salt.

Snail poultices were used when I had a poisoned leg as a schoolboy and the doctor had given up hope of saving my life. My Gran picked snails and made the poultice, which drew the poison back quickly. I'm nearly 80 now.'

'My grandmother used to go to Mothecombe and on the cliff by Malthouse Point she picked seeds in pods, little black seeds. She dried them for bad eyes; she put one in the eye overnight and by the morning it would be OK. And I have seen her cutting off seaweed that grows on the rocks and slitting the bubbles and saving the oil; it was good for bad legs. You see, all these things are sent for a cause. My granfer said that he suffered from heartburn, as they used to call it, so they tried to find a little pond or water and catch a tiny frog and swallow it. He used to swear by it but I couldn't do it.'

CATCHING THINGS

'At one time, during the First World War, several children in the village were taken ill, including we four sisters. It meant a walk of four miles by someone to get a doctor. He arrived on his pony. We had all got scarlet fever and were ordered to an isolation hospital 15 miles away. Next day we were taken away by horse and cab, a nurse travelling with us. We were very overcrowded with eight children, a stretcher and the nurse inside. Passing the school we saw the teacher and the other children waving to us. After some time the cab stopped, the horse was tethered and the driver and nurse went into a pub, leaving us on our own. The windows got steamed up so my sister opened one of them. The driver was very angry and said we were "letting the germs out". Our stay in hospital lasted seven weeks.'

'I can remember the dread of catching scarlet fever because patients were sent to the isolation hospital. However, I changed my mind when a friend who had straight hair like me, came back from the ordeal with curly hair, having had her hair shaved off while she had the fever.'

'Whilst at school, aged six, I caught ringworm on the head, from a fancy dress costume borrowed from a school friend. It itched badly and was cured eventually by electrical treatment (so-called X-ray). My head was shaved and marked with blue pencil in quarters. I lay on a table, my face covered with velvet and a sheet of lead. I was very frightened by the flashing blue light and the crackling.'

'During the polio scare of the 1950s all children were banned from bathing in the river at Brampford Speke. Some took no heed and one youngster having stripped and spent all day in the river and the sun, feared he had contracted the disease as his skin became so red.'

HOSPITALS

'In 1908 my mother was operated on for appendicitis. She did not go to hospital but had her operation on the kitchen table. About 45 gallons of water was boiled and two doctors and a nurse attended. She was kept in bed for three weeks.

Our hospital in Tavistock was called the cottage hospital, managed and supported by the local people. Once a year there was an Egg Week when the farmers would give ten or twelve dozen eggs to be sold for charity. There was also a scheme called Penny in the Pound where people would pay to the hospital a penny from every pound of their wages, and this entitled them to treatment if they were ill.

Sixty-eight years ago, at the age of five, I had my tonsils out. My mother took me to hospital in a taxi at 8.30 am. I had the tonsils removed and we were fetched by the taxi again at 4 pm. We walked the last half mile home as my mother refused to pay the extra that the driver wanted to take us down the farm lane.'

'Tiverton was our local hospital. Doctors took either private or panel patients. People would come to my father, the local vicar, for a "recommend" worth either one guinea or ten shillings and sixpence, which was paid from the harvest collections or from donations from the local gentry. These recommends were needed if the doctor considered a hospital consultation was necessary.'

'I knew very little about hospitals until the 1940s, when I was married and had a little boy of 18 months who needed a double hernia operation. I was living at Mamhead then in a particularly isolated spot. My son was taken into Dawlish cottage hospital and we had to pay for a surgeon to come out from Exeter to do the operation. The Matron was extremely strict. Crying babies and children were removed from the ward when the specialist was about because everything had to appear perfectly organised. It seems barbaric today, but we were not permitted to visit my son during his stay. That was bad enough, but I still had to wash all the dirty nappies he produced while he was there!'

'My war service ended in 1944 after being sent back from Alexandria (Egypt) with tuberculosis. After four months in Palestine in an Army hospital I finished up in Hawkmoor Sanatorium in Bovey Tracey (my parents lived, still, in Moretonhampstead nearby). The winter of 1944–45 was a rather bleak one. Food was poor and in short supply, the weather was cold and we had few comforts. Books were scarce, newspapers were shared between many of us, no radio and no occupational therapy of any sort. I spent eight months there in a chalet which was open on one side to the elements. It was a very cold winter and our regime was spartan and consisted mainly of bed rest. The lucky ones (I was one) had surgery, an artificial pneumothorax. After weeks of lying flat in bed one was allowed to sit up for a time and also go to the lavatory, great excitement! If one gained weight and one's temperature dropped, gradually the time up increased. We had few visitors as it was a fairly isolated place and transport was extremely difficult at that time. It was a tragic disease as it attacked mainly the young. There was even a children's block which was an enclosed place – mostly they died, as did a large amount of the young women I was with. I finished my treatment eight years later after the birth of my first child.'

DOCTORS AND DENTISTS

'I remember my grandfather having to put a black metal "Dr" sign on the gateway into the post office if the doctor was required for anyone in Sparkwell. The message would go through from the post office and the doctor would call there for the address.'

'Most people paid to see the doctor; if you didn't you were "on the panel" and seen as poor. There was no appointment system, you just went and waited your turn. You could wait for hours. The doctor used to come and see my grandmother frequently and he used to say that many people didn't know they were prescribed alcohol in their dosages. He used to say, "A glass of sherry in the mornings and a tot of brandy with hot milk at night would save me a lot of calls." They were a very brisk breed who came straight to the point.
    Dentists were even more frightening. I had my first tooth out when I was two and a half and I can still remember the large brown

mask that went over your mouth and nose to "put you off". My grandmother had a tooth out at home and I heard her screaming.'

'Dr Ayshford also practised dentistry. When I went to have a tooth pulled, Dr Ayshford told me to hold onto the chair, then he pulled so hard that I and the chair were pulled all round the room.'

'Dunsford Fair has long since passed into history and few people now remember it in all its bustling prime during the years between the wars.

An outstanding feature amongst the many side shows which helped to make up the entertainment side of the fair was a serious dental service. This was in the form of an itinerant black man (probably the only black man parishioners ever saw in their lives), whose stock in trade was a collapsible stool and a formidable pair of forceps.

He was a friendly, persuasive fellow and having set out his stool in the field and started his sales talk, a small crowd would gather, and eventually, after much "I will if you will" talk, some unfortunate sufferer would come forward to the cheers of the crowd. After having indicated the offending molar or molars, the patient sat on the stool, the "dentist" stood behind him (I never saw a woman come forward) and, having persuaded his victim to open his mouth wide, he thrust one hand into his patient's mouth to act as a gag, applied the forceps to the tooth indicated and with a wrench and a pull the offending molar was held aloft to the onlookers. They gave a clap and a cheer to the patient who sat nursing his jaw, but nevertheless feeling proud and relieved.

To anyone who may be wondering why someone suffering from toothache or kindred tortures did not go into Exeter for treatment by a qualified dentist, we have to remember that in those days every able-bodied man worked, and to take a day off for such a minor thing as a toothache, plus the cost of dental treatment, was often out of the question. One had only to wait until early September and Dunsford Fair when the visiting "dentist" would yank it out for only a shilling.'

THE LAST JOURNEY

'My grandfather kept bees. He believed they were part of the family and had to be told all the family news. When my grandmother died, he said to me, "Maid, we must tell the bees mother's gone." So we did.

When someone passed away in the village, the church bell would toll. Everyone rushed to their doors and windows to listen. Three tolls for a man, two for a woman, then the person's age was tolled, everyone silently counting.'

'I had a puzzle one day when I was delivering a large chest of drawers to a Membury farmhouse. There was a choice of two staircases but, although there were several large chests already in the room, it didn't seem possible that they could have been taken up either staircase. After spending some time trying to persuade the chest round the corners of the staircase, and not wishing to give up because the other pieces were in the room and they hadn't been erected in situ, I enquired if there was another entrance to the room. I was then informed that beneath the carpet there existed a large trapdoor, known as a coffin chute, used following an upstairs death to convey the body downstairs in its coffin.'

'When a death occurred it was the custom to lower the blinds in the house, especially as the funeral cortege was passing. As our house was near the churchyard I remember many darkened hours.'

'Until the 1930s there was a Mrs Emmett living in the village and she was the midwife and the layer out of the dead and she was called upon for advice on sickness. Her pay was little and she always wore a man's soft cap and a spotless long starched apron, and she never refused help.

Funerals were at the church and coffins were carried under sling from house to church, all the people walking behind in twos, next of kin being first and then according to nearest relative. Although the undertaker had a lovely bier made of wood and polished and striped, the villagers had a real hate of this and it was hardly used. At one time a man died on the outskirts of the village and the bearers walked, say, half a mile, rested the coffin on the road and sung a verse of a hymn. This they would repeat until they reached the lych gates of the church and at each point of rest four fresh men would do the carrying. On the following Sunday the mourners would again attend church walking in twos to and from the church.'

'Invitations were issued for the funeral, with a thick black edge, and instructions on what to wear on the bottom and sometimes black gloves were sent to the mourners. Horses with black plumes pulled the hearse and this was a sight of great solemnity.'

'Back in my young days, when someone died at home he was not removed to a mortuary but was kept in the house in the coffin until the funeral. This took place usually five days after the death. The family went into deep mourning. If the men did not have a dark suit they would go to the local tailor to be measured for one and it would be ready for the funeral. They would wear bowler hats, which was the usual head dress in those days. The women would wear black for a year and during the second year, maybe, grey or mauve. If people did not have black clothes they wore a black armband on their coats and jackets. This was worn on the left sleeve. Later it was succeeded by a black diamond-shaped patch. While in mourning people did not go to any form of entertainment, such as dances.'

CHILDHOOD &
SCHOOLDAYS

GROWING UP

How much freedom we had as children 40 or more years ago, spending hours away from home quite safely and happily and without our parents worrying at all. Some of us grew up in the country, some on the coast, but all have memories of a childhood in which the sun always seemed to shine – despite knowing that times were often hard for our families.

AT THE STATION HOUSE

'In 1912, when I was five years old, my father, a London and Great Western Railway booking clerk at Richmond, was appointed stationmaster at Bow in Devon at a salary of £80 a year with free house, light and coal. Our furniture must have looked lost in that large, rather gaunt house adjoining the platform and I only clearly remember the warm, semi-basement kitchen. I started school, by train to Crediton and quite a long walk there to the girls high school where I was terrified by all the other children at break times after home life as an only child.

Only 18 months later my father was promoted to Eggesford and my memories of the four years we spent there are clearer and very happy ones. I could still go daily to Crediton where I settled in and made some friends, particularly a girl whose family farm was quite near our station, giving wonderful opportunities to help with haymaking. Our house, again by the platform, looked much more attractive with climbing roses, clematis and wisteria. We quickly got used to the roar of the nearby waterfall and, as my father had to issue the salmon and trout fishing licences and we could provide the odd bed when the Fox and Hounds Inn was full, we often got a share of the catch. There were always gifts of rabbits, game, poultry and, one year, three turkeys at Christmas (two passed on to grateful relatives in Exeter!) and my mother soon learned to pluck and draw to cope with this enormously changed way of living.

The station was very much my play area as our garden was away from the house and so I came in for a bit of spoiling by some of the passengers. The owners of Eggesford House several times sent their carriage for me to spend a day with them and I went home loaded with flowers and soft fruit.

The war made little impact on us beyond the felling of hundreds of nearby conifers to provide poles. All this changed, however, when we moved to Feltham in Middlesex where, although there was no rationing, I remember queueing at the butcher's for a joint.'

GRANNY AND UNCLE JACK

'Uncle Jack was a miller. He owned a cottage with white roses in the front garden and the mill complete with millpond, the leat and the waterwheel. He also kept a few cows and some pigs. I spent many days and nights at Crowden Mill as company for my cousin Olive. We slept in a double bed with an iron bedstead with brass knobs and a deep feather mattress – soft and warm. We played in the stream and under the bridge and in the orchard, knowing every tree. One particular sweet apple, golden in colour, was known to us as "Pig's Snout" because of its shape. The millpond and leat were out of bounds but the slats of the waterwheel, when not working, were used by Granny to cool and set the home-made butter. When she heard Uncle Jack say he was going to start grinding the corn, she would shout to us girls, "Quick maids – go down to the wheel and get my butter."

Granny always dressed in long black skirts, wore a "barras" apron in the morning to do the dirty work then changed into a long white apron. On baking days Uncle Jack would bring in the faggots of wood to heat the cloam oven. When it was hot Granny would scrape out the ashes with a long-handled tool and then in would go the bread loaves, followed by saffron cakes and cutrounds, plate pasties and fruit pies. Finally a large tray of apples from the apple room went in and cooked slowly in the cooling oven and came out whole. The large whitewood kitchen table was a sight to behold and such delicious smells filled the kitchen by the end of the morning. We sat on forms or in the window seat and Uncle Jack sat in the high-backed settle by the open fire. Olive and I had stools to sit on in the hearth and we could look up the chimney and see the sky.

Uncle Jack had to swallow two raw eggs before each meal to "line his stomach" – we watched him and shuddered. I suppose he had an ulcer. He was a kindly man always covered in white dust from the mill and at the end of grinding we were allowed in the mill to ride up into the granary store on the full sacks of flour – Uncle Jack handturning the pulley.

Granny spoilt us by putting sugar in our tea and feeding us slices of bread spread with clotted cream and sprinkled with soft brown sugar – delicious. In the autumn Granny took me blackberry picking – she carried a hooked stick to reach the biggest and best and we walked miles. I've always loved blackberry time and I still follow

Granny's rule – "If they wet your fingers – drap 'em!"'

TAUGHT HOW TO COOK

'At the age of 14, in 1928, I went to live with my great aunt and uncle, Mr and Mrs Fulger in Okehampton. They were Mayor and Mayoress of Okehampton for several years. A very strict Victorian lady, she wore a long black serge skirt and black Victorian silk blouses with scores of press studs or hooks down the front. I remember helping to fasten them up. She wore leg of mutton sleeves.

I was taught how to cook, always to put on a starched white pinafore, and how to set a table properly with the good silver etc. I had to be in bed by eight each night.'

COUNTRY DAYS

'The summer evening after-school days are the ones I linger on, in the "safe out of sight" days. Going for tiddlers with friends, a tuppenny net, a jamjar and a load of optimism. Starting back for home with a jar full, arriving home with half the water, half the tiddlers, and one sock. The other downstream long since, because, of course, I always almost drowned. We blackberried, we gathered windfall apples, more bruised than a schoolboy's knees. We took them home with pride, but we were bramble-scratched and weary and showed our wounds like old soldiers, and cried bitterly at bedtime when our legs were washed.'

'In the 1930s the centre of my universe, when home from boarding school, was the kitchen of our farmhouse.

This room, with its stone floor, had a pump and trough in one corner, our only water supply, a brick-faced copper for the Monday wash in the other, and a large open hearth from which one could glimpse the sky.

The peace of this world was enhanced by the homely sounds of cows mooing and munching in their own-named stalls whilst their milk frothed into the pails, the incessant calling of rooks from the tall elms and the wag-at-the-wall warning to my hard-working mother that yet another meal was needed for her hungry family and farm hands.

Life was fairly spartan with cold linoleum covered floors, a lavatory, with two holes, at the bottom of the garden and oil-filled lamps.

Around these lamps we would gather on winter evenings to play cards, listen to the wireless or to Mother reading from Dickens, Scott, or the more digestible and amusing Jan Stewer. Then it was up to bed by candlelight, a quick brush of teeth from water in the jug and ewer on the marble stand and sleep to the sound of owls.

Summer memories are always of long happy busy days helping in the hay field, leading the horses, stooking the corn or feeding the elevator to make the rick. And everywhere was that delicious smell of dried grass and the sound of bees.

Later as a day girl in my teens I cycled three miles daily to school and in my free time roamed the countryside along with the dogs.

Life has indeed changed!'

A FEW YARDS FROM THE SEA

'I was born at Hope Cove in a cottage just a few yards from the sea. My grandfather and uncle lived next door (in the cottage with the cat on the wall for those of you who know the village now), and in the cottage on the other side of us lived a married uncle and his wife. Opposite, in two thatched cottages lived my mother's uncle, aunt and cousins.

The village was about a third of its present size. Yes, everyone knew everyone else, more or less!

This was the year that the breakwater was built. Mother used to tell me she took me down to the beach every day that summer, it being lovely weather, and watched the work in progress. I have definitely got salt water in my veins! My father was in the Navy, two of my mother's brothers were fishermen, and grandfather had been a fisherman and a seaman, and had travelled as far as Australia and South America, one of the crew of a small trading sailing vessel. I remember Grandfather sitting outside the fishermen's cellars with his binoculars, watching the fishing boats coming and going, and I expect keeping an eye on us children as well as we played on the sands. I was lucky to have two cousins of about the same age as myself and we spent every day on the beach in the school holidays. We hardly went away on holiday – why should we? We had everything we wanted on our doorstep. I used to feel very sorry for the visitors who only had two weeks holiday by the sea – I couldn't imagine living anywhere inland or in a city. There were about ten fishing boats manned by local families, working mainly for lobsters and crabs, and mackerel in the summer. Spider crabs were also caught but were of no use commercially so we often had one of these from one of the uncles. Nowadays I believe spider crabs are exported to France where their delicious sweet meat is more appreciated. The boats were clinker built, and registered SE (Salcombe).

99

The lifeboat was very important, it was a rowing one. What hard work! In the crew were my father, uncles and mother's cousin. I often think what a tragedy it would have been for our family if the lifeboat had capsized. I remember hearing the maroon going off in the night, and my father going out to man the boat.'

BRIXHAM CHILDHOOD

'I grew up in the fishing village of Brixham in the 1920s, spending the first twelve years of my life there.

Although my father was a farmer, his father had owned a trawler and skippered it. My brothers and I were regaled with exploits of his fishing forays in the North Sea. It was fascinating to watch the fish being brought in and unloaded on to the floor of the quay. We never ceased to be excited by the sight of seagulls, which flew in by the hundreds, catching and swallowing large fish whole. The smaller fish would be discarded and then the auctioning would take place. No large co-operatives in those days! All this took place under the watchful eye of William of Orange whose statue was and still is a landmark on the quay in Brixham.

I remember the lovely fish my mother cooked. My grandmother would take a deep, rush bag to the door and a pedlar would fill it to overflowing with choice Dover soles, dabs, plaice, gurnets, ray (or skate) etc; he never weighed them. We were sometimes sent down to the fish quay with the bags. Here a luscious crab could be got for a shilling, which my grandmother cooked by plunging it into boiling water alive, much to our consternation.

On bank holidays or in the school summer holidays we would walk to Broadsands from Higher Brixham where we lived on the farm. In those days the beaches were practically deserted and we spent long, happy hours playing in the seaside pools or picking bucketfuls of winkles which our mother cooked for tea. Mansands was out of bounds to us, being considered far too lonely and desolate.

Another secluded beach we used to play on was called Mudstone. Walking down to it with the warm sand trickling through my bare toes was wonderful. It was sheer bliss if I had been given a penny to buy an ice cream cornet from the rough wooden hut above the sands. We paddled in the sea with our summer frocks tucked into our knickers.

We walked everywhere in those days. No school buses! It was quite a walk to Hillside College in Lower Brixham, the school to which I was sent at the age of six. One memory I have is of standing in the school drive waiting to see the Prince of Wales, later the Duke

100

Brixham children had dancing lessons from Miss Helen Mitchell in the 1920s, and performed for guests at the local big houses.

of Windsor, pass by. We all had little bunches of wild flowers to throw at his car as he drove past. He had been on a visit to the Brixham Seamen's Orphanage where the children of fishermen were cared for should they have been unlucky enough to have lost their fathers at sea.

I also had ballet lessons from Miss Helen Mitchell, reputed to be a former pupil of Pavlova. We entertained in the big houses when there were guests. One of these was Lupton Court, then the family seat of Lord and Lady Churston. Lady Churston had been Denise Orme, a well known actress then. She organised pageants and fetes for charity involving the village children as well as us. Four of us danced in front of Arthur, Duke of Connaught and his daughter. He presented us with boxes of King George V chocolates with his autograph on the lid. We were very proud of these. Another event we danced at was a fete at Greenway House, later the home of Agatha Christie.'

GOING TO THE LANDSLIP

'One of my fondest memories of childhood is of going to the "landslip" to see my granny. She had a cottage in the cliffs between Lyme Regis and Seaton. She made cream teas and at holiday times would get as many as 200 people. They were huge teas with a big

101

piece of white and brown bread, dough cake, slab cake and dishes of butter, cream and jam, all for one shilling and sixpence. It was served beneath the trees on tables made of tree trunks. The family all helped and we had our tea when everyone else had gone.

Water was dipped from a "well" in the garden. It was really a little pool about two feet across, into which water ran down from the cliff. It had to be carefully dipped so as not to disturb the sandy bottom.

As children we liked to go down to the very rocky beach. If visitors were few my aunt would bring tea down to us. When we got older and wanted to swim we would go further along to Charton Bay. Then it was always on Sundays and we took lunch and tea. The water ran down the cliffs and Dad "hid" the kettle for the next time. We loved collecting sticks for the fire to make it boil.

During the war two German prisoners escaped from their camp at Seaton and spent several weeks living in the cliffs. My granny and aunt used to smell their food cooking, but it didn't seem to worry them.'

NEVER THE SAME AGAIN

'My childhood was no doubt the envy of many city children. The youngest of four, I was born in a small terraced house in Ilfracombe. My father was a postman. When I was ten months old we moved to a large guest house overlooking the sea and harbour, with only a sloping field between our house and the sea. It is not surprising that most of my early memories are of the sea in all its various moods, of sheep grazing in the fields, visitors by the score during the summer months and glorious days of haymaking. The farmer had no tractors, only horses and carts. He must have been a very tolerant man, putting up with the capers of many children when it was time to "save" the hay! We were allowed to "help" with making the haystack and our reward was to help eat the food brought by the farmer's wife, and to sample the cider brought in small churn-like cans. One of my own rewards was to ride, bare-backed, one of the horses the three miles to the farm and then to walk home again!

In the "season" our mother seemed always to be busy cooking. Visitors in those days always had three cooked meals a day. Many years went by before any of these visitors realised that there were four children in the house! The criteria was that children should be neither seen nor heard and woe betide any child who made a noise! With the beach and the fields in sight of the house none of this mattered to me. Hours were spent turning over small rocks in pools catching unwary crabs or in searching for tadpoles in a muddy stream. Frogspawn was not a very popular thing to take home! I also loved to climb trees and to explore the stone wall which cut across the top of Hillsborough. The stream has long since been covered in and no farmer saves the hay in those fields. Indeed one of them is now a car park and the other has a go-cart track and pitch and putt course. Not nearly so interesting for an inquisitive youngster!

In summertime life was one long holiday. Winters were different. Our parents had more time for us and hours were spent in front of the fire listening to the wireless, learning to knit or sew. Early evenings could be spent playing with friends in the gaslit streets.

Before my father had a vegetable garden, produce was brought to us by horse and cart from Combe Martin. I can recall milk being delivered that way, too. There would be churns of milk on the cart and this would be served with a ladle into your own jugs. My mother used to take her bucket and shovel to clear up the droppings left by the horses. Marvellous stuff for the geraniums! Sometimes I would be sent to a farm at Hele Bay to collect skimmed milk in a can. It's a wonder the milk ever reached home for I would swing it high over my head and yes! there were times when I was too slow and got drenched with milk and was soundly berated for being so careless!

Servants in hotels and boarding houses came mainly from Wales. The first White Funnel steamer of the season would be crowded with people looking for work and the last steamer of the season took them all back again to Wales. That was a truly wonderful sight with the boat lit up and everyone singing *Land Of My Fathers* in Welsh. I have seen as many as six of these paddle steamers tied up alongside the pier in Ilfracombe.

As we children grew older we had certain chores to do. Helping turn the handle of the wooden-roller mangle was one of them. Another was to scrub down the blue slate flagstones of the back steps and passageway.

With the start of the Second World War many changes took place. No longer did the White Funnel steamers come. My mother's hotel (it had doubled in size by this time) was commandeered by the Army for the Royal Artillery. There were evacuees everywhere and many more hotels were taken over. We were not able to roam the hills and beaches any more and gun emplacements were built. In 1942 I was old enough to join the WAAF as most of my friends had done. Life would never be the same again.'

MY FIRST BIKE

'I had acquired my first bicycle – I had spotted it in a neighbour's porch, negotiated the price (£1) and paid for it with my pocket money over the weeks until it was mine – a Rudgewitworth (Rolls

Royce of bikes) with a black enamelled chain case picked out in gold, and a stand to keep it upright! It also had a very superior bell, or so I thought, and it lasted me until after I was married, when my husband gave it to our German POW much to my annoyance – it is probably going strong now!

Our gear for cycling was shorts or divided skirt when I was younger but in my teens we always wore skirts – no slacks available and jeans were unheard of. Sometimes I borrowed a pair of my brother's flannel trousers but had to creep into the cellar and change on my return as we had a rather strict great-aunt living with us. I can't recall the biblical passage she quoted but I think women in trousers were definitely beyond the pale. I was also warned not to whistle, "A whistling woman and a crowing hen will both come to a bad end!"

In spite of these restrictions I managed to enjoy myself with our Youth Fellowship. We used to pile into one of the little trains and hike or bike around Dartmoor and the surrounding countryside. We took sandwiches and a bottle of lemonade, sometimes popping into a country pub for cider – very daring this, but OK in the country. There was no food in pubs then, except perhaps a tired pork pie so I think things have changed for the better. Our lives were very unsophisticated but we enjoyed life and I count myself lucky to have had such a happy childhood.'

PLAYING ON THE BOMB SITES

'I was born just after the Second World War and I can remember playing on bomb sites. One day there were a group of us playing in the bombed house near the railway line in the Mutley area of Plymouth. Suddenly we heard a noise, looked up, and could see only a pair of black boots and navy trousers. We had been caught by a policeman! After giving us a good talking to he sent us off home with a dire warning about ever going on bomb sites again – somehow we never did.

I can also remember the lamplighter coming round every evening and lighting the gas street lamps. I think this ended in Plymouth in the early 1950s.'

HOW WE LOOKED

Following fashion was not an overriding concern for many of us when young – it was hard enough trying to break free from the Victorian attitudes still imposed by the older generation! For some, of course, hand-me-downs were the only clothes we had as children, but many a mother struggled to put a curl in her little girl's hair and to see her nicely dressed.

FIRST PAIR OF TROUSERS

'I grew up in Silverton in the early years of the century, and boys and girls wore dresses until they could toddle. A first pair of trousers was an event. Christening gowns were handed down in families, and were lavish with lace and trimmings.'

REMEMBER RAG ROLLERS?

'Do you remember rag rollers? When my sister and I were very young, in the 1920s, we had our hair done in ringlets. Mum used to use strips of calico from old pillow-cases, cut in about twelve inch lengths and two inches wide, then, taking a lock of hair, dip a comb in water and comb through. She would then place the strip on the bottom of the hair, fold over and roll up, tying a double knot, to the nape of the neck. We would sleep with ten or twelve of these round our heads. The little fold over, at the bottom of the lock, was like the tissues they use in salons today. I can remember even Dad helping Mum if we were going late to bed. Next morning the rag curlers would be taken out and Mum would comb the locks around her finger, leaving ringlets of hair, and the two front ones would be tied up high with ribbon. We only lived a five minute walk from the school at Stockleigh Pomeroy, so we went home for midday dinner, after which these curls had to be combed again. Many a shout of "whoa" you would hear, as with running and racing about, it would get very tangly.

When we were, perhaps, about nine onwards, we plaited our hair. We used to have bows of ribbon at the bottom of the plaits which were forever falling off, until some little slides with springs that would grip the hair were bought and these would stay on all day, if not pulled too hard.

When my sister was 18, the era of putting up the hair began. Plaited or twisted coils of hair would be made into rounds like chelsea buns, fixed with hidden hair pins two inches or longer, which held the hair in place, either in one or two buns in the nape of the neck, or over the ears like earphones. Sometimes when wearing a hat, it would press the pins into the ears, which wouldn't be very comfortable.'

OLD FASHIONED WAYS

'I was born late 1915, the eldest child of somewhat elderly parents and my childhood was restricted and frustrated by old fashioned ways.

Long after my contemporaries were allowed to wear knee length socks, I still had stockings held up by suspenders attached to a liberty bodice and knickers which buttoned on because elastic at the waist was supposed to be bad for the circulation. When I developed out of this horrible garment I was not permitted a brassiere and girdle like my friends, but was strait-jacketed into a corselette with bones up the front from pelvis to sternum, intended to improve posture and keep the tummy in, but effectively preventing bending for any of the exercises in the school gymnasium. At this time knickers had elastic top and bottom and most girls kept a handkerchief up one leg. A button hook was needed to do up instep-strap shoes.

My grandfather was extremely Victorian and autocratic. Women with short hair were thought to be Jezebels. So while other girls were bobbed and waved, I had my mouse-coloured hair scragged back into a thick pigtail which made my compulsorily worn school hat ride up at the back. The hair ends were periodically singed with a taper which was believed to keep them from splitting.

About 1930 we spent our summer holiday at Looe. By then I had out-developed my simple all-over bathing suit and Mother could only buy a backless one, which would have been anathema to my prudish aunt. So while she watched from the hotel balcony, I would walk into the sea backwards waving to her until the water was deep enough for me to submerge. Then, after swimming, I would surface facing shorewards and come out without admitting the indiscretion. This same aunt was horrified when the Lido was built in Plymouth. She thought it encouraged all sorts of immorality, with couples spread out to sunbathe on the Hoe. I was never allowed to go near the new swimming pool, let alone take a boat past the Lions' Den where the men were allowed to dip in the nude. I had a gooseberry bush version of sex education, with puberty described as a punishment for Eve's sins. For years I thought

106

that further enlightenment was provided by the vicar when newly married couples went into the vestry at the end of the service.

In those days nice little girls did not ask questions about such taboo subjects and were expected to be slavishly obedient. Today's child would not understand the feeling of guilt when I took scissors and removed the bones from my corselette or the courage it needed to refuse to let myself be measured by the Spirella lady for a fully laced and boned adult corset!'

KNICKERS TO MATCH

'I was a child of the 1920s, the "knickers to match" brigade. My mother, as did most mothers, made my dresses, and when buying material always bought with "enough for knickers" in mind. I must have been a disappointment to her in appearance, having a small pale face which she pinched to bring the colour to my cheeks, and hair of the straight mouse variety. She spent hours curling my hair with tongs, which usually finished up with the smell of charred hair and my tresses stuck to the instrument of torture. All her efforts were for naught – I remain to this day with hair of straight mouse. I suppose I looked thinner than I was because my mother indignantly informed others I "undressed well". She fed me regularly on Virol and in my teenage years surely wished she hadn't.'

ALWAYS NICELY DRESSED

'On Sunday evenings in summer in the 1930s we always went for a walk to the park to listen to the band. We wore our Sunday best. I had a mustard coloured pinafore skirt and matching bolero jacket and a white blouse with yellow flowers on it. My sister's outfit was exactly the same except it was dusty pink. We wore white ankle socks, white sandals and white sailor hats.

Although we were quite poor my sister and I were always nicely dressed. We had short straight hair which was always parted in the middle and tied up at either side with ribbons to match our frocks. In the winter we wore brown leather gaiters which came up over our knees and had buttons all the way up the sides, which had to be fastened with a button hook. Sometimes a piece of flesh would get pinched between the button and the button hook. Ouch!

During the Depression when times were hard, a friend of my mother's who had been a tailoress made me a dress from an old skirt. It was dark brown, princess line, with long sleeves. It had a pink satin Peter Pan collar and cuffs. I *hated* that dress, though I realise now that it must have been very smart and beautifully made.

107

One dress I did love was a "Shirley Temple" party dress of white organdie, with a three-layered collar edged with coloured piping, red, green and yellow. I had a book called *Shirley Temple and her dolls*, which I read so often I can still remember it to this day. I can remember being taken to see Shirley Temple in the film *A little princess*.'

CAREFUL!

'We walked to the convent school from Colebrook. When we did sports such as high jumping we had to tuck our skirts into the elastic at the bottom of our long knickers. We were not allowed to do handstands and if we were caught showing our knickers we had the bamboo stick across our legs.'

BOOTS AND CLOGS

'I grew up on a farm at Cotleigh. I remember wearing brown lace-up boots which had been worn by all my three sisters, who were older than me. I also wore wooden clogs as you could have them for the farm without coupons.'

TREATS, GAMES AND CHORES

When outings and parties were few and far between, they became something to remember. Making a little pocket money and having a halfpenny or two to spend at the village sweet shop was also a treat. The games we played varied with the seasons and came around with comforting regularity – though some of the pranks we got up to are perhaps best forgotten! Every child had chores to do at home or at school, accepted as part of life and usually unpaid.

ONCE A YEAR TO CREDITON

'In the 1920s we'd go perhaps once a year to Crediton (five miles away from our home at Colebrook) with my mother. We'd walk down to Yeoford station two miles away and catch the train. After shopping, there would always be a treat. A visit to Labbett's Cafe for a cup of tea and a plate of buns, plain buns, and ham sandwiches. The ham was on the counter with a big glass dome over it. We'd gobble them up.'

FOLLOWING THE LAMPLIGHTER

'I had to walk the two and a half miles home from school in Plymouth, usually with a friend. What we enjoyed was following the lamplighter on his round. He carried a long pole with a shielded light at the top, which he poked into the lamp and lit the gas mantle. I was early home from school on the days we caught up with him, as he scurried along so quickly.'

MY FIRST PARTY

'My first party was on 11th January 1936, when I was nine years old. Dressed in a long pink dress, with matching shoes, my Dad took me two miles on horseback in the pouring rain. Local children had invited their friends and we played games and enjoyed a lovely tea before receiving presents from the tall Christmas tree. On reaching home later, Mum told me I skipped round the room saying, "At tea I sat between Herman and Peter and Peter gave me his paper hat!"'

THE FIRST GRAMOPHONE

'I remember hearing a gramophone for the first time. I was supposed to be sitting but in fact was kneeling on a chair with my ear to the horn. Every so often I felt my hair being pulled. They told me it must have been the man in there. I could never figure out how he got in there, I thought he must be a wizard.'

A HA'PENNY TO SPEND

'When I was about seven, if my friend, Mary, and I had a ha'penny, it was big spending power. We went across the field and down the road to the sweet shop. It was the local shop really, but it was tuned to kids' ha'pennies. All the way, we were working out what we would buy.

Spearmint balls lasted a long time and we had to keep taking them out of our mouths because they changed colour as we sucked. Coconut shreds covered in chocolate powder tasted good. Two everlasting strips, long thin strips of brittle toffee. Palm toffee, banana splits, or raspberry, were all cracked up with a little hammer. A liquorice scout pipe, a pretend smoke, then eaten, stem first. Sweet cigarettes were quite grey by the time we ate them. A bag full of liquorice allsorts, with a special request for some pink coconut rolls. Pontefract cakes, liquorice telephone wires, a bag full of liquorice comfits (a real favourite because the red ones were licked and used as lipsticks). There were sherbet dabs, sherbet fountains, sherbet lemons or satin cushions, raspberry drops, acid drops, dolly mixtures and jelly drops. Such a choice! What would we buy? Aniseed balls were ten for a penny, a bargain if you liked them. Coconut mushrooms were a favourite, or jelly babies (who dared ask for all boys!) Peardrops, or a gobstopper, which was taken out many times to look at because of its many changes of colour. Chewing gum was taken out of the mouth and stretched to see just how far it would go. Love hearts, all had a sentimental motto on them.

This was all window shopping, we still had not decided what we were going to buy. Perhaps we would go to Mrs Hemmings, who made toffee apples on a Thursday afternoon, and we would go and knock on her door and have one of those, all sticky and warm. Maybe we would hear the bell of Cassaluci's ice cream cart. It was painted yellow and pony-drawn. We could have a cornet or a ha'penny yo-yo (a round wafer about the size of a digestive biscuit). It was nearly as much fun to work out what to buy as to actually spend our money!'

PLAYING PRANKS

'In 1922 my family moved from Plymouth to live in Yelverton. My parents bought a large house in Harrowbeer Lane with wonderful views from Cox Tor to Peak Hill.

Our bathroom window looked out onto the back yard and had a convenient flat roof outside the sash window. Here we would take up station with our bicycle pumps and a bucket of water and wait for the first person to come out of the back door.

The railway from Plymouth to Tavistock passed in front of the house and became a feature of our lives. The embankment was a treasurehouse in spring and summer with primroses, marguerites and wild strawberries to pick. There was always an element of adventure as we were never certain when the next train would arrive. A railway signal stood high on the emban'ment and each day a man would walk up the line from Horrab idge station to place an oil lamp to illuminate the signal. My two elder brothers were crack shots with an air rifle and would regularly reak the glass in the lamp – eventually the stationmaster gave up r lacing it. At the time a policeman called when we were out and asked the maid if there were any guns in the house – she showed him a small toy gun and he went away satisfied the culprit was not in our house.'

'When we were children at Kingston we used to do naughty things. My brother was out one night with other boys and he told them to rap-tap our house. They did but he was up in the bedroom with a big jug of water which he poured on their heads. It was a dark night.

Another thing they did was to make a parcel with a long string, hide away and wait for someone to pick it up, pull the string and have a good laugh.

My two sons Harry and John and their friends were in here in the evening before going out to the bonfire on Guy Fawkes night, and one of the boys went into the back kitchen. We used to have a Lidstone range for cooking in those days and when he came out into the front he must have lighted a firework and as he came past he threw it on the range. My goodness, uncle was sitting in the armchair in the corner. It frightened the lot of us, leave alone the soot, we were like Turks. What a laugh it was, but the boys scooted I can tell you.'

'Virtually all the boys in or around our age group had nicknames. Albert was Cuffer, Roger was Iron, Leslie was Louso, George was Ellis and Frank was Teddies; great characters and friends. We were, from time to time, involved in rap-tapping. One thing that always puzzled me was that the local boys usually issued warnings to the intended victims, so if the pin and button were not inserted with the utmost silence, or if you were too close to the wall of the cottage, then a bucket or similar container of liquid would be emptied from an upper window and I don't think it was always clean water.

There was an astonishing piece of faking by Eric Triggs whilst engaged as a golf caddy on Bigbury golf course. Eric announced that he had discovered a daisy and buttercup growing from one stem on the golf course. So cleverly did he do it, that the great discovery went to, I think, a section of the Plymouth Museum and finally to Kew Gardens before the deception was revealed. It did receive press coverage at Plymouth and I think on a national basis.'

GAMES WE PLAYED

'All of us walked to school before the First World War. The boys used to meet up in groups. Everyone had an iron hoop and a bar with a hook on the end (I've still got mine at home now!). We walked and ran along bowling our hoops and guiding them with the bar. When

111

we got to The Honest Heart at the top of Kentisbeare, some of the boys used to let their hoops go rolling down the hill. There was trouble sometimes when a hoop went in through the open door of Miss Miller's shop. If the hoop broke we took it to Mr Moulding, the blacksmith, and he'd mend it.

We also took tops with us we had made out of cotton reels. To spin them we drove a hob (nail) into the hole at the bottom of the reel.'

'Our farm at Uffculme was near the busy A38 and the road took one past what used to be Uffculme Downs – now quarried away. On the Downs were the remains of trenches dug during the First World War and used for volunteer training. We used to play in them and I can remember my father showing us a nightjar's nest there. We caught minnows and later swam in the river Culm.

Everyone wore hats, even to go to the village. On the post office counter there was a moneybox supporting some Missionary Society. It was in the shape of a negro head and bust. The arm was movable and if one put a penny in the outstretched palm it could be transferred to the mouthpiece where it was swallowed.'

'I cannot remember that we were ever bored, either after school or in the holidays. There was always something to do, walks, tree climbing – yes, we were all tom-boys – to mention but two of our youthful activities. Sometimes we – the local lads as well – kindled bonfires in the old quarry at Cheriton Fitzpaine, roasting potatoes and having sing-songs, often being told that we could be heard in the village three quarters of a mile away!'

'Games were mostly played on the streets, pavements or school playground. There was a season and ritual for most games. Bowling hoops in winter, and skipping to rhymes handed on by the older girls in the playground. Tops were gaudily painted. A great excitement of those days in 1920s Moretonhampstead was the writing down of car numbers – six to ten a day was considered good going! The boys played "last across the road", but I remember this was stopped when a little boy got killed.

The enormous bonus of childhood between the wars was the perfect freedom that country children enjoyed. We could walk without adults anywhere – catching tadpoles, primrose picking, climbing trees in the woods and visiting friends on farms miles away.'

'Out of school games at Clayhanger included something called "bumping in the back". Other games were playing shops (with buttons as money) and playing schools, usually with an older sister being the teacher and using a rolled up newspaper to thwack her younger "pupils".'

WIDENING HORIZONS

'In my youth in the 1920s there were few opportunities for youngsters to widen their horizons. In the early 1930s Mr Edward Cave, heir to the baronetcy at Sidbury Manor, started a Scout troop with a Mr Froome as assistant Scoutmaster. A whole new world was opened up for those who became Scouts. The early camps took these boys as far afield as Pershore, Abingdon and Southampton, their transport being one of Mr Len Lockyer's lorries, the cost for two weeks away being ten shillings.

The girls of Sidmouth were able to attend a branch of the Girls Friendly Society, which met once a week in the village hall. The younger girls were known as Candidates, the older ones as Associates. The Rev Prendergast's wife, together with Mrs Mannington and a Miss Morshead, gave much of their time to these girls.'

'My parents were active members of the League of Nations and I vividly remember an entertainment in the local hall (Moreton-hampstead in about 1928) when I was six years old. It was organised to depict the horrors of war. One scene was my father reciting Southey's poem *The Battle of Blenheim*. I was the child who discovered the skull! In another scene I was supposedly dying from poison gas with my mother, while my stage father, complete with First World War gas mask, wept over me. The most memorable scene for me, however, depicted an empty stage with a backcloth of the sea, while below the stage in a cellar was a male voice choir singing *Jesu lover of my soul*; this gradually faded away as the men supposedly died in a submarine. All rather simple things by today's standards but effective.

Most children I knew belonged to the Band of Hope and adults to the White Ribbon Club, supposed to educate us to the horrors of alcohol. I do remember, as a very small child, lying in bed and hearing many drunken brawls in the street, so perhaps it was a necessary crusade.'

'The Ballard swimming pool in Plymouth may not conjure up many thoughts to people who go there to swim but to me and many other pre-war young boys the name Archie Ballard will always be remembered with affection.

Archie was a small hunch-backed man with very few distinguishing features. He was a very rich man, his money it was said, being made during the First World War. He thoroughly disliked females of any age and he particularly hated Lady Astor.

He had a magnificent five-storey boys club built, this being destroyed during the major blitz on Plymouth. One floor of this building was a magnificent gymnasium, another a full-sized cinema and yet another a concert hall.

Boys from the age of ten upwards to 16 could attend the club any night except Sunday and take part in the activities, for which they received a new silver threepenny piece, a large sum of money in an age when wages were about £2 a week. Most nights the gymnasium was used; hundreds of boys supervised by service keep-fit instructors controlling the many activities such as club swinging to music, team games etc. Archie would sit on a carver chair raised on a small stage and watch the proceedings with a very large bag of sixpenny pieces by his side and from time to time would reward one boy or another for effort and the winning team of each game with sixpence each.

Christmas week there would be a special performance of the local pantomime and every boy who was registered would be given a Christmas pudding on one floor, a box of chocolates for his mother on the next floor, and on the next two floors could choose a gift for his parents and sisters and one for himself. Other times when you arrived there would be a showing of the latest film or a special performance of the stage show from the old Palace Theatre and on those nights we would be given sixpence.

In 1937 we all had to sign in a special registration book each time we attended which was a departure from the norm. Then on Coronation Day for King George VI everyone who had made ten appearances or more was given a Westminster bankbook containing £5, a most princely sum. Six months later we all had to bring in our bank books and if you still had the original £5 in it an additional £1 was added to try and persuade people to save.'

DOING THE CHORES

'In the 1930s the children at Molland used to go picking whortleberries and blackberries, which they sold to provide money for buying clothes, and they had nutting expeditions in the autumn.'

'Girls were expected to do numerous chores before and after school – feeding poultry, collecting firewood, laying the "morning sticks" for

114

the first cup of tea, trimming lamps and clearing up after Monday washday, which involved using the precious hot water for washing floors, scrubbing milking stalls, and washing chamber pots. Boys worked equally hard – the thatcher's son at Dunkeswell was up at four o'clock in summer to help thatch ricks. As a young child he was strapped onto the roofs his father was thatching to get him used to heights. The dairy farmer's sons milked, bottled and delivered before they went to school.'

'Life was very hard as a young boy of nine or ten during the First World War. I had to take the milk in 17-gallon churns to the GWR station with a pony and jingle before going to school, having to walk a mile each way. Sometimes my great-uncle would meet me halfway with my lunch.

At about eleven or twelve we had moved to the other side of Tavistock. I had to help with the milking by hand and then go into the field to catch the horse (sometimes taking two of us as he had to be cornered). Then I had to take the milk to meet the dairyman at Drake's Statue by horse and trap, had to put frost nails in the horse's shoes in the winter to get up Crease Lane. Had to take the horse and trap back to Crease Farm and then run back to the grammar school in Plymouth Road, walk home to lunch and back again and home again in the afternoon (one mile each way).

When I lived with my widowed mother and great-uncle, my brother and I (aged eleven and eight) were sent into the fields to cut thistles and stinging nettles with a scythe and I had a small hook on Saturdays. We also had to load manure into the cart and take it into the fields and spread it from small heaps with a fork. We had to take turns in the turning of the chaff-cutter and the turnip slicer, by hand. We also had to turn the mangle on washdays for Mother after she had boiled the clothes in the copper. I left school at 14 to run the farm with my mother.'

'My earliest recollection in the 1930s of doing a chore for my parents is of taking our Sunday roast dinner to the local bakery at South Zeal, where between 20 and 40 roast dinners were cooked in the big bread ovens. The many dishes were pushed to the back of the oven and then retrieved by a long-handled flat wooden spoon. The journey to the bakery was over cobbled pavements. Another chore was to collect the cream dishes from the locals on a Saturday to be filled by my mother so that clotted cream could be delivered for the Sunday treat for tea. Our kitchen had permanent bowls of milk, sometimes four or five at a time, cooling on the stone floor, having been simmered on the oil stove until a firm yellow crust formed. The crust would be skimmed off and the skimmed milk sold for a penny a pint.'

'The girls at Clayhanger all had chores to do. These usually involved bringing in wood for the stoves, drawing water from the well and washing dishes. Some earned money for doing chores for others – blackleading the teacher's stove and cleaning her silver earned two shillings and sixpence in the 1930s.'

'At weekends we had chores to do, without pocket money. I became an expert brass polisher, working away at door handles, letter box, stair rods and clips, fire fenders, poker, shovel, brush and stand, and my grandfather's sword which hung over the door. We picked and bunched flowers to send to London, and also sold them to people from Plymouth when they came on Sundays to visit our Party field where there were donkey rides, swings, seesaws, roundabouts etc. To a lot of people, this was the treat of the year.'

THE BEST YEARS OF OUR LIVES?

Perhaps for some of us they really were the best years – they were certainly different to today's schools. Most children walked long distances to school, in all weathers, and the cane was all too often the threat hanging over the heads of those who were late or who misbehaved in class. Many schools were still 'looked after' by a local benefactor, usually whoever lived at the big house in the village.

GETTING THERE

'My mother, aged 84, recalls walking three miles to Sandford school and three miles home every day, and wearing black boots and an apron – brown boots on Sundays.'

'It was an education living in a cottage on the edge of Whitchurch Down in the mid 1930s. My sister and I at the age of five years, together with about twelve other children who lived in neighbouring farms and cottages, had to walk two and a half to three miles across the moors to the village primary school in Whitchurch. We started out each day at 8.15 am in all weathers. School commenced at 9 am – we really enjoyed school and there were very few absentees. The headmistress recorded in the log book that she noticed that the country children's shoes were always clean and shiny.

When we were very young our mothers accompanied us until we met up with the rest of the country children or until we reached the end of the moors where we met the road leading to the school. If we were at this point and heard the school bell ringing we knew we had five minutes to reach school or we were in trouble for being late. Most times we were in school early hoping that we might be allowed to toll the bell which was in a granite arch on one side of the school roof, but usually the teacher pulled the rope.

There was a variety of wild flowers to be seen, ling and bell heather, gorse and bracken on the high parts and wild orchids, marsh marigolds, meadowsweet, old man's beard and many more in the valley of the Taviton Brook. The moors were stocked with Highland Cattle (long horns and coats), a few Devons owned by the cottagers with common rights and pure Dartmoor ponies. There were a few geese, a small number of sheep, rabbits, hares, but no badgers and a great variety of birds.

I feel very privileged to have lived during the 1930s and to have seen and enjoyed the moors at their best.'

'"Granny, did you really ride to school on a horse in the olden days?" To my city-bred grandchildren for whom horses are simply for recreation, life in Devon 60 years ago seems remote indeed.

I began to learn to ride when I was four. My big sister put me bareback on her pony and told me to hold on tight and follow her as she ran ahead. If I fell off I was told that you had to have a dozen falls – or maybe 20 – before you could ride. As I progressed I was put, still without a saddle, on to an ancient mare called Scotchy who was reputedly 30 years old. The reason for starting to ride bareback was to teach me to grip hard with my knees and not depend on stirrups. Sound advice perhaps but most uncomfortable when trotting on Scotchy who, because of her great age, had a sunken back behind extra high withers.

When I was promoted to a saddle Scotchy and I went up on the down with big sister. She continued my equestrian education by cantering her pony through a maze of gorse bushes. Scotchy followed, twisting and turning to avoid the gorse. I hung on desperately, not wanting to fall off into the prickles.

When we were old enough my younger sister and I used to catch our ponies – Scotchy was no more, thank goodness – in the field, get the worst of the mud off them and give them a few oats. Then we would dash into breakfast, out again, saddle up and off we went, our school satchels swinging on our backs. Through the village at a quick trot, then galloping over the down to the inn where we stabled our ponies. A quick walk across the green and we were just in time for school prayers.'

BEFORE SCHOOL DINNERS

'We used to bake potatoes in the oven for lunch at Filleigh school. We scrubbed them and scratched our names on them. Twice a week, a rice pudding was made and sold to children staying midday to cover the cost.

Tuesdays and Thursdays were soup days. This went well until two senior girls preparing it put in daffodil bulbs instead of onions with the vegetables. Several children were ill and had to be taken home, but we all survived. I wish I had kept the report which was in the newspaper – it was blown up out of proportion but we had a good laugh.'

'We didn't have school lunches in those days at Sparkwell and more often than not I would walk back up Cemetery Hill and meet my Mum who had a walk of three quarters of a mile from Drakeland, and she would have something warm like a pasty or an egg custard. Children living in other directions also went to "meet their dinner" some days of the week.'

BY KIND PERMISSION

'At Sidbury Manor, by kind permission of Lord and Lady Cave, tea was given to the children after the sports at the Manor grounds. It was served on trestle tables in the big stable yards. Children from Sidford village a mile away were collected and returned by two large hay carts, drawn by lovely shire horses, each beautifully groomed, tails and manes plaited and braided in colour, harnesses and horse brasses beautifully polished.'

'The family who owned the mill at Exton lived in a very large house in its own grounds; we never got to know them. We did see Mrs Mallett once a year on Shrove Tuesday when the children of Exwick school went to the house with our teachers. We all marched up the drive, lined with daffodils, and she would be waiting with her maid to present us all with one penny, such riches for children then. But

118

Mr Snow, one of the school governors, could better this. Once a year he came and gave us sixpence each.'

'During the summer at Brampford Speke, some of the boys acted as ball boys for tennis parties at one or other of the large houses in the village. Captain and Mrs Porter provided a Christmas party and tree in the Hall with a gift for every child in the village. The Porters also gave prizes for the best sewing and the best work.'

'My schooldays in the 1930s were spent at Drakes School, East Budleigh and at that time there were three teachers to over a hundred children. Every three years, by kind invitation of Lord and Lady Clinton, we went to Bicton House for tea, games and a Christmas tree, when every child received a present. It only happened every three years as Otterton and Colaton Raleigh also each had a turn.'

AN UNRULY LOT

'We had three teachers at Coldridge at the time of the First World War and they were very strict. If you were caught talking to each other in lessons, the master would give you a good whack in your ear without warning.'

'My brother cut sycamore twigs, cut the skin off and notched a "v" shape and we had lovely whistles. He also used to cut sticks and strip them for canes for the teacher to use – he was often the first to get it too! Cotleigh was a very strict school and we were caned if we were late, though it was a long walk up hills and down again.'

'The headmaster at Stockland caned me once, so the canes went into the coke stove that winter and no one ever knew who did it. He also had a little apple tree. The following year it bore one apple and he used to watch this apple grow, until to his horror one day he found only the core left on the tree! I was a nice lad really.'

'Holcombe Burnell school was built about three quarters of a mile from the village of Longdown, next to the church and the Barton. Of course we had to walk to school in all weathers, through lonely woods. The school had a very large catchment area of about 15 miles. It was a well built brick building, but was very lofty, where all the heat went on a cold day. It was heated by a big combustion stove. The head teacher had her table by this stove and if it was a wet day, her clothes were draped all over the guard, so little warmth, if any, reached the infants who were down at the other end of the room. There was a total of 32 to 35 pupils, of these about twelve were infants and 20 older children. It was distracting, having two blackboards, but I think it was a blessing because we could watch the most interesting one. One distraction during lessons in the summertime was our old friends the hornets, which nested regularly in the school wall. I don't think anyone was ever stung, perhaps due to the fact that one brave boy was given the task of killing them, with the aid of a ruler and compass.

We were a rather unruly lot of children. I remember one girl who used to throw inkwells at the head teacher and those in the way were well splashed with ink, for which we were unfairly punished by our parents. We had gipsies at our school, and on one occasion a gipsy boy was badly treated by the dentist. He came out swearing vengeance, picked up a stone and threw it through the window, missing the dentist, and the stone came out through the front window, breaking another window. This poor boy was cross-eyed so perhaps this saved the dentist's life. This boy and others of his tribe never brought any food with them in the springtime, they lived on birds' eggs, of which there was a large supply up in the church tower where many jackdaws nested.

There were a number of things to distract our attention; the animals on their way to and from the farm, and the days when the Foxhounds met nearby the mistress was quite likely to lose half her class. Another break or distraction was the visit of the parson, as ours was a church school. Whilst he was saying the prayers, with his eyes shut tightly, the children would slope off in ones and twos.

The sanitary conditions were a joke. The water in the pump came out in spurts for about five months of the year and it smelt terrible. I am sure it came from the churchyard. During the dry season we had to fetch water for washing and painting from a stream about 200 yards away. The lavatories were never flushed until choked, and smelt terrible in hot weather. One of our tasks was to go out into the woods and collect leaf-mould for the headmistress's garden. She was afraid of insects and snakes and there was always one or the other to be put in her path. One form of punishment that the teacher adopted, after her cane was burnt, was to send someone out to cut a stick. We used to cut a small notch in it, so after one swipe the stick was useless.'

SCHOOLS BEFORE THE FIRST WORLD WAR

Strict discipline, wet clothes steaming in front of the stove, large classes of all ages and learning by rote – memories of schools at the beginning of the century.

ATHERINGTON SCHOOL

'I was born in the village of Atherington in the year 1907. I started school at four. There were two schools in the village at that time, one controlled by the chapel, the other by the church. I went to the chapel one first, then when a new school was built at Umberleigh, one and a half miles away, it was closed and I went to the church one.

The vicar came once a week for the Scripture lesson. We attended a service in church on special days during the year. We were not allowed inside the door unless our heads were covered. We would tie knots in the corners of our handkerchiefs to wear if we had no hats. About four times a year a Scripture examiner would come and ask us questions, then we would have a half day holiday.

The school ran a Penny Bank, and to every five shillings saved the vicar would add sixpence.

There were two rooms, one big, the other smaller, and three teachers. It was heated with tortoise stoves. The bigger boys would fetch the coal from a shed. In winter we would run a certain distance to warm ourselves but if slippery or snowy we put the desks in the centre of the room then did a hop, skip and jump to keep warm. During the dinner hour we were allowed to push the desks against the wall so that we could arrange sets of eight to dance quadrilles or lancers. There was no music, we used to sing la-la to the tune required. Girls always had two afternoons a week for needlework. We made our clothes, always white aprons. The school provided the material, we paid for the finished article. The first lesson was run and fell, followed by feather stitching, French knots, crochet, embroidery and drawn thread work.

We wore black knitted stockings. During the First World War boxes of wool skeins arrived and certain lessons were stopped to wind the wool in balls and knit socks for the soldiers.

A very special day was 24th May, Empire Day, when we wore sashes representing the Empire, parading the village with Britannia in the centre. We also used to go to the village square the days when the foxhounds met there, and learnt many of their names.

A school attendance officer came once a week in his pony and trap. Anyone missing, he would visit their home to know the reason why.'

STARTING IN THE INFANTS CLASS

'I started school at Elburton aged three years and ten months, in September 1912. There was one trained certificated mistress and one r· onitress with no training, working in one large square room with high windows in three walls (no outlook). Heating was by open fire from 1st November to 1st April. There was a gallery of backless wooden forms for new entrants, iron-framed desks seating five or six pupils. Slates and slate pencils were used by all, with a damp sponge for cleaning the slates.

The day for the infants was from nine o'clock to noon, with a break at 10.45, and from two o'clock to four with another break at 2.45. At five to eight the bell rang and pupils assembled in the playground, entered through the door marked "Infants", hung their coats on a peg in the corridor and marched into school. At nine was morning assembly with a hymn and prayers. Registration was very important – a teacher could be dismissed for errors in the register.

Number tables were chanted in unison led by the teacher. For reading the class stood in a semi circle, toes to a chalk line, and read off a wall chart. Each page showed similarly spelt words illustrated by a coloured picture; C-A-T spells cat, B-A-T spells bat etc. Each line was repeated at least three times. Writing was done in longhand on slates – down strokes thin, up strokes thick, and the pencil was not lifted until the stroke was complete.

For drill we stood by our seat. The joints were exercised as we chanted "Wrist joints, elbow joints, neck joints, knee joints . . ."

In singing, a wallchart showed the scale in tonic-sol-fa. We sang it up and down from doh to doh. The mistress struck her tuning fork on the desk and gave us the note for doh (there was no piano). We sang the alphabet – "Come little children and listen to me, and I will teach you the ABC" and nursery rhymes.

The last lesson in the afternoon the monitress read stories to us, such as *Dick and his donkey* or *How Jim went fishing*. There were no books for the class.'

LUCKY TO HAVE BUCKETS

'We were lucky to have buckets at Down St Mary school, as these were only installed about 1900 after much arguing between the church school heads and the school managers. Before that it was "holes" and two shillings and sixpence per quarter was paid to caretaker Mrs Brookland to add earth or ashes and empty them twice a week. This was for the girls – the boys had galvanised iron to wee against.

In 1903 the teacher was paid £65 per annum and the assistant £20. The cleaner and caretaker's salary was fixed at £4 10s 0d a year and this would include lighting the fire weekdays and on Sundays for the Sunday school and scrubbing the floor four times a year. In 1895 the children had had to sweep the school themselves and light the fires when they arrived, often wet and cold.

In 1906 it was stated that a brother and sister, John and Annie, were "not fitted" to receive instruction at the school. They were declared deaf and dumb and a hindrance to the other children.

My 86 year old aunt remembers going to the same school wearing my Dad's boots when they were too small for him. She wore mostly long dark clothes to keep out the cold and an apron to keep them clean.'

THROWLEIGH AND GIDLEIGH BOARD SCHOOL

'I started school in 1914, immediately after my fifth birthday on 17th February, not waiting for the beginning of a term. This small rural school, opened in 1877, was then called Throwleigh and Gidleigh Board School and had two classrooms for children five to 14 years. The school was situated exactly one and a quarter miles from Throwleigh and Gidleigh villages and the hamlet of Murchington. This meant that most children had a long walk to school in all weathers, wearing hobnailed boots as the roads were just covered with granite stones. There was great excitement, periodically, when the stone-cutter came to cut up the heaps of granite boulders, already brought there and left tidily in heaps (like potato clamps) along the side of the roads, these "wide places" forming lay-bys today for our cars. We children, of course, had great pleasure climbing over these and sliding down to the detriment of the tidy rows and of our hobnailed boots.

Then came the time when workmen came to spread these stones, the water-cart to wet them and the steamroller to roll them in, and for us to be sent to the village blacksmith to have the metal toe-protectors (scutes) and nails on the soles of our boots replaced.

Because of the distance from home this meant, of course, that we had to take packed lunches, and in the summer, bottles of cold tea. There were taps and running water for the wash-hand basins in each lobby but this was from a *very* large rainwater tank, augmented by water pumped by the caretaker from a well which supplied excellent pure water. Drinking water had to be fetched from the "pump house" and kept in enamel jugs – cold tea in our own satchels was more easily available when jugs became empty or someone had failed to fill them as the pump house was always locked and out of bounds.

Hot cocoa was made for us in the winter. The water was warmed in a large iron kettle (I have it now and it has been frequently used for picnics on our lovely moor, by my friends and their offspring of two generations). This kettle was perched precariously on an open grate to boil and the cocoa was made and distributed by the older girls (13–14 years) before both members of the staff left us unattended to go home for their own lunch. (One walked a mile each way.) This lack of supervision during the hour and a half lunch break continued until 1930 when a new infants teacher was appointed and I became the head teacher.

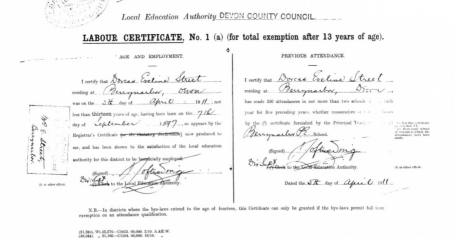

Dorcas Street of Berrynarbor, aged 13, needed this Labour Certificate in 1911 to enable her to legally find work. The teacher had to confirm that she had attended a certain number of days at school.

What fun we had walking to school in those days in spring, popping the seedheads of stitchwort and eating the tangy young leaves of sorrel dock. And don't forget the feasts of "bread and cheese" – the white flowers and young green leaves of wood sorrel. Also bird-nesting, naughtily knocking the heads off foxgloves, and inflicting our presence on the workmen in the fields – haymaking, harvesting the stooks of corn or planting and lifting potatoes – and pinching and eating raw turnips!

I wondered why a "John Bull" type retired farmer, with his little Pekinese walking in front of him (just under his tummy) was always at the top of the school hill as we left each evening. He ambled along the road, gently swinging his cane and muttering, "Nasty little children, horrible little children." When I returned as head teacher in 1930, I had the answer. He was protecting the many seedlings he had planted in the hedges and adjoining fields – horse chestnuts (still there), scots pine, copper beech, laburnum and four lovely Lombardy poplars. These, alas, disappeared after the 1947 winter. He also had flowers to protect, for he had planted a horse chestnut in the middle of a T-junction to commemorate Queen Victoria's Golden Jubilee and had planted a garden around it, protected by a wooden fence. The tree is still there but the surrounding area provides a good turning point for cars today.'

WHATEVER CAME TO HAND

'At Dalwood the master and mistress were a Mr and Mrs Bennett. We had to obey orders. Mrs Bennett would throw whatever she had in her hand, usually the block of wood with thick felt on one side used to clean the blackboard. It would hit very hard. Mr Bennett used the cane. He used it on my sister's hand. She was left handed and was told she had to use her right hand but she couldn't so she had the cane. It cut her hand, making a mess on her exercise book, and there was a storm about that.'

SCHOOL AT DARTMOUTH

'At the age of six I started at a little dame school in Dartmouth – I had had to wait until my sister was five and we could walk the two miles each way together. Besides reading and writing (starting with pothooks), I can remember hating sums, loving history and geography and fainting when we were told about the circulation of the blood. Every morning we had to show our hands and nails and a clean hankie, and were given marks to enter in our Toilet Book. We soon learned to have two hankies, "one to show and one to blow".

Children at West Buckland school in 1914. Village schools coped with children of all ages, from as young as three to those about to leave school at 13 or 14.

Then when I was ten a grammar school was opened in Dartmouth and off I went. There were never more than 80 pupils during the seven years I was there, and only five members of staff. By today's standards it was pitiful, but how happy I was. When I was 17 I went to university thanks to the grounding I was given.

Our school uniform consisted of the usual navy blue gym tunic, with a white blouse, over thick navy brushed cotton bloomers and black woollen stockings. In summer we wore blue dresses with white collars and cuffs – and always the inevitable liberty bodice.

The school had a tennis court used for netball – for tennis we went down to the municipal courts in Duke Street. Hockey entailed a very long and steep walk to the top of Jawbone Hill – it's a wonder we had the energy to play! Swimming involved another long walk to Castle Cove at the mouth of the river. There wasn't a prouder girl in southern England than me on the day I received my "Colours" for tennis, hockey, netball and swimming!'

SCHOOLDAYS INTO THE 1950s

The next generation of children would have seen very little change in the schools since their parents and grandparents attended. It was not until the 1950s, and then only slowly, that schools began to move into the 'modern' world. However, many a Devon child has good cause to thank the teachers of those years for the education they received.

PRIVATE SCHOOL AT PLYMOUTH

'I was at private school in Plymouth from 1920 to 1933, and strange as it may seem, they were among the happiest years of my life.

The school was run by nuns from the convent of St Mary the Virgin, at Wantage, and was Anglo-Catholic, but religion was never made the be all and end all of our lives.

Discipline was good and uniform had to be worn – gym tunic and white blouse, with "navy sleeves" worn separately to protect the cuffs. Thick woollen stockings were worn, winter *and* summer, and the memories of playing a heated game of tennis on a hot summer's afternoon lives with me still! The sisters were dears – and as we grew older, we realised that there was a great sense of humour among them. Saints' Days were always recognised, with a service in St Peter's church, and in Lent we went to church every Wednesday morning. We had our own chapel at school for various religious classes.

In those days heating was minimal and we all suffered from chilblains, but somehow managed to run and jump at playtime without a thought for our fingers and toes. At break-time there was always a stall where you could get a bun and a cup of cocoa (a halfpenny each) or if you could afford it, you could go to the sweet stall, where, for twopence, you could buy a marvellous selection of goodies. One of these was a cushion of hard, sweet, very pink crisp, in a coating of chocolate – which I have never seen anywhere else, in spite of trying to find one for years!

The only thing wrong with the school, to my mind, was the fact that we were not allowed to go to the "pictures" in term time, and to such a cinema fan as I was this was punishment indeed, as all the films I wanted to see came in term time, or so it seemed.'

CALLED BY THE BELL

'In the 1920s at Stoke Canon we were called to school by the school bell; the time was told by the church clock and the paper mill hooter, no one I knew at that time possessed a watch.'

THE DALTON PLAN

'Our headmistress at the all girls school in Cambridge Road, Ford, had been to America and had brought back a system of teaching called the Dalton Plan. We were all given a card divided into four weekly sections and headed with each subject. The school bell rang at nine in the morning and we went into whichever class we wanted, where we worked until break time; we then left the work we had done to be marked and our card was crossed off for the amount done. We had what were called "assignments" for each subject, and the whole assignment had to be completed each month, the card was then signed by the teacher. When the whole card was completed it was taken to the headmistress for a new one. If we had taken more than a month to complete the card, it meant a telling off. I really enjoyed my time at that school and left at the age of 15.'

SCHOOL AT ILFRACOMBE

'St Philip's and St James's school was mixed, with about 35–40 pupils in a class. Classes had the same teacher for all subjects, except when woodwork or domestic science etc were involved. The headmaster took his own mixed class, his desk in the classroom serving as his office. This being a C of E school, the day's work included Scripture, and the Vicar of Ilfracombe came in once a week to enlighten us. There would always be a lady teacher who could play the piano for morning prayers and hymns. There were six classes, designated Standard 1 to 6. Once a year, in September, all the classes would move up a room, leaving the teacher behind to cope with the next lot. Everyone in Class 6 would leave to make their way in the outside world.

School started each day promptly at 9 am and finished at 4.15 pm. There was a break of two hours for dinner, twelve noon till two. No school dinners in those days, everyone went home, except the country children and they brought sandwiches. A hot Horlicks drink made with water was available at the mid-morning break for those who wanted it, at one shilling per week.

The annual prizegiving day was held at the Scala Cinema, when books were given out to those who deserved them, and sometimes, in our eyes, to those who didn't, all preceded by a suitable selection of songs for the benefit of parents and big-wigs. Before returning to school in the New Year, there would be a special treat for the children of both schools. This was an afternoon at the pictures, showing a Laurel and Hardy plus a cowboy film, with perhaps an ever popular Popeye. Then we would all march in a long column accompanied by Father Christmas to the Alexandra Hall for buns and jam and cream and things all set out on a battery of long trestle tables, each table presided over at one end by a stern "I want no nonsense from you lot" lady complete with pinny and hat, who would dispense tea from a shiny brass and copper urn. Following the tea and cracker pulling, there would be entertainment from the stage by local talent, perhaps some community singing, then off home clutching a paper bag containing an apple, orange and a bar of Fry's chocolate, usually eaten before you got there. I do not know who paid for all this, maybe a town fund of some kind.

School holidays never seemed to come soon enough, especially the four weeks off in August. Apart from a week at camp with the Scouts, all our time was spent on the beach. When the sun shone you could earn a few coppers by helping people to carry hired deck-chairs to a sunny spot and set them up. Then spend same at the beach kiosk on a tube of wine-gums, hoping to get lots of black ones! There would be fishing in the rock pools for "bullheads" with chopped up limpets for bait. The catch (if any) carried home in a jam jar, were always dead by next morning and consigned to the dustbin. Another cash earner was the retrieval of tennis balls knocked over the high-wire of the nearby courts by enthusiastic players. On Saturdays there were the trains and paddle steamers to meet with your barrow, on the lookout for people struggling with luggage you could help them with. Games of cricket took place in Rapparee Field using tennis balls which somehow had been "lost", and at haymaking time we were always there to assist by getting in the way. The carefully built stack of hay in the corner of the field didn't stay that way very long. Ideal for attacking and defending, you see. We were ever on the look-out for the Pleasure Ground Constable, who seemed always to appear on the scene when we were enjoying whatever we happened to be doing. Just the sight of his tall figure approaching and we scattered.

There were the "lovers" to spy on in the long grass and bushes of Hillsborough, cigarette cards to collect and swap. We would help the local boatmen with their craft and perhaps be taken out for a trip, find ways and means of getting onto the pier without paying, play marbles and conkers, and fetch seaweed from the beaches for fertilising the family allotment, all in their proper season, of course. So much to do.'

THE COMING OF WAR

'Were they the "good old days"? I think they were. In the 1930s walking to school as I did along the country lane from Watcombe to St Marychurch, I remember the quiet serenity. Watching the farmers ploughing with the horse, and seeing them layer hedges, hardly disturbing the nesting birds and other wildlife. I remember the spring flowers along the hedgerows, cowslips in abundance. No fear of speeding cars and unsavoury characters.

I attended the small church school at St Marychurch. Teachers were respected whether inside or out of school. Whenever we saw a teacher outside of school the girls would have to curtsey and the boys touch their caps and woe betide anyone who did not do this. At senior level, wearing a school uniform was a privilege – it meant something and we were proud of it.

At the outbreak of war, all the windows of our school were covered with a mesh for fear of shattering glass if there was an air raid. Sadly there was a lightning aircraft attack one Sunday and the church was hit with the loss of many lives.

My first job was as secretary to the Medical Officer of Health at St Marychurch. I visited the school clinics with him distributing orange juice and cod liver oil to help against lack of vitamins in diets. Scabies and dermatitis were very prevalent with the children at that time.'

'When I started school at Awliscombe most of the boys and girls were still wearing boots and the girls wore aprons. I rebelled and would not wear boots or an apron, something I am constantly being reminded of by my eldest sister.

We learnt to write with trays of sand, and also to know our ABC and numbers without paper and pencils (much cheaper). We spread a thin layer of sand in individual trays and then formed the letters in the sand with our forefinger. After the teacher had inspected them we gave the tray a shake and started all over again. Our infants teacher was very athletic and we spent a lot of time on PE and games. During the summer we competed at Honiton Sports Day and one year we won the shield and were presented with a complete full-sized cricket set. Each summer after that it was always cricket in one of Mr Pring's fields, with girls and boys taking part.

I remember very well the day war broke out in 1939. We were at home and had to be very quiet while our parents listened to the wireless. From then on we had to remember to take our gas masks

130

with us wherever we went. At school we had regular gas mask drill and I can still remember the smell of those masks!

Each school was allocated drinking chocolate to supplement rations. We had a large cup of cocoa each which had been made in a huge saucepan of milk heated on the large black heater that heated the school. During school holidays we were encouraged to make large camouflage nets to cover army lorries. We had to cut and thread strips of khaki, green and brown hessian into the nets. During the summer and autumn we picked hips from wild and garden rose bushes to make rose hip syrup. This was rich in Vitamin C and distributed to mothers with babies and young children. We were paid a small amount for all the hips picked.

At school we learnt reading, writing and arithmetic but very little else. These subjects were learnt mainly by the whole class taking part. We had lots of mental arithmetic instead of using pens and paper. We had to work things out in our head. We also chanted our times-tables until we knew them by heart. The same with spelling. We were asked at random to spell a certain word. I don't remember whether paper was rationed or if it was easier for the teacher, so that she didn't have many books to mark.

The girls were all encouraged to knit and sew during handiwork lessons. In fact many of us remember knitting one teacher's underwear! We used very small needles and very fine, soft Vyella wool with a silky thread in it, in pastel shades. Her vest and pants were all in pattern and shaped. They must have been very warm and comfortable to wear. We were encouraged to knit whilst she read stories to us – she knitted too.

The boys learnt gardening in the school garden, and I think they had to do the teacher's garden as well. Much of the time the boys were left on their own. The garden was not very close to the school and I think a lot of the farmers' apples went missing as well as the boys. One boy usually kept watch and whistled if they thought the teacher was coming.'

'During the war they kept the schools open in the summer holidays because fathers were away and mothers working in the factories so a lot of children had no one to look after them during the day. We didn't do any lessons, but had a wonderful time acting little plays, being read to and making things. I remember I made myself some slippers in blue material with yellow cross stitch embroidery on the front. I was about eight years old at that time.

To begin with we always used to take a tin of "iron rations" to school in case there was an air raid and we couldn't get home for a meal. But every day, when there hadn't been a raid, we would eat the iron rations on the way home. So the mothers soon got fed up with that lark.

We saved every scrap of waste paper at school. At the end of each day it was my job to take the waste paper bin from our classroom and empty the contents into a big sack in the cloakroom. I also had the privilege of collecting the headmistress's waste paper bin too. I liked this job because it got me out of the prayers which we always said at the end of each day.

Our favourite game in the playground was a skipping game with two "enders" turning the rope. Everyone else stood in a line and took it in turns to run into the rope, skip four times and out again, to the chant of "Up the Mississippi, if you miss a beat you're out". This game would go on non-stop for the entire playtime, day after day, week after week. We also played a very complicated ball game, bouncing the ball against a wall and doing various actions, always with a rhyme to go with it. We never played whip and top in the playground, though we did play it in the street at home, there being no cars in those days. I can remember the very first person in our street to get a car, after the war. We thought they were *very* rich!'

STILL NO MOD CONS

'In 1950 Goodleigh school had very few of the mod cons that are taken for granted nowadays. There was no mains water, so no flush toilets only the bucket variety, which were very smelly, particularly in summer. Water for drinking had to be fetched each day from the village well. The bigger boys took it in turns to take the water bucket down, and then carry it back up the hill between them.

One hot July afternoon one of His Majesty's Inspectors arrived. The headmistress, Miss Claye, asked him if there was anything she could get him. "I should love a glass of water," was the reply. "I'm afraid that is the one thing I can't give you," Miss Claye said, "but I'll send the boys down to the well." Off went two of the boys with the bucket, and in due course the thirsty HMI got his drink of water.

The other mod con that hadn't reached Goodleigh in 1950 was electricity. This meant that on a dark winter's afternoon activities such as reading and writing had to come to a halt well before home-time. The art of story-telling (as opposed to story-reading) came into its own. I have happy memories of many a winter's afternoon sitting round the fire (yes – a real fire!) for a long session of stories, poems and songs.

The most magical time was Christmas, when we had our concert. The infants end of the school was transformed, with a real stage. The performance was in the evening, so that all relations and friends

Stoke Canon primary school pupils in 1951. Many schools were still without basic facilities, but changes were in the air at last.

could attend. Miss Claye and I arrived first, and the school was, of course, in pitch darkness. Then, one by one, the families began to arrive, each father with his storm lantern, which he hung on one of the waiting nails on the schoolroom wall. By the time everyone had arrived the whole room was glittering with the lights of all the lanterns.

But at last the day came – sad or happy, I'm not sure which – when electricity came to Goodleigh. Miss Claye decided that we should have a little ceremony to mark the occasion. She chose Jimmy Balsdon, the youngest child in the school, to switch on the first light. It was the one in the entrance porch, and the switch was high up out of Jimmy's reach, so I had to lift him up. A little nervously he pressed the switch down. Then, for the first time in his life he saw electric light. He looked down at me, his face shining with delight, "Tez like moonshine, Miss."'

THE WORLD OF WORK

Little
Torrington

ON THE LAND

Farming has always been one of Devon's most important 'industries', but how it has changed over the last 50 years. Mechanisation has replaced the horse and in many cases the labourer as well, while even the cows in the fields have undergone a change in breed!

THE FARMER AND HIS WIFE

'Farmers carried on the traditions of their forebears and there was very little change until the tractor began to replace the horse. A few cows were kept and milked by hand, the milker wearing a coarse apron made from sacking and an old cap, whilst sitting on a three-legged stool with his head resting on the cow's warm side and the bucket held between his legs. It was not unusual for two or three people to do the milking, even when there were only ten or twelve cows. The farmer, his wife and children would all be involved. Someone would feed the calves or walk the cows in from the fields. There was seldom anyone passing on the roads then and a dawdle along the lane allowed the cows an extra feed, but woe betide you if you had let the cows eat the ramsey (wild garlic) as it would taint the milk and no one would want to buy your butter or cream.

In the winter there were the turnips and mangels to be taken round and put in all the feed mangers. These were carried round in "mauns" (large wicker two-handled baskets) and the hay to be carried round was kept in the barn above the cowshed and thrown down the hatchways. The cows were kept tied up with chains round their necks, in stout wooden stalls with plenty of straw bedding (or on Dartmoor, bracken would be used), so they would be comfortable all night and contentedly chew their cud. Next morning, after milking, there would be a lot of cleaning out to do, all by hand with a fork (eavil). The milk was used for feeding the calves, and the rest brought indoors for the women to separate and when the cream was cold, to make into butter. The whey was used to feed the pigs, as well as any household scraps or potato peelings.

Home-grown oats and barley were ground with an engine to work the mill and used for feed for all the animals, including the fowls (never called chickens then, that was only for babies). They were shut in at night and let out to roam in the morning; there was always a cock with them, so there was a lot of crowing and cackling. As

136

soon as they were let out they rushed off to the hedges to their own special place to lay. Whenever we heard a hen cackling we had to try and locate the nests as magpies were usually keeping an eye for a fresh egg. Sometimes the fox would take both hen and eggs and sometimes we would get a pleasant surprise when we thought a lost hen had been taken by a fox, she suddenly appeared with a lovely brood of chicks. They would have to be caught and put in a coop with a wire run, otherwise the chicks would not last for long.

Although women worked hard and often alongside their husbands, there were many things that the men kept them away from. If there was a bad calving, women were sent indoors, or to fetch another farmer to help. With pig killing a local pig-killer would come to do the job. Rabbit was another fresh meat we had in quantity, as my father was a good shot and rabbits were so numerous that farmers waged a constant battle against them; they did so much damage to the corn and grass that farmers were obliged to keep them down.

Some farmers would do the gardening, but my father preferred to grow as much as possible in the fields, so usually had a few lines of peas and beans and always plenty of potatoes, turnips and greens. The winter work for the farmer included hedging. I don't remember any wire round the hedges. Trees were cut down for the large amount of firewood that was required and the smaller brushwood cut and bound up with twisted hazel ropes into faggots, then brought near the house and built into wood ricks, for use as kindling sticks later. The hedges were then dug out at the bottom and stoned and turfed up to about five ft and finished off with a laid hazel bush, so were quite stockproof. As fields were so much smaller, there were more hedges and this work took up most of the winter months. If there were too many rabbits about they created havoc with this sort of hedge and their burrowing soon brought them down again. A farmer could not manage without a lot of help and support from his wife, or if he did not have a wife, a housekeeper, as so many jobs needed both. He brought the milk in after milking and she would then put it through the separator and make the cream, then had the big job of making the butter by hand. It took a long time to turn and a cool hand was needed. The wooden butter pats shaped it into squares or rounds and possibly stamped it with your personal stamp, the shape of an acorn or clover leaf or rose was sometimes used, and all was wrapped up to keep cool until market day.

Housework took up so much time for the women, getting up by candle or lamplight, stoking up the fire to boil the kettle and fry the hog's pudding, bacon and eggs in the frying pan balanced on the

137

trivet over the open fire, to give the family a good breakfast, before seeing them off to work or school. Packing up dinner baskets with pasties or bread and cheese or dripping. Then the dishes would be washed in a bowl on the table and drained on a tray, all to be wiped and the water carried outside.

The lamps would need more oil and the wicks cleaned and the glass chimneys too, if the lamp had been in a draught and had "smeeched" and gone black.

Then it was upstairs to make the beds. The feather ties needed a good shake each day and were turned once a week. An enamel bucket with a lid was used to empty out the china wash bowls and chamberpots and carried downstairs. There may be time to do a few outdoor jobs now, let out the fowls and the ducks, hoping to get their eggs before they go off to the pond and lay them in the mud. Now it's time to start the dinner, roast pork, rabbit or a good stew with mainly vegetables and dumplings. But if the men are threshing or harvesting they will want "drinkings" carried out to them, so must make a batch of pasties and some dough cakes to satisfy their appetites. Then make the tea and put it into the copper "harvest kettle" with a potato in the spout so the hot tea will not scald your legs while carrying it to the fields. If tea was needed outdoors, a big potato cake could be made with plenty of mashed potato, a few currants, sugar, egg and a little flour. A lovely tasty snack, if eaten while warm and often made for the children when coming home from school.

After dinner everything would be washed up and put away. The floors must be swept and most days needed scrubbing. It was a matter of pride amongst most wives that their stone floors should be really "blue". When all was clean and tidy, Mother could, if she was lucky, have a little time to herself, but this was used for her daily "change". Carrying her own large jug of hot water to her bedroom, she would take off her working apron and have a good wash, change her dress and put on a cleaner overall and do her hair. This invariably was the time to do the mending and sewing. Before we were old enough to be useful helpers, my father usually had a boy to help with the farm jobs. He would live in and my mother would treat him as one of the family and look after him. This would be part of his wages, so she always had his washing and mending to do too, so she had a girl to help her. She came daily, walking from the village a mile away in all weathers, six days a week. She did everything with my mother, so when in the afternoon my mother was sewing, she would sit on the table, either helping to sew or cleaning silver or peeling apples for chutney. Always busy, but I can well remember this was the time for a gossip!

Most girls from the village expected to get a job like this, but the amount of work required of them varied according to the personalities of their employer. Ours treated us like an older sister would, bullying us at times and continually telling us "old wives' tales", but she was very "touchy" and would often threaten to leave, but never did until a medical condition forced her to give it up. But she always remained very proud of her association with our family and it was spoken of at her funeral.

Farming was the only work that I knew as a child, as all my relations were farmers. In fact, my grandparents lived in the big farm with a lovely big house, less than a mile away and two other uncles and aunts in other farms only two miles away. So we led very insular lives and had little knowledge of the world outside. There was a great feeling of pride in the family. Farming was going through a very bad time in the 1930s depression and no one had money. My father worked so hard all day with everything to be done by hand and just with Duke the big carthorse. I know they were always struggling and after a hard day's work, he would take his gun and get as many rabbits as he could to take to the market to sell so that Mother had a little cash to buy necessities. She would have made the butter and washed the eggs and packed it all into the big square market baskets covered with white cloths.

Mother would have polished my father's best brown market boots and laced-up leggings and brushed his Harris Tweed coat and Heldon cord breeches, putting it all out ready for him to wear after he had done the morning's milking, so as to be able to make an early start in the newly-acquired BSA Chummy car. Setting off for Newton market, she wore her best costume (suit) and felt hat, with Father carrying the heavy baskets in to the usual trestle stall in the butter market. My earliest memory is of sitting on a stall beside these enormous baskets. The shopkeepers would come into the market and bargain with the farmers' wives to buy as cheaply as possible and, as they could not take their butter and cream home again, they had to sell. I have heard them say that many times they only got sixpence per rabbit, as there were so many there. But they had to get enough so that they could get their own essential shopping. Although they were relatively self sufficient, they always needed flour, sugar, salt and currants. Later in the mid 1930s, farmers were delighted at the formation of the Milk Marketing Board. Then churns were provided for the milk and collected from the milk stands at the side of the road by big milk lorries and taken to the milk factories for bottling and distribution; this continued for 40 years, until milk tankers took over. Many farmers living near a station took their churns to the station and the train took them to the factory. Also,

139

as more hens were kept, the eggs were collected and egg packing stations were set up. This was the end of butter-making on most farms and only a few farmers' wives still had a market stall.'

MILK AND EGGS

'North Devon cattle were kept by most farmers. They had long horns and were on the whole docile. Cows were tied up for milking with chains around their necks. To milk them we sat on three-legged stools, on their right hand side, with the milking bucket between our knees. It was quite a restful job. Some cows would be "kickers", perhaps with sore teats. You would land on the floor, milk and all sometimes, when a cow kicked. Then there was the row of cows behind to beware of when you were on the ground, for they may kick as well. The shippen floor was cobbled, as was the yard, to allow water to drain away. In the late 1920s, selling milk to the factories became the general practice. Milk churns held ten gallons, but in my very early days I can remember 17-gallon churns. Most people would make butter. There was a period when our cream went to a butter factory in churns collected by lorry. We used a yoke made of wood and shaped to fit our shoulders to carry buckets. From each end of the yoke there was a chain and crook to attach to the bucket handles. This eased the strain on one's arms.

The cows would be bedded up in the winter with straw. After they were milked and fed they would be let out. The dung would then be loaded into a wheelbarrow with a four-prong pick and pushed out into the yard to a heap. Eventually it would be loaded again with picks into a two-wheeled cart and pulled by a horse out to a field. Here it would be pulled out with a dungall (a four-prong pick, with the prongs bent at right angles) into heaps of about two or three ft in diameter at regular intervals in lines across the field. These were then spread evenly over the ground. Basic slag and some artificial manure was used as well. My father hadn't a manure spreader. I remember him sowing it from the cart, using two saucers to dip in the manure bag, while I drove the horse up and down the field.

Poultry were free-range. We kept a cockerel or two and from 80 to 100 hens. Sometimes they would lay out somewhere and after a time appear with a brood of chicks. Otherwise a hen would be set on eggs. The hen would be put in a coop, a box with bars which allowed the chicken to go out and scratch about. There were various egg collectors. My early memories recall them coming with a horse and trap. Egg boxes held 30 dozen eggs, with cardboard sections. Chickens were reared and the young cockerels were killed and sold; hens also, when they had come to the end of their useful life. The feathers were left on the wings, and feet tied under the wings. A very neat job was made by doing this.'

'A story was told to me by an 89 year old in the Drewsteignton area. She and a fellow farmer's wife were travelling to London by train. Passing through Wiltshire, she said in a clear voice to her companion, "Look at all those *margarine* cows!" The eyes of fellow travellers which had been hitherto on their reading matter, were raised in sudden interest. The two Devonshire ladies smothered their mirth. Back home cows were Devon Reds and Shorthorns – Friesians could never be good enough for butter!'

TIMES WERE BAD

'The depression in the early 1930s was bad. I remember my father saying in 1927 he made 56 shillings and sixpence for each lamb; in 1930 each lamb made only 26 shillings and sixpence. All of his costs were the same.'

'In 1919 my father came home after being demobbed and took up his original job as farm worker. The wages were very low but fortunately my father was a man of all trades, ie thatching, chimney sweeping, and killing and cutting up pigs and sheep for local farmers – this helped the family meat supply as he would get a pig's head or some offal for a few pence. During the next eight years our family increased to five. I was the last of the litter and was born just before the 1929 depression started. This meant harder times for everyone, as farm wages dropped from 30 shillings a week to 18 shillings. A pair of work boots for my father cost three weeks' wages.'

KEEPING TO THE OLD WAYS

'When we began farming at Iddesleigh 40 years ago, we had little money and only the most basic farm implements. My brother sowed one field with a "fiddle" – a box slung from his neck and shoulders containing seeds. As he walked up and down he pulled a handle in and out, scattering seeds in a wide arc, like a character from the Bible. Corn was cut and gathered, tied and stooked by hand. Hoeing was by horse. In winter water from the brook was warmed over the Rayburn to thaw the ice before calves could be fed. In summer churns were stood in the brook overnight to cool the milk. When reed was combed, all available help was called in, a huge machine thrashing away noisily all day.'

'During the Second World War it was difficult to get tyres for cars and trailers. We had a 1929 Morris Cowley touring car and trailer, and luckily the tyres were the same size. It got so difficult that the trailer tyres were stuffed with hay, releasing the good tyres for the car and going to town.

Our first field of hay was cut with a scythe and we turned it with wooden rakes. We tried to hire a horse and cart to make it into a rick but we couldn't, so we rigged up a tarpaulin behind the car and dragged as much hay as possible at a time until the field was cleared.

The following year we bought a horse, and made a cart. Tractors were almost unobtainable until the War Agricultural Committee released some. We then became the proud owners of a Fordson tractor!

During that dreadful winter of 1947 we literally lived on fat bacon with potatoes and swedes. The frying pan was on permanent duty. We all kept fit and carried on our outdoor work; it lasted for eight weeks. We were well oiled internally!'

'To get the cow in calf meant a mile or so walk to the one farmer at Peters Marland who kept a bull, and this could take a good half

Sheep shearing at Upottery using hand-powered shears. In some areas the water the shearers washed in would be scented with rose petals.

day. Cattle and sheep used to be driven on foot to any of the three markets in local villages; pigs were transported by horse and butt and usually delivered to the buyer, which could be several miles away.'

'On our farm at Sandford stood a very old round thatched ash house. This was used to contain the ashes from the fires, which were left to dry and then mixed with lime, manure etc to form fertilizer for use on the fields. This ash house has been very well preserved and is one of the few still in existence in this country.'

ROSE PETAL WATER

'My mother told me how, with her sister, she picked rose petals and put them into a trough for the sheep shearing team to wash their hands in, to take away the smell. I have heard there is a Shearing Rose.'

WORKING WITH HORSES

'My uncle, a farm labourer, walked every day from North Tawton bridge through the Hams to Newland and from there to Beacon Cross, Halford and on to Rowden Farm where he started work at seven o'clock. This was a journey of at least five miles. He ploughed with a horse-drawn one-furrow plough all day long. He once ploughed 21 acres in 20 days. He lighted his way home in the dark by means of a candle in a jamjar. On Christmas Day he did the same walk to feed his horse.'

'In the 1930s we had four to five carthorses at Ruxford Barton, which were used for all the jobs tractors now do, as well as in the poundhouse, where apples were turned into cider and the animal walked round and round to work the press. There was continual worry over the health of these horses. Too much corn given to them could produce colic, a serious illness.'

'In the late 1940s I would come home to Cheriton Bishop for my holidays and help out with the farm work. In the summer, immediately on my return and if the weather was right, my instructions would be to take Madam, the large shire carthorse, to the far fields to rake the cut hay into rows. My job was to put on the heavy harness, blinkers and all – "and don't forget the traces!" – for the rake was already up there in the highest field, to be utilized when we got there. With all extraneous impediments looped around the collar, I would climb aboard, usually from an obliging gatepost,

143

and off we went to our work. It was a slow progress. Madam was one of two horses we worked at the time and was the largest, kept for heavy slow work; the other, a black called Queenie, was much smaller and lighter but older, so was kept for taking the milk down to the milkstand by eight in the morning, and all sorts of lighter work with a flat cart.

Madam plodded slowly away through the fields to the last one, where I dismounted to open the gate into the hayfield. Shutting the gate to prevent the milkherd coming through, I backed the mare into the hayrake. She was an amiable creature, luckily, as the shafts were heavy and the harness clumsy. Once everything was fixed, the girth checked, the traces firmly fastened and the breaching adjusted, we were off. Then followed hours of slow plodding. It was a sloping field – coming down the slope the tines of the rake were dropped and lifted to make the neat parallel rows of hay; going up the slope the rake was raised to save the drag on the horse. Turning at the top by the hedge, Madam knew well she was heading towards her stable and until she settled to the job in hand it took quite an effort to hold her from charging down the hill. The hayrake was made for someone a good deal larger than I and it was hard work to handle the heavy lever as well as the reins.

But the view was breathtaking. Cheriton Bishop was away there on the hill and the tiny vehicles on the A30 were visible. The first post-war holidaymakers, albeit not numerous, were driving to the West, using their precious saved-up petrol – whilst we were quietly getting on with producing milk for the nation.'

THE CHANGING SCENE

'It was late in 1945 when my family moved into Okenbury at Kingston. The main part of the farmhouse had changed little since Elizabethan times and was large, cold and damp.

At that time, tractors were coming into fairly general use but there were still many working horses around. We ourselves had two remaining, used mainly for carting and odd jobs. The stable was magnificent with cobbled floor and twelve separate stalls, each with its own manger and hay rack. But of what use was such a stable in an age when mechanisation was rapidly taking over?

Our herd of British Friesian cattle caused quite a sensation when it was installed at Okenbury. All the local herds then were South Devons, and a British Friesian had never before been seen in Kingsbridge market. The auctioneers thought these strangely-coloured animals were a great joke, little realising that in a few years' time most of the dairy farmers in South Devon would have opted for Friesians instead of the much lower yielding, dual-purpose South Devons.

At that time many herds were still being milked by hand. We were using one of the early bucket-type milking machines, where the cows stood in their stalls in the shippen and the milking machine cluster was clamped on to each cow in turn. The milk then had to be passed through a cooler into twelve-gallon churns, which were collected daily from the farm by lorry, the driver leaving behind an appropriate number of empty churns for the next day's milking. Milking machines developed rapidly over the next few years and our twelve-stall stable became first an "abreast" type milking parlour and finally a "herringbone", which it remains to this day. Milk churns were phased out during the 1960s and farmers had to install refrigerated bulk tankers.

In the years after the war most farming operations were very labour intensive and there were ten permanent men on the staff. In fact, with part time helpers, Okenbury provided a whole or part time living for 50 men and women in and around Kingston. Over the years economic circumstances have forced increased mechanisation, and social and economic changes have meant employing less part time and full time labour. Even so, on an acreage which has gradually increased, five full time men were still employed at Okenbury in 1990, a very different situation from the bare minimum labour force employed in "prairie farming".'

HARVESTING AND THRESHING

Before the days of the combine harvester the threshing machine used to travel from farm to farm during the winter, threshing corn from the ricks. Harvest time, threshing days and – before modern silage techniques took over – haymaking, were all great times in the farming calendar. They were days of hard work, but also of great happiness, and hold nostalgic memories for most Devon folk.

HAYMAKING AND HARVEST

'At haymaking time it was customary to start mowing the grass early in the morning to benefit the horses before the heat of the day. The horses were out at grass overnight and it would probably take half an hour to fetch them in and tackle up. One year the farmers at Mooracre and Lower Creedy met in the pub and had a bet as to who would be first out mowing in the morning. The winner "cheated" by keeping his horses in the stable overnight, thereby saving himself half an hour.

Before myxomatosis rabbits were a very real pest and most farms were overrun. Ferreting, shooting and snares were necessary to keep their numbers down. Corn crops were badly affected where the rabbits would eat all the young shoots for four or five yards out from the hedge where their burrows were. When the ripe corn was being cut with the self-binder any rabbits in the crop would be too frightened to come out into the open and run for the hedge, so as the uncut crop became less and less the rabbits would end up in the middle of the field and only run out when the crop was a few yards wide. It was a great attraction for the youngsters of the parish to turn up in the cornfield at that time with their sticks and dogs to catch the rabbits. When farmers were cutting their corn, word would quickly go round the village and then it was a case of deciding which farmer would finish first because the rabbits would not come out of the corn until the last half hour or so. If the youngsters gauged it right, they could be in "at the kill" on one farm and then still have time to get to a neighbouring farm before that farm had finished cutting the crop. It was always a great disappointment if the farmer failed to finish cutting his crop before dark, because all the rabbits would escape in the night.

146

Harvest time, although hard work for those involved, was also a "fun time". Carrying the sheaves of corn on the carts and making the ricks, or sweeping the hay to the hayrick and then sitting around having tea in the field usually resulted in the tedium being broken with wisecracks, banter and leg-pulling. At the end of the day there was always the satisfaction of a job well done though sometimes the unexpected would happen. The sheaves of corn on the cart would slip sideways and the cart would tip over, perhaps, throwing the horse on to its side. The only way to stop it thrashing around and injuring itself was to sit on its neck until someone else could unfasten the harness.

In the days when most farms made their own cider the workers would fill their firkins at the farm cellar in the morning to last them all day, though at harvest time they would often work overtime just for the extra cider. The firkin was a small wooden barrel holding about a gallon.'

MAKING THE HAYRICKS

'At harvest time many workers started the day at 5.30 or 6 am to get the grass cut to start it drying for hay. As soon as the swaths were dry and the seed-head rattled they were turned over using long-handled forks, then they were spread out to dry and finally raked into rows by a horse-drawn hayrake. If rain threatened the hay was piled into large "pokes" (heaps) to keep it as dry as possible. When it was ready to be gathered in, a haysweep, a large comb-like instrument, was pulled by a horse with the horseman following to guide it by long reins up and down the rows. This was taken to the rick which was normally made in the corner of the field. It was "tipped" and then put onto the hayrick by men once again using pitchforks or else by "grabs". This last was a tall pole on which were hung large mechanical grabs that were raised or lowered by a horse pulling the ropes. When the grabs were in position on the rick the rickmaker, who was usually the farmer himself or some elderly experienced workman, would shout "tip" and the person controlling the horse that worked the grabs, who was usually the farmer's or the workman's wife, would pull the ropes that released the hay.

Hay had to be made "sweet" by twining hay and making a ring with it and then a boy and girl kissed through the ring, which was thrown onto the rick to prevent it burning from spontaneous combustion! Huge baskets of food were brought out to the field by the farmer's wife and family with kettles or jugs of hot tea and bottles of home-made lemonade. This latter essential of the day's activities was called "the drinking".'

'SWEET-HAYING'

'At hay harvest times at Bantham, when the women took the drinkings to the field, the men would run after them with a bundle of hay in their hand and rub their faces, to say they had "sweet-hayed" whoever it was.'

THRESHING DAY

'Threshing day was a big day on the farm both outside and inside the house.

About 20 men were needed to run the whole thing; two men travelled with the thresher which long ago was run by coal but later turned to steam. At about 7.30 am men would appear from neighbouring farms and some would start stripping the ricks, which meant taking off the thatch and spars which had been used to keep the ricks dry.

Lunch time was at ten o'clock and was looked forward to with great anticipation, with the owner of the engine asking my husband, "Are they making potato cakes?" and the answer was always, "Yes". They were made as follows. Cold boiled potatoes were mashed with

Haymaking in South Devon in the 1920s. This, together with harvest time and threshing, was one of the great communal efforts on the farm.

148

flour, salt, sugar, dried fruit and egg. A huge roll was made and cut into slices to be fried, turned well each side, then opened with a little butter inserted and sent out hot for the men. They were very much enjoyed.

Netting was put around the rickyard so that rats that might be in the bottom of the ricks could not escape before being caught by the dogs. One dreadful day a rat got up the trousers of our young worker, to be beaten with a stick by the owner of the machine! Needless to say, he never again went threshing unless the trouser bottoms had been tied very tightly.

Lunch over, indoors we were preparing for the one o'clock meal, which was boiled ham, swede, potatoes and a suet pudding with apple and jam tart to follow. The table was laid for about 20 men, on another table the tea cups were laid out. The whole thing seemed effortless because there was so much room for everything to be dealt with.'

'At one o'clock the men would come into the kitchen of our farmhouse at Beeson for the usual threshing lunch, which was always roast beef, Yorkshire pudding, roast potatoes and vegetables, followed by apple pie and plenty of cream. Believe me, that beef, being a big joint, was wonderful. Plenty of cider was drunk but no one got the worse for wear. Tea again at half past four and then one man came home to do the milking and the others carried on until dusk.'

THE THRESHING TEAM

'Threshing time was a busy time on our farm at Exminster. My father was joint owner of a threshing set and this outfit would be away from the farm for a week or more at a time, working on outlying farms. Early on Monday mornings, my father and I would drive the men to a railway station, in a pony and trap, perhaps to Ide and they would then spend the next week working from one farm to another in the Christow, Teign Valley area, returning to their homes the following weekend and lodging locally during the week. Farmers' wives worked hard producing food, which was carried out to the fields to feed the extra workers.

When our own threshing was in progress, my father and neighbouring farmers would hire extra hands from the Industrial School at Exminster, at one shilling per day. These hands were young offenders, who were placed in the school for corrective training and to be taught a trade – carpentry, tailoring, farming etc. These boys wore uniform and caused no trouble in the village; they were under

149

strict discipline and attended church regularly, sitting together in specially reserved seats.'

CIDER MAKING

At one time every farmer in Devon probably made his own cider, in varying quantities – he would not have attracted many helpers at harvest time without it! Some farms also provided apples for the commercial cider makers, such as the Whiteways Cider Co of Whimple, as this account of cider making in the 1920s recalls.

'The best known cider makers in Devonshire for many years were the Whiteways Cider Company of Whimple. From trains on the main railway line from Waterloo to Exeter, passengers have seen acres of well maintained apple trees planted in regimented rows. But these supplied only a fraction of the apples required for the company's mass production of cider. Further apples were bought from farmers and juice was imported from Normandy. The product was widely sold in bottled form but was sometimes dismissed by connoisseurs as "ladies' cider" or "sweet cider". In draught form this cider was available in some public houses at the discretion of the owners – usually brewers who saw it as a cheap competitor for their beer. Only the free houses could sell genuine farmhouse cider, a much more potent drink known locally as "scrumpy".

My recollections of boyhood in East Devon in the 1920s suggest that most local farmers produced cider by traditional methods. At that time my father, grandfather, an uncle and two great-uncles were farming in the Sid Valley and I think that all produced cider.

I have clear memories of cider making at Ridgway Farm, Sidbury, with plant dating from the 19th century. The farm had three orchards, of which the biggest was naturally known as Big Orchard. It was on irregular ground, unsuitable for cultivation, and contained a filtration tank which was the main source of the village's water supply. The second orchard had been systematically planted with orderly rows of dessert, cooking and cider apples. It was, for reasons I have been unable to discover, known and shown on maps as Ping-Pong Orchard. The third was small and has since

Cider was an essential 'perk' for Devon farmworkers, as this happy band of barley harvesters on a farm near Dartmouth in the 1920s would testify.

been built over as part of the David's Close development. Sixty years ago one corner was fenced off for the carter's hens and pig. On one boundary stood an uncompleted house used for storage. This gave the orchard its name of Pinchloaf and local report had it that a Victorian baker had started to build a house but had run out of funds. The implications of the name are perhaps slanderous!

Each autumn the apples were shaken or knocked from the trees and transported to the apple chamber, a large room on the first floor above the poundhouse. In one corner was an opening through which the apples reached the mill. The crushed fruit fell into a trough and was carried on a large shovel to the dish of the pound. This was strongly constructed of oak, with a central metal screw down which a hatch could be lowered under great pressure by means of a ratchet and a windlass. The apple pulp was spread on beds of straw, the ends of which were tucked in layer by layer to a height of about five ft. The apple juice was soon gushing from the lip of the dish of the pound into a large oval trough known as a trunnel. Thence it was carried in buckets and strained into a nearby oaken vat holding about 300 gallons. When the cheese of apple and straw had settled, it was pressed. When it flattened and spread the hatch was raised, the cheese was trimmed with a hayknife, the off-cut put on top and the pressing repeated. After several such operations the remaining cheese would be broken up by hand, remade and pressed for the last time. The residue was then spread over a field out of reach of cows, whose milk it would have tainted. The pigs gorged on it and reached a state of happy intoxication.

The apples had not been washed and some were rotting but as the juice fermented all impurities rose to the surface and were skimmed off. After a few days the fermented cider was clear and could be transferred to casks. These were of three sizes – hogsheads of 54 gallons, tuns or butts of 108 gallons and vertical pipes of 130 gallons. The cider, with no additives or dilutants, was periodically racked into casks for sale.

What happened to the cider? Some was sold to a free house at Sidmouth. There was a buyer's market and the landlord could strike a hard bargain, selecting the best cider and expecting delivery (by horse and cart) for about a shilling a gallon. This was the price at which several villagers brought their five-gallon barrels to be filled. A surprising amount was drunk on the farm. By tradition each workman took one gallon a day in his firkin or stoneware jar. All the casual workers at the hay and corn harvests and the annual threshing expected to be liberally refreshed, both in the fields and at the farmhouse suppers to which they returned. Many visitors to the farm were offered cider (mulled with ginger in the winter). If an apple crop exceeded that needed for a year's supply of cider, the surplus was delivered to the Whiteways factory for about £3 per ton, probably well below the cost of production and transport.

What has since happened to the orchards? These have been "let down" and the land restored to other uses. This process was accelerated at Ridgway by a series of fierce autumnal gales which toppled hundreds of trees in the late 1920s. During one of these storms my mother's sister was killed by a falling tree in Station Road, Sidmouth, while riding in a pony-trap. She threw into a ditch the baby son in her arms. He was concussed for days but survived. So did her husband, who was leading the frightened pony by the head. The pony was killed.

Why do I have such vivid memories of cider making over 60 years ago? Because to a small boy it was one of the most exciting activities in the farming calendar, and he was allowed to stay up late and help. Grinding the apples and making the cheese required more men than worked regularly on the farm so it was necessary to recruit casual help to make up a team of five or six. Thus each cheese was usually made in the evening with the apple chamber and poundhouse illuminated by lanterns and candles in alcoves. The motive power was provided by a light horse in the yard outside the poundhouse. It was harnessed to a pole attached to a large horizontal cogwheel which was highly geared to a rod passing through the wall and connected directly to the mill. A small boy could keep the horse moving steadily around in the near darkness. Later he would be promoted to shovel apples into the mill. Then a petrol engine was installed to drive the apple mill and other machinery. At about the same time electricity became available (direct current generated at the local mill). Cider making lost its excitement. The horsewheel has long since disappeared. The poundhouse and the adjoining stables have been converted into a desirable thatched residence. The cooper no longer comes to repair casks. The horse (a family favourite with a craving for lump sugar) lived in peaceful retirement for many years but came to a sad end when it was found on its back in a deep ditch and had to be shot. And good farmhouse cider is now hard to find.'

A LIVING FROM THE SEA

Devon's fishermen wrested a difficult and dangerous living from the sea, making their own nets and crab and lobster pots. It was often a family concern, son following father, and whole communities had a keen interest in the first sighting of fish out to sea. There were other maritime occupations too, such as the Coastguard.

A HARD LIFE

'Life up to the 1930s was very hard for the fishing community in Budleigh Salterton. The herring industry used to be very big; six to eight boats from Salterton alone were capable of carrying 30,000 to 40,000 herrings a boat. The price the hard working fishermen received for the catches was as low as ten shillings a thousand.

Pushing off at three o'clock, out all night in an open boat and returning next morning, everything was done by hand. There were no machines to help pull up the boats. Big holly poles, which were called ways, were pushed under the boat. These were well greased, then with the help of a capstan fitted with four bars you walked around to pull the laden boat up the beach. The herrings were stored in grape barrels and carried up the beach. Many people waited until the early hours to help pull up the boats to get herrings to help feed them through the week.

That was winter fishing that went on to February or March, then the crab and lobster fishing started.

Every pot was hand-made of willows, which was a skilled job and it took all day to make *two* pots. Willows were bought from Taunton. Crabs and lobsters were plentiful then, but the price the fishermen received was tuppence a pound for crabs and a shilling a pound for lobsters. "Potting" started about three o'clock in the morning. Every fisherman had their own fishing grounds, the knowledge being handed down from generation to generation.

Evening was the time for mackerel, caught in shoals off the beach – sometimes 10,000, sometimes an empty net – and hauled in by the fishermen and anyone else who happened to be watching or passing. If you were able to sell them, you made two shillings a hundred, if there was no sale for them they were dumped back in the sea.

After the war the herrings disappeared and fishermen started scalloping. The catch were sent mostly to Brighton and other places, the fishermen being paid two and sixpence a dozen. Having to pay the cost of sack, carriage and telegram to say they were arriving, that was very little money for the labour that dredging for scallops entailed – some difference to today's prices.'

Fishermen, like Mr Legassick pictured here, made their own crab and lobster pots using locally grown withies.

154

ONE FOR THE BOAT

'In Beer the principal male work was fishing, scratching a living from a boat. The family owned the boat and two men worked it. They fished according to season, sold the catch and split the proceeds into three shares – one for each worker and one for the boat. The boat share was of great importance as from it was bought replacement nets, ropes and other gear.

From Easter till September about half the boats went shellfishing (crabs and lobsters) whilst the balance trawled for white fish – dabs, plaice, soles, skate etc. The catches were sold by auction on the beach daily and the merchants had the whip hand, the fishermen had to take whatever was offered. From about November the Atlantic herring in its migration was appearing in the west channel and the boats went herring drifting. This was night fishing and the boats rode to a fleet of five to seven nets each about 30 ft long, which were tested at each slack of the tide. The catches were good, 20,000 to 30,000 fish were common. The prices were not good, varying from five to ten shillings per *thousand*. In the shops, herrings sold at twopence each.

The crab and lobster pots were made locally. They were half-orange shaped and were woven from withies, each man making his own. A good pot would last some four years. Nets, too, were frequently made in the village, white twine being used and the weaving done with a "palm" needle. After making, the nets were barked in a boiling mixture. This preserved them and also coloured them a dark red.

I can remember counting 26 boats on the beach when I was a boy. We lads were expected to take a turn about the capstan to wind the boats up onto the beach. The herring stopped coming this way about the end of the Second World War.'

SIGHTING THE FISH

'When a school of fish came near Burgh Island, old Fanny Barnes used to put out a white sheet to let the Bantham fishermen know.'

'A beautiful sunset in November at Budleigh Salterton, glowing colours of red and yellow setting behind dark brown cliffs, calm seas, high tide, gulls swooping. It's about 4.30 pm and herring boats are being pushed down to the water's edge, laden with nets. People watched from the Parade and the back of the Cliff Path. The boats would be back by 9.30 pm laden with thousands of herrings. People would be down on the beach to meet them, having seen them

155

coming in – knowing they must be carrying a lot of fish because the hurricane lamps on the mast heads were low in the water.

We fishing families were on hand. My father did not go herring catching so he would be getting the wooden casks ready and packing the fish in, covered with sacking. They would go on the 6.30 am train to Aberdeen. They made this journey from Devon because there were no herring fields in Scotland at that time. I was often allowed to be up quite late because I was with my mother who was helping to put the sacking on top of the fish casks.

We also used to smoke some of the catch in a shed quite near the beach, over bamboo sawdust which used to smell lovely. Another welcome smell was when we came home from school and mother was frying fresh herrings. We were quite poor and the fish was a good substitute for meat. If the weather was too rough to go to sea, we knew Christmas would be bleak for all the fishing families. The local shops would allow credit, and when herrings were plentiful, and you could sell them, they would be paid.

The doctor attending fishing families didn't want payment. My grandfather would pick out the very best of the catch for him – this was his way of paying.

Summer time would be mackerel fishing time. Visitors and family alike helped pull up the nets onto the beach, filled with fish gleaming in the sea like silver, splashing. I can remember seeing people carrying them home, fingers threaded through the gills of the fish, and seeing the pillow case from a baby's pram being taken off and used as a temporary bag!

My grandfather used to catch the train at 6.30 am to get to Ottery St Mary with two large baskets on his arms, and went selling fish door to door.

We gathered winkles from the rocks, mussels and crabs, and after storms collected cuttle fish and seaweed for the garden.'

NICKNAMES

'It was a delight to go down to the beach at Sidmouth when I was young in the 1920s, as there was so much of interest in the activities of the fishermen. They were always working on their boats and repairing their nets, which were spread out to dry in what seemed endless sunny days.

Our friendly fishermen had odd sounding nicknames, like Scrummer Smith, Tinker Harris and Dappy Pinn. The latter, being blind, could not actually catch fish but could still hawk them around the town on his barrow, which he pushed while calling out, "Crab-o, crab-o and herrings alive-o." Tinker Harris would also cart his fish around the town, calling out "Veesh all live-o" and "Mack-er-e-al"! But the best fish of all were the ones purchased straight from the boats for only a few coppers. I well recall going home with a mackerel on each finger of both hands and Mother frying them up for tea. Never have I tasted fish so good since.'

A NAVAL TRADITION

'My grandfather who was born in Plymouth in 1859 was part of a naval family where by tradition, like myself, most of the sons left home to join the navy as boys between the ages of twelve and 15 and the girls went into service.

In his days the Coastguard Service was actually part of the navy and not a separate service as today so it provided the chance of a break from sea service and the opportunity for a family to be together in one place, albeit usually on some remote headland. Until about 1950 being drafted to a naval ship often meant being separated from one's family for as long as three and a half years so a posting to a coastguard station was most welcome.

The lives of both my grandfathers can be traced to various coastguard stations all around the British Isles including Southern Ireland, and eventually as they became older and nearer retirement they were moved to stations nearer their natural homes. My maternal grandfather was moved eventually to Prawle coastguard station and from there to his final station at Challaborough where he was the officer in charge until his retirement.

In those days there were just the five coastguard cottages and the coastguards used to walk the cliffs between the Erme and the Avon both by day and night to keep watch. With 13 children and no transport both my grandparents had to "make do and mend" in the old naval tradition, my grandmother besides doing the cooking, cleaning and repairs also made the girls' clothes. My grandfather when not walking the cliffs would grow all the family vegetables, make and repair all the family shoes and make the clothes for the boys.

The coal for heating and cooking was brought in by boat and tipped on to the beach at high tide to be gathered up by the children when the tide had gone out. Once a month those not on duty would launch the coastguard cutter and sail with all the families around the coast to Plymouth for a day's shopping and a change of scenery. Unfortunately, if the wind dropped then the cutter had to be rowed back in the evening, not an easy task.

The younger children walked up the hil! to school and church at Ringmore or even across the fields to Modbury but when they

157

reached about the age of ten they were sent out to work, the three boys joining the navy at twelve at the Greenwich school, some of the older girls going into service. My mother I know worked as nanny for the Evans family.

Life in those days may have been hard but they seem to have been happy and able to survive, most of them living to good ages.'

IN SERVICE

From farmhouses to the big house of the manor, servants were in demand right up to, and after, the Second World War. Many young girls found that a life in service was the only option available to them when they left school.

AT THE BIG HOUSE

'I worked as house-cum-sewing maid at Ashridge Court in the 1930s. Sir Ashley and Lady Biggs were very good employers; kind and thoughtful towards their staff. We were provided with good living quarters and whenever Lady Biggs went away, she always brought back a gift for the servants – chocolates or something for the servants' hall.

The staff consisted of a head gardener, second gardener and seven under-gardeners, a cook, parlourmaid, housemaid and kitchenmaid. In addition a local woman went in two days a week to do the washing, ie Monday for washing and Tuesday for ironing. The servants all had separate rooms and every other Sunday and one afternoon a week off.

I rose at 7 am and took the morning tea to her Ladyship at 8 am. I also made dresses for Lady Biggs and all the servants' uniforms. The latter were made from material known as Tobralco. I remember one particular garment I made for Lady Biggs which had a cape and was worn to open a fete in the rectory grounds at North Tawton.

Bridge and shooting parties were held at Ashridge Court and once a year there was a meet of the Eggesford Hunt. Local people were often invited for an afternoon outing and tea.'

'Huntsham, in my memories, was all linked with Huntsham Court when all the farms and cottages belonged to the estate.

My parents moved to Lake Cottage in 1917 when I was a baby. My father looked after the lake. He went out in a little boat to feed the fish and ducks, and generally helped with other jobs on the estate.

There was a carpenter, mason, plumber, two woodmen, two gardeners, groom and chauffeur. There was a steward who gave them their orders daily at 7 am. Now you should be able to picture how beautifully the village was kept.

At times, workers seemed an "Aldridge" family affair. My mother did the laundry for the house, a brother did over 50 years service as chauffeur and other jobs. His wife helped through busy times; another brother was under-keeper. My father's brother and his son worked in the gardens and I had three sisters that were kitchenmaids at different times.

I worked at Huntsham Court for Sir Gilbert and Lady Acland Troyte from 1931 to 1935. I was just 14 years old when I started. My wages were £1 10s 0d a month rising to £2. Morning and afternoon uniform was worn. I was a housemaid. Other servants were cook/housekeeper, kitchenmaid, butler and lady's maid. Time off was 3 pm to 9 pm every Wednesday and the same time on alternate Sundays, plus alternate Sunday mornings to attend church. Time off increased to 10 pm. You did one another's duties when the others had their time off.

I started work at 7 am – front stairs and the stone hall, morning room and through to the office was my responsibility before breakfast. At nine o'clock the bell would ring for all servants to attend prayers in the morning room, led by Lady Troyte.

Upstairs were my next duties. There were five bedrooms on the front landing; Chintz Room, East Room, Pink Room, West Room and Lady Troyte's. All had open fires and washstands, so work varied according to the number of visitors. The lady's maid would help make the beds and do all the dusting. I would do grates (with blacklead), then washstands and sweep all the carpets on hands and knees with a dustpan and brush. (Later a carpet sweeper was provided.) There was no electricity, just gas lighting.

Then there was the back landing, work room and bathroom to clean daily plus cleaning all brass twice a week and scrubbing the back stairs.

There were numerous other jobs: mending household linen, jugs of hot water taken to the bedrooms three times a day, hot water bottles, folding counterpanes, keeping the fires going when in use. All servants were responsible for doing their own bedrooms.

There was no telephone, so telegrams were numerous, delivered from the post office and to be handed on a silver salver.

The kitchenmaid had to be up to clean and light the old range before the cook appeared to get breakfast. The kitchen table was scrubbed, and half the floor, every morning before her Ladyship went to the kitchen to give orders and arrange menus with the cook. A bell was tolled at 8 am and 1 pm, a duty usually done by the kitchenmaid, to remind outdoor staff of meal times.

On ordinary days my work ended about 10 pm, but when there were visitors and dinner parties, it would be much later.'

'Women and girls who worked in domestic service at Courtenay House near Powderham Castle in the 1920s were paid £14 a year plus their keep. Each servant was allocated a pound each of butter, sugar and cocoa, which was then taken to the servants' hall for them.'

'I left school at 14 in 1946 and went into service. My sister and I got jobs in the same big house. She was cook and I was housemaid. Our pay was ten shillings a week. Our working day was from 7.30 am to 8.30 pm but we had two hours off in the afternoons. We had one day off a week and two weeks holiday a year. I worked there for ten years and only had one Christmas at home, on my 21st birthday.'

IN THE FARMHOUSE

'I was born in 1910 and grew up in Okehampton. I was the eldest of five children, three boys and two girls. Times were hard in those days and I went to work on a farm at the age of 14, although my teacher would have liked me to stay on at school. I went by pony and trap to my new home, some distance from Okehampton. The farmer's first words were, "My word, you are not very big for 14!"

I was expected to work both indoors and outdoors, in all weathers and at all times. I helped to feed the pigs and learnt to milk the cows by hand. I helped to lamb the sheep and also helped with the hay and corn harvest. In between this I did the job I was really engaged for – cleaning and cooking in the house.

My wages were four shillings a week and of course my food and lodging too. In fact I lived as one of the family. We sold butter and other farm produce in Okehampton market. Butter was tenpence a pound then. I was pleased to have such a good place to live and felt I was doing a very useful job. My family were pleased to see me well placed and of course it was one less mouth to feed. I stayed on at the farm until they retired. I never got married.'

FROM SERVANT TO DAILY

'When the Tamar Valley mining boom collapsed in the 1890s fathers left their families to seek work abroad. The daughter of one told me she never saw him again though he regularly sent money home from Australia to his wife and children.

She had little schooling and was forced out into full time residential domestic service at 13. Her mother came with her to the interview to make sure that the establishment was respectable. The regime was harsh – up before five to light the kitchen stove and other fires, clean the downstairs rooms, carry hot water and early morning tea to the master and mistress and any visitors. After breakfast there was housework and help in the kitchen throughout the day, including plenty of polishing of brass and silver. She was finally released to her truckle bed after serving a last hot drink at about 9 pm. Her food was kept separately and strictly rationed until her mother complained of its inadequacy. On her half day off each week she walked eight miles home from Sampford Spiney to Gunnislake and back and she gave most of her wages to her family. No wonder she married young to escape the drudgery.

But life thereafter did not treat her well. She had and survived TB; her husband became a First World War casualty, having been thrown from a runaway horse during training (through a plate glass window in Tavistock); her son was lost from his ship in the Second World War.

She slaved as a daily help for many years, doing other people's dirty work with cheerfulness and little reward – cleaning floors and fireplaces, slops and sinks while her various mistresses did some delicate dusting and chatted. But she had a subtle pride and would never use the word "Madam" or call the children "Miss this" or "Master that". "I'm as good as they are," she'd say. In spite of a poverty which led her to exist on bread and dripping for several months to pay for her husband's headstone, she refused to ask for state help. With many of her generation, she had an antipathy to what she thought of as charity.'

MINES, QUARRIES & CHINA CLAY

Devon's rich land has also yielded valuable stone, china clay, copper and other minerals. There are still memories of the men who worked the quarries and the mines in the past.

IRON ORE TO MOLLAND

'A local farmer's daughter, now 90 years old, remembers the wonderful sight of the iron ore taken from the mine being drawn by a team of four horses with a very long waggon up over the winding stony hill to Molland station. The mine was closed in 1918.'

THE COPPER MINES

'At the end of the 19th century Mill Hill, a small hamlet near Gulworthy and a few miles from Tavistock, consisted of 24 cottages in blocks of four each, built by the then Duke of Bedford for his workers. You would find an alarm clock in every house as they were occupied mostly by miners working at Devon Great Consuls mines, plus a few farm workers.

The miners had to be underground by six o'clock. If they were late they missed the step on and off worked by an engine to take them down the pit, and would have to climb down by ladder and miss a shift and lose a day's pay. They carried their crib in a white calico bag – sandwiches or pasties, teddy (potato) and meat and onion; bacon or toad in the hole; turnip and mutton; a hobbin or a teddy cake or fish pie. They had tallow candles for lights. The miners were paid partly in "chips" – tokens that could be exchanged at the mine company's shop – hence the pub called The Chip Shop.

Leaving work at two o'clock, they had a two mile walk home, then a wash and a meal and a pipe of baccy and it was out to their gardens. These were well kept and every yard was planted with enough fruit and vegetables for the family through the year. The flower garden at the front was generally cared for by the women. Saturday night the men would slip off for a pint, or take the family to Tavistock to listen to the Salvation Army band in Bedford Square and buy a *War Cry* from that grand old Salvation Army warrior Dick Perry, who could be seen any day around the streets of Tavistock in and out of the pubs with a bundle of the *War Cry*. Very few could resist his happy approach.

I remember the Friday when the Old Age Pension was paid, the old women with frilled print bonnets waiting for the money to be brought from Tavistock and when it came they wept and clutched the note saying, "Good old Lloydy George, thank the dear Lloydy George!" One may smile, but that came from grateful hearts as their men, some 80 years old or more, had had to walk to the mines every day – now life would be easier and they could do part time. But one day the men were told the Devon Great Consuls mines were to be shut down and they would lose their jobs. Many of the men left the village and settled abroad and never returned.

The slate quarry kept working a little longer. They employed just a few men, but the slates were of good quality and later the quarry was used by a firm making blocks from the waste from the slates thrown aside in the past. The DGC mines were taken over by a German firm and worked for about two years for wolfram before the war – which was exported to Germany at a time when Britain was cutting down on defence.'

CHINA CLAY

'My grandfather, John Olver, built Claymoor House at Sparkwell to house his family of nine children, on land adjoining the Smallhanger China Clay Works, which he started in the 1860s. My father (born in 1872) worked here until 1915 when he inherited half the works and one of his brothers had the other half. My father lived in the farmhouse on Smallhanger and farmed about 40 acres, at the same time mining clay – men from Sparkwell were employed on the works and one on the farm. Only horses were used – ever – until my father retired in 1952.

The clay was mined by gravity, a man using a pick (maybe two men) on the face of the pit which sloped from perhaps 70 ft to the bottom, "picking" the lumps into the stream of water, fed from a pond. At the bottom of the pit the clay, being lighter than the sand and gravel, would continue. The sand and gravel would be constantly removed by horse and cart and moved about half a mile to the sand-dumps (still visible), but the white stream containing the clay went in pipes about a further half mile to settling pits, and after some weeks (depending on the weather) when it was solid enough, was shovelled in lumps of about twelve inches square (like enormous sugar lumps) and put on shelves in drying sheds to be dried by the elements (a north-west wind was excellent!). Before the 1940s the clay was taken by waggon and a team of horses to Plympton station and thence to the potteries in the North, but by 1940 a lorry was used on hire instead of the waggon. We had one of the first telephones on the Cornwood exchange (12) where we picked up and a Miss Vivian would ask for the required number – Mother would perhaps have a chat, then we were put through. When it was Plympton station, we ordered "a truck and cover" in case rain came when the clay was loaded for its journey.

My grandmother did not like people to see her, so was always driven in a closed carriage. In fact, the road from Claymoor to Sparkwell was specially made up and cut so that she did not have to be driven through Hemerdon village!'

QUARRYING

'Quarrying has gone on at Beer since Roman times. The stone, Beer Freestone, was easily worked as it could be cut by a handsaw. The basic size was a four ton block, which was hoisted by sheer-legs on to a low-loading flat cart, or latterly a lorry.'

'There was a stone quarry on the outskirts of Bittaford and when they were going to blast the rock they would give a five minute warning. If we were in our friend's garden, which was near the quarry, we used to rush into their outside toilet for cover and often we would hear the lumps of stone landing on the corrugated roof.'

'Between the wars whetstone was mined at Blackborough, near the gliding club, and taken to Saint Hill where it would be shaped "like a fish" for sale. One man would turn the grinder while another shaped the stone. They were then sent to miners in Wales.'

'Some men at Abbotskerswell worked at Decoy clay pits and they had to walk to work along the field paths between the villages. Shifts were 6 am to 2 pm, 2 pm to 10 pm and 10 pm to 6 am.

Other men worked in the quarry at Stoneycombe. They worked from 7 am to 5 pm. They had to walk about a mile and a half each way. If it was raining they were sent home again without loss of pay.'

OTHER WAYS WE MADE A LIVING

From picking strawberries to making ropes, from woollen mills to lacemaking, there were dozens of other ways we made a living, some now only memories.

TOWN AND VILLAGE INDUSTRIES

'Occupations for women were gloving at home for a factory at Torrington, and domestic work. For men agriculture and clay mining at Claymoor, for potteries and export, also making bricks and pipes with the poor clay. The Marland white brick can be seen all over North Devon today.

In the 1930s when my husband was at the local school by the church, the schoolchildren would look out of the window to see the steam lorries of I Baker and Son and Devon Trading pass loaded with bricks or pipes.

At Woolaton there were steam engineers called Hutching Brothers who repaired road rollers and the steam engines that pulled the threshing machines, also blacksmithing, shoeing horses and mending farm machinery.'

'At Crediton before the Second World War my father had various jobs, mainly working for Carr & Quick delivering by horse and cart. Later he worked as a checker at the local milk factory. Women's work was in service, dressmaking, shops, factories and nursing. Other occupations in the town included a tannery, printing works, farming, building, carpentry (the firm of Dart & Francis specialising in church carving) and factories – Bristow's sweet factory and two Jackson's Lozenge factories (Jackson's were the largest employers in the town).'

TAILORING

'A retired tailor recalls his apprenticeship in Kentisbeare under Fred Manning for five years, earning three shillings a week. He would give twopence to his mother to buy five cigarettes. From there he went to Aylesbury as an improver for twelve months and then he worked for two years in Wimbourne. When he qualified he went to work in Wellington for E H Thomas and cycled the ten miles to work each day. He was a tailor there for eight years and then went to work in Pinder & Tuckwells in Exeter, to which he travelled by train from Cullompton. At that time they employed 44 tailors. During the war he was called up for munitions work but after peace came he went to work with Hoskins of Honiton. He would make individual garments in Honiton but when at Exeter he made coats at a cost to the buyer of £2. Suits would cost £2 10s 0d.'

NURSING

'It was the 1920s and I really wanted to be a nurse but I didn't have a grammar school education so I couldn't become one, even though I had had plenty of practice helping my mother when all my brothers came along. When the midwife came at the birth of one of my brothers she told me that I would make a very good nurse, would I like it? Of course I said yes. So she wrote to the Superintendent at Exeter. I needed £100 security so I asked the vicar of Cotleigh to help as I had always been in the choir. I was about 22 years old when I qualified as a district nurse.

I travelled everywhere by bicycle in my first district – Axmouth, Rousdon, Pinhay, Combpyne etc. We had half a day off once a month, if we were lucky. Out of our wages we had to pay for laundry, lodgings, and buy black stockings and shoes. People paid subscriptions for our services, if they could afford it.'

'Life was hard for probationer nurses in 1940. We were on duty from 7.30 am to 9 pm with a two hour break. Often lectures and classes occurred during that break, so there was no real rest. We wore stiff uncomfortable dresses with starched collars and only nine inches from the floor in length. We had to help senior nurses with treatment of patients then clean the dressing rooms. There was plenty of sluicing of soiled sheets to be done as laundries wouldn't take soiled washing. Patients were kept in bed for weeks so "pressure area" treatment took a lot of the junior nurses' time. On night duty we had to cut loaves of bread by hand ready for breakfast. We tested urine samples on an open bunsen burner. We made cotton wool swabs by hand in our spare time! We washed crepe bandages by hand and got them dried ready for use again. We slept in a nurses home in a small single room with no heating. Our flannel would be frozen on the watering jug in the morning. We just didn't seem to notice.

We had to be in the home by 10 pm unless a special pass was granted. This was only given on rare occasions.

We were happy, we went to the pictures when we had a day

off. There were always a few of us off together. We shared a communal sitting room with our own "year". Senior nurses did not socialise with the juniors! This was not allowed. A ward sister was treated with great respect and her orders carried out without any questioning.

My mother was a district midwife in a small country town in the late 1800s. The conditions in which babies were born were dreadful. She would go to a small cottage on a bicycle and find nothing ready in the way of clothes for the baby; she would first have to boil the water. The mothers were in poor condition and ignorant of any hygiene. They weren't even clean themselves. Neighbours helped one another at such times. Often there were too many around!

Sometimes she would be fetched by pony and trap to go to an outlying farmhouse. It would often be hours too early but she just had to stay to be brought home again. There were only oil lamps to use for lighting and sometimes only candles.'

'Since I was about five years old I had wanted to be a nurse. Now it was 28th August 1946 and I was 17 years and one week old and my dream was about to come true. I was too young to start general nurse training but one could commence orthopaedic training at 17 years old and I was off to Mount Gold Orthopaedic Hospital in Plymouth.

It was heavy work – patients with TB spines were nursed in plaster beds and TB hips were nursed in plaster hip spicas. In almost all weathers, except pouring rain, the whole side of the ward was opened and the beds pushed out onto the balcony – fresh air was all part of the cure!

What student nurse of today would believe that we made all our own plaster of paris bandages. Now every sterile dressing comes pre-packed – no packing the stainless steel drums with dressings, which then went off to be sterilized by steam under pressure, and we had to make the cotton wool balls and fold the gauze swabs to pack the drums.

The hours were long, 7 am to 8 pm with two hours off each day and a half day each week. The pay was low at £3 a month, but we lived in and all meals on duty were provided.

I completed my orthopaedic training in two years and then my general training in three years at Torbay Hospital. How grateful I am that I learned to nurse and care for patients without having to feed a computer. Modern medicine is wonderful, but I do believe a little tender loving care goes a long way towards a cure.'

WHEELWRIGHT AND BLACKSMITH

'Before the First World War Mr Thomas was the blacksmith at Kingston and sometimes he would let us in to watch the horses being shod. He worked very long hours, often we would hear him striking the iron as late as ten o'clock. He didn't stop to go home for tea but fried his own on the smithy fire. Then at the end of the day if there was a horse that the farmer hadn't collected he would just let it loose, give it a slap and send it home. The horse would always get back to the farm all right.

My father was the village carpenter, wheelwright and undertaker for many years, with the help of his two brothers. They made all the carts and waggons for the farmers in and around Kingston. It took them all day to make all the spokes for the wheels and afterwards they were taken up to the blacksmith to finish off with iron bands.

The village children would spend hours in the workshop watching a coffin being made. I can remember the excitement of having the remains of the lining material to dress my wooden doll. In the corner of the workshop stood a wooden Aunt Sally, kept for village fetes.'

'Our blacksmith at Bantham was a wonderful man who could mend anything as well as shoe horses. He used to say he was the hardest working man in the parish, "Men bring me their tools when they leave work and then want them ready for next morning." He used to make dolls out of pieces of wood, burning holes for eyes and mouth. He once repaired a man's wooden leg and I've seen him pull a tooth for someone who couldn't get to the dentist.'

LACEMAKING

'Lacemaking came to south-east Devon from Flanders in the late 1500s. It is rumoured that at its peak some 400 women worked in the craft at Beer, but by the 1920s and 1930s this had dwindled to a few old ladies of whom my grandmother was one. The lace was pillow lace. A pattern was pricked out on a pillow with ivory pins and the cotton worked on these pins. In some ways it was a sociable occupation as I have seen Grannie put a candlestick on a high stool and she and three other ladies sat around this light with their pillows on their laps and gossiped. It was poorly paid though. I remember being sent by my Gran to take a piece of work to the woman who bought lace and bringing back a florin (two shillings) and the old lady looking at the money so sadly and saying, "Is that all?"'

'From the age of ten, when she left school, my mother lived at the post office at Sidbury with her great-aunt. My mother spent more and more time assembling Honiton lace motifs by mounting them on net or joining them with needle-made bars to form articles such as collars, fronts, lappets, handkerchiefs and wedding veils. In 1901 she helped to join together Honiton lace motifs for the lace which adorned peeresses' robes at the Coronation of Edward VII. I can remember the last two ladies in Sidbury who made Honiton lace for a living. They were a Mrs Bessie Pinn and her daughter Alice. The art of Honiton lace is still kept alive at the Lace School at Winslade, Clyst St Mary.'

'Lace classes were held in the evenings at Sidford, taught by Miss Pinn who would walk from Sidbury carrying her lantern in winter to see the way. These classes were held in the Sidford Hall.'

'Many years ago, whilst a pupil at St Peter's church school, Budleigh Salterton, I was asked if I would like to learn how to make the fine Honiton lace. It was entirely voluntary and several girls were interested enough to put their names forward for the Monday morning classes with Mrs Whittaker to instruct us. We all thought what a nice easy way to start the week, but we were in for a surprise! Our class started immediately after assembly and continued, with a mid-morning break, until twelve noon. Lace classes were held in the Staff Room so I don't think Mrs Whittaker and her girls were very popular with the other teaching staff some Monday mornings.

Our lace bobbins only cost a few pence each in 1948 and Mrs Whittaker was able to furnish us with a pillow, pins, cotton and (most important) a needle pin. My eyesight in those days was perfect and we were always able to work in a good light even on a dull winter's morning. Mrs Whittaker was very strict with us – definitely no talking. Anyone who had volunteered to make lace thinking it would be a "fun period" had another think coming. We made a number of pieces that were sent away for exhibition at different venues. I remember being told I would be able to earn seven shillings and sixpence per hour teaching lace, a small fortune to me then! Although strict, she was a marvellous teacher, and would either stand behind you or sit alongside and demonstrate a stitch. She would then undo it and say, "Now let me see you do it". She ensured you had grasped the stitch before she moved to someone else. We learned how to handle the fine thread as little as possible so as not to make it dirty, and when we had finished our lesson were taught to make an envelope out of our blue cloth by folding the bottom up over the bobbins and securing each side with pins.

Mrs Whittaker travelled to school by motorbike, wearing a leather

169

flying helmet and a man's greatcoat, with high legged leather boots. The boys were fascinated by her and her large motorbike and were always willing to give a helping hand, then they would cheer her and make various engine noises!'

FRUIT AND FLOWER PICKING

'A train packed with 30 carriages of fruit from the Tamar Valley, mainly strawberries, steamed through Bere Ferrers in the 1920s on its way to destinations all over the country.

Two and a half tons of raspberries would be picked and packed into tubs for jam making. The "lady pickers", as they were quaintly called, were paid three shillings and sixpence a day for working from 5 am to 3 pm, and supplied many Plymouth shops with produce.'

'Weare Giffard was well known as a strawberry growing village, and many villagers grew them on the south-facing slopes behind their cottages. In the picking season they picked into straw baskets called skips, which were set in trays and the carrier took them up to the train at Torrington.'

'As a child of about seven or eight, during the 1930s, we lived opposite a paper mill where my father worked. The emblem of this firm was the primrose, and each year (until the start of the Second World War) for about three weeks from the end of February, workers and their families were asked to gather primroses.

Each weekend, whole families went out picking the flowers, carrying food with them, and we were no exception. On sunny days we wandered around the countryside seeking out the flowers, and time flew by. So keen were the pickers that, at weekends, we were limited to 300 bunches per family. During the week, wives and men on shift work would also go out every day.

In the evenings, as soon as we had finished our meal, we all sat around the kitchen table bunching up the flowers. Each bunch had to contain 50 flowers with five leaves and was meticulously counted. The bunches were then taken to a hall across the square, where six or seven ladies packed them into boxes (two bunches per box) to be sent all over the British Isles to each of the firm's customers. A large mail van (sometimes two) was sent out from Exeter each day to collect the boxes, the local post office being unable to cope.

The reward for gathering the flowers was one penny per bunch and as most of the men were on short time working, and very few mothers worked, the money earned from this enterprise became an essential part of everyone's income, and in our family (eight of us) this extra money meant weatherproof winter shoes, or boots, for all.'

'Both apples and tomatoes were expected to be picked ripe, so the fruit was inspected every two or three days in the harvesting season. In the tomato houses this was no problem but in the orchards there could be no picking if the apples were wet with rain or dew. Sometimes the work went on till late into the evening when they had dried off. Different varieties ripened at different times and, for the late apples, wind was a further hazard to the crop.

Apples had to be very carefully handled. They were hand picked, stalks on, into large baskets and taken to a shed where they were carefully piled on shelves ready for sorting and packing. At night there were often attacks by mice who gnawed in for the pips, leaving little mounds of messy, pulpy flesh. During sorting, "mousy" or blemished apples were discarded onto a heap which went to the cider makers, while perfect apples were rolled onto a special tilted table, meeting slots of increasing size till each could go through into its appropriate section. The apples were then packed in standard wooden boxes, cleverly designed to take the same weight of apples (20 lbs I think) whatever the size of the individual fruit. There was a different packing pattern for each size.

The pinkest and prettiest apples could be held back for the top layer and polished, but all had to be of the same general quality. Apples for the lower layers were individually wrapped in small squares of tissue paper, lifted by a rubber thimble on the middle finger. With practice this became a speedy operation and seeing a nicely packed box ready for nailing down gave great satisfaction.

Some slightly less than perfect apples were sold loose and ungraded on the local markets. Windfalls were also sometimes sold rapidly and cheaply. Gleaning by the pickers was permitted. At picking time there was a glut and prices low, so it was a matter of judgement how much to lose to the mice before the price went up.

Tomatoes too were graded for size and packed loosely in twelve lb chip baskets, lined with tissue paper of different colours for rapid identification of the grades. The pinks and whites with eight or ten to the pound brought the highest wholesale prices because the retailing greengrocer could give the most accurate amount when weighing out a pound of fruit. He was always expected to give over rather than under the weight asked for and, with larger tomatoes, this meant having to give two or three ounces too much without scaling up the cost to the purchaser and thus reducing his return. How different now, when calculating scales charge for every fraction of an ounce. Irregularly shaped and very small tomatoes were graded separately

171

and sold more cheaply. Green tomatoes found their way to market when the plants were stripped at the end of the season and used for chutney making.'

'The first King Alfred daffodil was propagated at Newton Poppleford and I worked as a teenager for Mr Harry Hill, the gardener. I used to prepare and bunch this new variety, which was then loaded onto a cart and taken to the railway station en route for Covent Garden.'

'In the 1920s nearly every cottage in Dittisham had an orchard on which grew plum trees. The plums were of a special variety called Ploughman and they had a ready market in the surrounding towns of Paignton, Torquay, Totnes and Dartmouth. Buyers also came from as far afield as Plymouth, and I remember that one year when the plum crop failed in other parts of the country a buyer came from Covent Garden in London and bought up the greater part of the village crop. He paid fourpence a pound. At one time plums were sold at so much a hundred and that meant my sisters had to count every plum. They did this by picking up five plums in each hand. Doing this ten times totalled 100 plums and then one plum was placed on one side as a tally. As a buyer might want as many as 5,000 plums, you can see what a tedious business this was. The plums started to ripen about the beginning of August and the gathering went on for about three weeks. All the family took part in the work; Father and I together with anyone else who was around did the picking, the girls did the sorting and packing, while Mother brought us lemonade and cake during the mornings and tea, bread and butter, and cake in the afternoons. The day's work took about twelve hours.

My father rented an orchard from the rector for £5 per annum. This orchard was under Binhay Copse and right on the riverside. When Father inherited Otago on the death of Uncle William he gave up Binhay orchard as Otago had its own large orchard. The biggest crop from that orchard that I can remember was four and a half tons and the biggest gathering in one day was seven hundredweight. One year our plums made £90. Multiply this by seven or eight and you get some idea what an important part of the family income the plum crop was. Fortunately the crop gathering was finished or nearly so before Dartmouth Regatta took place on the last Thursday, Friday and Saturday in August.'

ROPES AND NETS

'My grandfather, Nicholas Cook, made many types of ropes for farm purposes. Horses were used for most of the farm work and ropes big and small, short and long, were in great demand. He lived at Molland Cross when he started, then he moved to Heddon, Filleigh. My father was born in 1890 and when old enough, he learned and took on the task of ropemaking.

My grandfather broke his hip after being knocked down when loading bullocks into a lorry going to market. He was 85. Doctors agreed to let it knit on its own as he was too old for an operation. He lived in a bedroom at the farmhouse until he was 92, spending a great deal of his time sitting making rabbit nets, pig nets for covering trailers, weaving circles at the end of harness for horses etc. He was a grand old man.

My family have sold goods in Barnstaple Pannier Market for many years – I guess for more than 100. We took a huge wooden box, about six by four ft and four ft deep, from which we sold many types of farm ropes – baler cord, wool cord, binder cord, small balls of twine, rabbit nets, trailer nets, sheep and horse and cart ropes etc. I helped my father make ropes and sheep halters used at shows for leading, horse harness etc. We also repaired ropes, including bell ropes. We did all the turning to make them by hand.'

SHOPS AND OFFICES

'In 1933 I became a fully qualified shorthand typist/book-keeper. The salary was £3 per month. After deductions I had about £2 9s 6d in my salary envelope, and gave my mother £2. I remember silk stockings were sixpence a pair in Woolworths and they were very good!'

'In the late 1920s I was apprenticed at a draper's. The first two years I got two shillings and sixpence a week, the third year (improver) fiver shillings a week, and when qualified ten shillings a week. The hours were 9 am to 7 pm except Friday and Saturday when we worked till 8 pm, and we had a half day on Wednesday. I cycled nearly three miles to catch a train at 8 am, and any spare time in the evening I spent dancing until 2 am. What a life.'

THE POST OFFICE

'As I lived at the post office at Ottery St Mary, my father being the postmaster, I had firsthand knowledge of "the mail" from 4.30 am when the large mail van came, to the evenings when all the letters were taken down to the station for dispatch. The letters came in large sacks with leaded seals. These were then sorted and put in the various rounds. There were nine postmen, and each had quite a long distance to travel on their red bicycles. These were very heavy

173

models with a large basket contraption in the front for the larger parcels. The postmen were dressed in heavy black serge suits and wore hats, rather like top hats but lower in the crown with shiny peaks. They wore very large black boots.

My father, for a very low salary, was expected to provide the premises, heat and light, besides paying for two counter staff. My mother also helped, thus saving expense, especially on the days when the assistants had time off. How she coped I can't imagine.

After leaving school I joined my father's counter staff. I wasn't too happy with selling stamps and making my book balance with my money in the drawer. I liked best the receiving and sending of telegrams. These were handwritten on pink forms, and for special occasions greeting telegrams were available, these to be written on gold monogrammed paper for which there was an extra charge of sixpence. The ordinary telegrams were worked out at a penny per word. When the opportunity arose I was invited to join the staff at the Telephone Exchange. This was in a terraced house at 5 Jesu Street, in the front room. Just three switchboards, on a large frame full of rather complicated red and black wiring. I liked this very much and by the time the war came I was "officer in charge". I can remember, although these were very serious times, many amusing things including when we first practised operating in a gas mask and tin hat. The speakers were built into the masks and very quickly became unbearably hot. I had detailed instructions as to what I must do when the Germans had invaded and were approaching the front door. A bell had been fitted in preparation for this event. I must open the door as far as the bolt would allow – should the Germans be there, quickly shut the door, whip out as many wires as possible, hastily grab all the files and nip out over the back wall. I never did find out what I was to do should a German be in the back garden!'

'We lived in a small farm hamlet several miles from the nearest village on the edge of Exmoor. Our postman always came on ponyback. We never saw him off his pony. When he got to our gate he would give a "hallo" and if we weren't there his Devonshire hollers got louder and the letter was thrown over the gate.

His round took all day. Midday he would stop at a hotel and do a few jobs in return for his dinner, then start homeward picking up mail on the way back. If we had a letter to go and it was dry weather, a stick with a slit cut in the top to put the letter in was stuck in the hedge by the gate so all he had to do was to lean over and get the letter, without getting off the pony. What always amazed us was he never really drove the pony with the reins, but just hooked them over his arm. The pony knew the way just as well as the man.

En route were many drinking troughs which the pony just walked to if needing a drink.

Christmas time if there were parcels, there was a trap hitched up to the pony.'

'The telephone exchange at Manaton was manually operated and in a small village the postmistress would know all her clients' numbers by heart, and often much of their business too as listening in was easy. I remember making a phone call to my aunt one afternoon and being told firmly, "It bain't no manner of use ringing her at home now, I've just seen her crossing the green. Maybe she've gone to tea with Mrs X, shall I try there?"'

'Father was the country postman, which meant he started at 5 am on the moors. He had a shed in one village, where he ate his dinner and his horse went in the field. He wore a uniform of navy blue jacket and trousers, piped with red. He had a heavy waterproof black overcoat, which he wore in the pony and trap to keep warm.'

'I started work as a Messenger for the Ilfracombe post office in 1935. It was a 48 hour week with starting pay of nine shillings a week plus a shilling a week cycle allowance. Uniform consisted of a tunic with a high button-up collar, long trousers (at that time my first pair ever), a pillbox style hat, black shoes, a short overcoat for cold weather and gloves. For wet weather there was a cycle cape and leggings – cycle clips, very necessary, were not supplied. The uniform material was a navy blue serge with red piping and brass buttons.

My first telegram was addressed to a High Street fish merchant, with the latest prices from Hull or Grimsby. High Street telegrams were always walked, but when we delivered telegrams to outlying farms it could keep us away from the office for an hour or more. These trips were very enjoyable in summer and even in winter it could be better than hanging around the office with nothing much to do. There would always be a sixpenny tip at one place, hot or cold milk at another, freshly made buns elsewhere. At one particular farm I was invited to join the family at the tea table and what a spread that was! I don't remember my excuse for being late back.

When the town football team were playing at home on a Saturday afternoon, a visit to the ground had to be made, coinciding with half time, to collect the latest score and report from the local newspaper reporter, to be taken to the newspaper office in the High Street for insertion in the stop-press column of the afternoon edition. The charge for this service was sixpence.

Summer time could be extremely busy with the town full of

holidaymakers. Two extra boys would be taken on to help out. Occasionally there would be a telegram for a boat in the harbour; this would mean a visit to the harbour office to find out where the boat was berthed, then a slosh across the mud if the tide was out, or a holler from the quayside if it was in, hoping the addressee was on board and could hear you!

A Boy Messengers General Examination took place nationwide at the age of 16. The result could determine if you became established as a postman, or appointed for indoor work as a sorting clerk and telegraphist, or whether you would be found suitable for transfer to Post Office Telephones – or perhaps made you decide to leave the Post Office entirely!'

THE BRUSH FACTORIES

'At the beginning of the century much of Axminster's industry was to be found in the two factories at the foot of Castle Hill. The brush factories – Coates and Bidwells – manufactured toilet and dental brushes. Over 300 men were employed both inside and outside the factories with 72 different kinds of toothbrushes being produced and 200 different patterns of hair brushes. By 1909 Axminster had become the centre of the brush industry and products from the two factories were shipped to many different parts of the world. They are no longer in Axminster, for the Coates factory moved to Chard in 1930 and Bidwells, which was founded in 1822, went bankrupt in 1955. My grandfather was employed at Bidwells, and my two aunts and my mother were French polishers of hair brushes.'

AMBROSIA

'In the mid 1920s the Ambrosia Creamery was opened at Lapford. Milk was collected in churns from the farms and brought to the Creamery where it was used to manufacture rice puddings, chocolate, baby food and butter. The Creamery also produced tinned cream – so the farmer's wife no longer had the hard work of turning the butter by hand and scalding the cream on her kitchen range. The rice pudding recipe was patented by a local chemist. The people of Lapford were sorry to see the Creamery close in the 1970s.'

WOOL AND FLOUR

'The town of North Tawton was very dependent on the wool factory for some years. It was owned by Shaws of Halifax. Originally folk working there had to start at six and a hooter sounded at half past five to waken the village. At eight o'clock all had three quarters of an hour to go home for breakfast and Ethel (89) remembers being frightened as a child by all the people rushing home and back at breakfast and dinner times. The women wore clogs and shawls then. Leonard remembers one man who worked at the wool factory calling in at The Globe (now The Copper Key) on his way to work at six for a pint of cider and another at eight o'clock. The landlord always had the glasses of cider lined up ready on the counter.

Leonard started in 1919 at two shillings a week when he was 14 and one year later, got a rise of another two shillings. The hours were six to six, and six to one on Saturdays. Later on, when Ethel worked there, the hours changed to eight until five and until twelve on Saturdays. In 1919–1920 they built what was always called "New Shed". Ethel was the first to work a hanking machine there. In order to build the New Shed, blocks were produced on the site. They ground ashes from the boilers to make breeze blocks. Other harder blocks were also produced. Any surplus to requirements were sold to local builders and we know of two houses in North Tawton made from these blocks, which were known as Factory Blocks.

Apart from the wool factory there was a flour mill at Newland. This was also water powered.

There were reports that on one occasion George took home a flour bag from Newlands Mill – they were made of linen in those days. His sister made knickers from this and these retained the printed logo. One version of the story is that the knickers had "First Grade" down one leg and "Superfine" on the other.'

177

WAR & PEACE

THE GREAT WAR 1914–1918

Though the fighting took place far away, every town and village in Devon was touched by the war. Families struggled with food shortages and the worry for their men at the Front, while troops became a common sight for the county's children. Memories of the day it all began and the day it, at last, was over are still strong.

THE DAY IT STARTED

'I can clearly remember the day war was declared, 4th August 1914. I was at East Budleigh Flower Show and we were all able to look up to Woodbury Common and see the Somerset Yeomanry packing up with their horses to go to France.'

'The postman used to ride a horse from South Molton, spend all day in the postman's hut at West Buckland and return to South Molton late afternoon. On this important day he brought the news that we were at war with Germany. The men of the village all congregated round the postman's hut to hear the news and later several of these young men joined the services.'

'Stoodleigh held cricket matches at Stoodleigh Court, and they played Knightshayes Court once a year. They were playing in 1914 when war was declared, so the owner of Stoodleigh Court ordered champagne to be brought out. When asked if it was something to celebrate, he answered that many might not be alive to enjoy it after the war, so they should enjoy it now.'

LIFE GOES ON

'We came to Whimple in 1916 when Dad was posted to South Africa. The war seemed a long way off and everyone was worried about their relatives in the army or navy. The village women organised sewing classes and my mother did all the cutting out. I went with her and sewed shirt sleeves and knitted socks on wooden needles. There was enough to eat as most people grew their own vegetables, but townsfolk were not so lucky. Soldiers' pay was one shilling a day, with a separation allowance for wives of ten shillings a week and seven shillings and sixpence for a child.'

'Rationing was mostly done by price. Eggs were £1 a dozen, sugar four shillings and sixpence a pound, butter £1 a pound and bacon £1 5s 0d a pound. A loaf of bread was threepence and beef dripping sixpence a pound, so the poorer people had a lot of that.'

'Things such as food and coal got very short. Someone would come back from town and say, "Mr Dallyn has had some coal in", or a grocer would have some sugar or lard or anything in the grocery line. My Mum would put me in the pushchair and off we would go to Barnstaple, often to find they had sold out.'

'When the army pay was held up and there was no food in the house and no money, Gran Cottery cut the stumps of cabbages and cauliflowers, skinned them and cooked the inside pith with a few herbs and this was served up for children for breakfast before going off to school.'

'Many wounded soldiers were billeted on us at our farm near Dartmouth and departed, I'm sure, all the better for my mother's care. Because of all the extra work entailed by the soldiers, we had a nursemaid to take us out and there were also two maids and two farm workers living in the house. I also remember various "ladies" who came "to help with the milking" – mostly incapable, but wanting to do their bit. They would adjust their berets before our dining room mirror to prevent their hair touching the cow.

My father employed seven men and boys. Three went off to the war. One lost a hand, but returned to work for us for the rest of his life using a crook to fit the handles of various tools. Another was wounded many times, but also returned after the war to work for us. The third was killed a few days before the Armistice.'

MEMORIES OF TEIGNMOUTH

'Our nursemaid used to take us for walks along the sea front at Teignmouth, and we watched the soldiers doing bayonet drill on the beach. Sacks of straw were hung from the pier, and the soldiers used to charge these with fixed bayonets and blood curdling yells. We loved it. I also remember a ship being blown up on the horizon, presumably by a mine. I don't think we thought this was so funny.

Food rationing was not so well organised as in the last war, and I remember standing in queues with my mother for beef dripping and some lovely gooey stuff called honey-sugar. My mother, always full of initiative, nearly poisoned us all with cooked rhubarb leaves

181

instead of cabbage, but we thrived on stinging nettles. She also rented an allotment from a lady, suitably called Mrs Harvest, where my brother and I were allowed to plant mustard and cress in the shape of our initials – great joy.

We often spent lovely long hot days on the beach, and occasionally as a great treat hired a horse and carriage to take us home, as it was all uphill. I can feel the linen seat covers sliding about under us now, and the huge delight caused when the horse, in time with its clip clopping, emitted a series of loud rude noises, or better still, deposited steaming heaps in the middle of the road. We thought it quite hilarious.

I also remember, with sadness now, the pages and pages of casualty lists in the newspaper every day, and asking my mother, "What was in the papers when there wasn't a war on?"

There must have been a Military Hospital in Teignmouth, as there were so many wounded soldiers about, all dressed in bright blue suits and red ties. I suppose they had a uniform.

In nearly every house was a card with a cross on, displayed in the window, which I think signified that a member of the family had been lost. It must have been a horrendous time.'

THE TANK

'When I was about eight years old during the First World War our headmaster at Kingsteignton school told us he was taking us to see a war tank from France. We had to hurry back to school after dinner and take a small Union Jack to wave. The tank had to knock down a wall at Baker's Park in Newton Abbot and, after doing so, it stayed there until it was needed as scrap metal during the Second World War.'

PICKING AND MAKING

'Two ladies used to walk miles around Thurlestone with a box on wheels to collect vegetables for the sailors. The children would pick blackberries. There were always plenty of apples and the teacher would make jam for the troops. At Christmas every child took something to school to make Christmas puddings for the troops, and of course, all the girls used to knit socks, gloves etc.'

'People used to go on the moors to pick sphagnum moss. The children went to the vicarage where we picked it over and it was used for field dressings for the troops.'

'We collected sacks of horse chestnuts to manufacture explosives and sacks of foxglove leaves for drugs and medicines. The local Mothers' Union refused to make pyjamas for the wounded but would make nightshirts for wounded private soldiers. Horse sales took place in the village, when officials from the War Office vetted surplus horses owned by local farmers and landowners. If approved, horses were bought for war service.'

TROOPS ON THE MOVE

'A troop of cavalry were temporarily housed in the Barkyard at the bottom of North Tawton overnight. They left on a Sunday and went all through the town, which fetched everyone out to watch them and delayed the church service somewhat. This entertainment was enlivened by the antics of one particular brown and white horse which proved to be of circus origin. All types of horses were taken for the war.'

'Soldiers were billeted all over Tavistock. As a boy I used to see them running down Bannawell Street for morning parade and drill in Bedford Square. Soldiers who were suffering from shellshock were billeted at Mount Tavy House and some used to come into Tavistock wearing pale blue uniforms. Troop trains sometimes stopped at the London & South Western station and Canadian soldiers used to walk along to the viaduct and throw coins to the children in Bannawell Street.'

'In 1914 Lord Sidmouth let them have the Justice Room at Upottery for a convalescent home. The first to arrive were Belgians, about ten or twelve of them, and since they couldn't return home Lord Sidmouth let them stay in an empty cottage in Rawridge until they could go back after the war. Then the British soldiers came. My mother always had an open door for the soldiers and when they returned home one sent her some cutlery from his home in Sheffield and another sent her beautiful embroidered postcards.'

IT'S OVER!

'I was in school at Cullompton on 11th November 1918, when a school manager called the headmaster to say the Armistice had just been signed. We were told we could go home, a holiday for the rest of the day. In the afternoon lots of us schoolchildren marched around the village beating trays, saucepans and kitchen utensils, singing all the way, and finishing at the vicarage, where we were given tea.'

'It was November 1918, I was three years old, and in the middle of my lunch my mother came into the nursery and said I was to get my coat and bonnet on as we were going to church. So on with my button boots, velvet bonnet trimmed with a small piece of fur, and my coat (that was my Sunday best), and into the pony and trap and off to Uffculme.

I remember nothing of the service but I do remember going home and rushing upstairs to find that lunch had been cleared away and I had missed my pudding. I burst into tears and was only comforted when I learned that I was to have a chocolate biscuit for tea. And so the war ended.'

'Peace was declared whilst I was at West Down Farm, Littleham. I, with my sister and brother in law, attended a marvellous village celebration with bands etc. When the troops and horses came back from France, however, they brought with them a flu bug and several people in the village were very ill and died, including a farmer who left a wife and six children.'

'In about 1919/1920 Sir Thomas Dewey presented the local school-children at Sidbury with decorated mugs to commemorate the peace. They marched from the schools to Peak House where they assembled on the front lawn. With the local band in attendance they processed up the terrace steps where the boys received their mugs from Sir Thomas and the girls from Lady Dewey. The proceedings ended with the band leading all the children into singing the National Anthem and having the rest of the day off school.'

THE SECOND WORLD WAR 1939–1945

When war came again, this time Devon experienced the horrors of bombing and sudden death first hand. Many towns and villages suffered damage and loss of life, and many a night was spent in the air raid shelters or even in open country lanes away from built up areas. Special memories, however, are of the terrible bombing suffered by Plymouth and Exeter.

A MEETING IN THE DARK

'In 1938, at the time of the Munich crisis, they delivered us an Anderson air raid shelter and as my father, a naval reservist, had been called up, my brother and I set to digging the hole and erecting the shelter according to the enclosed instructions. Once the crisis had passed the shelter was relegated to being a storage shed for tools etc.

Our next door neighbour, who was of a rather superior nature, refused the offer of an Anderson shelter, explaining that there was no possibility or danger of war and that they would take their chances anyway.

Eventually the war did materialise and even then because the earlier months contained very little action people paid scant attention to making their shelters places of comfort in which to spend many long nights sheltering. During one dark February night in 1940, after days of heavy rain, the air raid sirens started to screech out their warnings over Plymouth at about two in the morning. We hurriedly dressed, gathered up our emergency equipment which included a torch and made our way to the shelter.

Opening the door we were amazed to see four people in nothing more than their scanty night attire standing in three feet of dirty rainwater with tools, deckchairs and other objects floating around them. On hearing the sirens they had panicked, rushed around to our shelter without getting dressed and in the dark without a torch, jumped headlong into the shelter. We declined their offer to make room for us in the water and returned to the house to enjoy our thoughts, my brother and I realising for the first time that the teenage girl next door had quite a nice figure.

Next day we dismantled the shelter and re-erected it after putting in proper drains, cementing the sides and putting in bunks, a table, emergency lighting and a *lock on the door*. Our neighbours had a special luxurious concrete shelter built, luckily in good time for the devastating air raids soon to be launched on Plymouth.'

SAFETY?

'In those days milk was delivered by horse and cart. During an air raid on Bovey Tracey the milkman was delivering to us and the noise of the raid made the poor horse bolt. Mother and I were covered in milk and the horse left a trail of milk straight up to the top of the road. I was put under the table for safety.

My sister was in a neighbour's house at this time. A German plane strafed the town and railway station. One of the bullets entered the living room of the house and went straight through our neighbour's arm and carried on through her wireless. My sister was duly put in a cupboard – for safety!'

IN THE PUB AT EXMOUTH

'A pleasant drink at a local hostelry was tragically interrupted during a Saturday evening in 1941, when an enemy air raid severely damaged Exmouth's town centre. Sadly a number of residents were killed.

The exploding bombs caused the packed pub to clear. Strangely, people were tripping at the doorway, and by torchlight an un-exploded bomb was seen protruding from the pavement. It was a 500 pounder.

I watched the bomb's removal, greatly admiring the courage and skill with which the unit performed its duties so successfully and cheerfully.'

BY THE TORBAY HOTEL

'During the war I lived in a public house, The Royal Oak, in Torquay. We often had hit and run raids. On one occasion I was playing on the flat roof when a German plane came over just clearing the roofs. I saw the swastika very clearly on the plane and was very surprised that I was not hit by aircraft fire. I saw the bomb come out of the plane. It landed by the Torbay Hotel where the amusement arcades now stand.'

NEWTON ABBOT

'We lived opposite to an ARP post and we knew when the air raid warning was about to sound as our lights dipped a few seconds before the wailing started.

One night when I had gone to bed and planes were about I heard a rushing noise which I thought was a lorry free-wheeling down the road, but when there was a great crump I realised it was a bomb. Another time when my sister was at home and sharing the same bedroom I again heard this rushing noise. While she was interestedly looking out of the window I was smartly rolling under my bed.

We could distinguish between hostile planes and friendly ones as the enemy engines made an intermittent wavery sound, "unsynchronised" we were told. On one occasion we had decided to go into the cellar during an alert (my schoolboy brother had carefully swept the coal shute because, he said, if anybody has to climb out that way he knew jolly well who it would be and he didn't intend to get his pyjamas blackened with coal dust. Luckily it never happened). Somebody remarked how pretty the moonlight looked shining on the wall. My sister, who was quicker on the uptake than most, nipped rapidly up the steps and wasn't surprised to see a huge flare gradually descending. The moon was on the other side of the house. That time we were very relieved to hear one of our own planes, which speedily dealt with the flare dropper.

We were about 30 miles from Plymouth and we could see the shadows of the flames from the fires there reflecting on the walls of our house. We could also see the glow from Exeter on that night in May 1942; we could smell the fire and we had scraps of burnt paper floating down even from that distance. My brother went to school in Exeter travelling by train each day and after the blitz the trains had to go up the Teign valley line as the main line was unusable. This pretty little country route no longer exists, a pity, it was a delightful way to travel.

When bombs were dropped on Newton Abbot one evening one of my father's ATC cadets was cycling along Queen Street and he was blown off his bike, his sleeves split right up. He was unhurt luckily but what intrigued him was the way the blast zig-zagged along the street, blowing in shop windows first on one side then on the other.'

BY THE RIVER DART

'In August 1942 my husband, then in the Fleet Air Arm, was spending a few days' leave with his family on their boat, which they had been allowed to bring out and moor (as a fixture and without her mast) in the river Dart at Dittisham.

The farm at Sandridge Park asked for volunteers to help with their harvest and the family all went off there and soon found themselves picking up sheaves of corn as they fell from the binder and learning how to stand them up six at a time, in stooks to dry.

Suddenly this peaceful scene was shattered by the roar of approaching aircraft. Two German planes appeared from nowhere and seconds later the harvesting party could see a stick of bombs falling further down the river and hear them exploding. They learned that one bomb had fallen on the Noss shipyard, half a mile downstream from their boat.'

'I joined the Land Army at 18 years of age and was sent to Stoke Fleming near Dartmouth, from Manchester. Coming to a quiet place after living in a city which was being bombed night after night, one was lulled into a false sense of security – until one day, alone in a field topping turnips, I looked up and saw two planes flying low in the distance. Dartmouth had been quiet up to then so I thought they were British and casually waved to them, then noticed they were German planes just as they swooped low and started to machine gun the field. I had never vaulted a gate before, or since! I tucked my head into the hedge of the next field with my rear end sticking out! The poor cows were chasing around. After the planes had gone over out to sea and it was safe to crawl out, I looked up to see the headmistress of the school opposite the field hanging out of her upstairs window calling out to me "was I all right?" I couldn't speak and just nodded. I went back down to the village and the farmhouse on jelly legs. Glass was everywhere and a bomb that hadn't exploded had been dropped behind the church. Then I learned that Dartmouth had been bombed and people killed.'

PLYMOUTH

'After over 50 years, I still have many vivid memories of the Plymouth Blitz, which lasted from 1940 to 1944. My family moved from Plymouth to Plympton (a distance of five miles) in July 1939, which was then a relatively rural area., By this change of location, we hoped to avoid the problems that an imminent war would cause, but this was not so, as it happened. In September 1940 I became one of the clerical staff in HM Dockyard, Devonport. The enemy raids started in earnest around that time, and one that I particularly remember took place in November 1940, which caused the oil tanks at Turnchapel to catch fire and they blazed for several

188

days. Plymouth was illuminated by the glare and the fire could be seen for miles. No one felt safe in such a situation.

The worst raids took place in March and April 1941, three or four nights in succession in both months. The dockyard was obviously a prime target, but Devonport and the main Plymouth shopping and business area were severely damaged. So many people lost their homes that each night they would trek outside the city in the hope of escaping any further misery. I vividly remember walking through what remained of Fore Street, Devonport, to get to the dockyard on one morning in April 1941, and seeing virtually no building left standing, the ruins still smouldering.

The greatest tragedy was that most of the destruction was caused by fire. Despite the gallantry of the firefighters, much of the city had to be left to burn itself out because the equipment brought in from other parts of the country would not fit the Plymouth hydrants. It had never been conceived that one area would have to deal with such a wholesale conflagration. During the period of 1940 to 1944, there were 59 raids of varying magnitude. Over 22,000 houses and business premises were destroyed or seriously damaged. The civilian casualties amounted to 4,500 of which nearly 1,900 were fatal.

It was very difficult on occasions to travel to and from work, especially after the heaviest raids. Help was rushed to Plymouth from all parts of the country and from all over the world there came messages of sympathy and admiration. Despite the difficulties of coping with everyday living, the spirit was unbroken – no one was going to allow Hitler to get the better of them!

My father built an air raid shelter in the garden under the greenhouse, to which we repaired when the air raid siren sounded. One night, we were particularly disturbed as incendiary bombs were dropped in hundreds in the fields all around the houses, but fortunately no high explosive bombs followed on.

Our bungalow was damaged by a blast from a bomb which fell on the road several hundred yards away. A German bomber had been hit by ack-ack fire and it jettisoned its bombs right across Plympton. We were having a brief holiday in North Cornwall at the time, and had to return in a hurry to deal with ceilings down, windows minus glass, etc. People were quick to offer help when needed – a spirit of comradeship existed which seems to be sadly lacking these days.

As a matter of interest, the house in Plymouth from which we moved in 1939 survived unscathed!'

'I was seven years old when the Second World War began. It meant nothing to me for some time, except for the fact that my gas mask, in its cardboard box, had to go everywhere with me – to class,

189

to the playground, to the bathroom, and to bed. Meals became uninteresting as my mother struggled to spin out the rations, but life continued much as it always had, until the night of the first blitz on Plymouth.

My sister and I had gone to bed, but woke when the siren went. We sheltered with our mother, as usual, in the cupboard under the stairs, hearing the planes droning overhead, the thunder of the anti-aircraft fire, and the screaming of the falling bombs. My father was helping to put out many of the incendiary bombs which were falling on our home and all around. Several times he came to tell my mother about the progress of the raid, and said it looked as though the whole of Plymouth was burning.

After an hour or more of incessant noise, my father said that the next-door building was on fire, and we must leave before it reached our house. He took a case of clothes in one hand and me in the other, and my mother and sister followed as we went into the night. Everywhere was light as day, for buildings all around us were on fire. Suddenly, a bomb came whistling down, and my father shielded me with his body against a wall as the bomb landed a short distance away. We tumbled into the car, and my father drove rapidly through the back streets of the city to my grandparents' house in the suburb of Hartley.

The sight of Plymouth burning was one I will never forget. As we sped past Central Park we looked over the whole city which seemed ablaze from end to end. Searchlights moved through the sky lighting up the barrage balloons and occasional aircraft. And still the guns thundered on. In the morning, Plymouth was a smoking ruin. As I went to school on the bus, the smell of charred wood and gas escaping from the fractured pipes lay over everything. Miraculously, some buildings had escaped the fire, but not for long. The following night, the raiders came again and finished off the total destruction of the city centre. I lost my home, my toys, my books, my pets, and I knew what it was to be totally destitute.

When the blitz of Plymouth was over, most children were evacuated to safety, and my class at school went down to three. My childhood at war became one of lessons interrupted by day-time raids, nights spent in the shelter, cycle rides in the countryside with not a car in sight, and queueing on Saturday mornings for off-the-ration food. It was a perilous time, in turns exciting and dreary, and utterly different from any childhood experiences before or since.'

'When I was about 15 and my brother seven, we were on our way to school when a stray Italian fighter plane zoomed low over us. We

190

heard machine gun fire. I took my brother's hand and ran with him to get inside our school. He now remembers this as an indignity – he was a large boy and did not run, normally! This was one of my earliest memories of wartime.

There are memories of sleepless nights under the stairs – getting hungry and quickly diving to the kitchen for a cold pasty. When we did get to bed I lay by my mother for comfort. She didn't remove her daytime clothes, even her shoes. Night after night of heavy bombing and wondering if we would be alive next morning. Then there was the time when I helped remove incendiary bombs that had come through the roof and being worried about the budgie when the windows blew out after a land mine exploded not far away. Memories of hiding under the table with my cousins – we giggled, not feeling fear.

All too clearly I remember trying to get to work through the city (Plymouth) amongst masses of hosepipes used by fire fighters during the blitz and of seeing firemen exhausted. Eventually reaching my place of work – E Dingle & Co, the department store. It had been razed to the ground. There were stacks of clothing, still folded, all smouldering by the pavements.

I was called up for war work to help produce the first Spitfire and later watched the Dakotas and gliders fill the sky on D-Day. Soon after there was a non-stop queue of ambulances bringing the wounded to a hospital nearby.'

'Bere Ferrers was packed with refugees and churches, chapels and anyone who had a spare room would have to take them in. The air raids would take place mainly at night. People from Plymouth would come to the village by train, sleep under the nearby hedges, return to the train in the morning and make their way back to Plymouth.'

'I came to work in Plymouth in 1944. By then D-Day was passed and the war had moved away, leaving devastation and shortages. The bombed sites had become colonised with buddleia and other garden escape weeds as well as numerous feral cats. The latter were tolerated to keep down the rats, but many found their way into the cooking pots because of shortage of meat. In the market the skinned, decapitated corpses were passed off as rabbits. Genuine rabbits were sold to the discriminating with their heads and skins intact. There was a small extra charge for flaying on the spot.

In spite of the cats a well known restaurant was closed down because of rats. An equally well known basement bakery survived its cockroaches for many years, on the theory that the insects had no chance to contaminate freshly baked bread and buns sold while still hot to the queues in the shop above. In those stressful times people were, in any case, less fussy. Many remember kitchens that had black beetles running harmlessly about at night, scavenging crumbs and scuttling away whenever a light was turned on. Some of the cockroaches caught in the bakery traps found their way to the Biology Department of the Technical College as much needed class specimens – a source which dried up with the coming of DDT.

Salvage of everything reusable was important and pig bins were provided in the residential areas for food waste. One day a friend received by post a generous gift of a chicken. Unfortunately there had been delay in transit due to bombings and rail disruption round London, so the bird was too decayed for human consumption. It was consigned to the pig bin on the corner. Shortly afterwards my friend began to worry that the rotten remains might poison the pigs and went to retrieve them – a very messy job from under later contributions to the bin. At that time dustbins were only emptied once a fortnight and they had been cleared the previous day. Hating to think of the odour in two weeks' time my friend took the parcel down town and, hoping to poison some of the rats, placed it under a pew in the ruined remains of St Andrew's church!'

EXETER

'My first term at Crediton High School for Girls exactly coincided with the outbreak of war – September 1939. My memories of catching the 8.20 am bus at Paul Street bus depot, Exeter (long since gone) are of packed lunch in school satchel; bus pass in wallet (paid for by parents in those days); crowded bus of girls and boys from CHS and Queen Elizabeth Grammar School for Boys; freezing feet and chilblains, and of course the inevitable square cardboard box containing the gas mask, always to be carried, come what may.

During the next couple of years Exeter suffered night after night of sirens – broken nights were the norm, but I was still, without fail, catching the 8.20 to Crediton, cycling to Paul Street first. When the wailing sirens started we had to get up and go downstairs to go either under the stairs, thought to be the safest part of the house, or later in the Morrison table-type shelter in our dining room, where the French windows were protected by a brick blast wall. Having acquired two new "sisters" as evacuees from Camberwell, quite a lot of fun somehow was enjoyed through the nights – the bliss and ignorance of youth!

When we now see refugees in open lorries in other countries I can well remember the very same thing, being taken into the country to escape the bombing of Exeter by the only available transport, a neighbour's lorry – Mum, sister and grandmother leaving Dad behind to do his ARP duties.'

'After the First World War my aunt became a nurse and arrived in Exeter in the early 1930s. She was a Queen's Nurse, the forerunners of today's Community Nurses. The work was mainly midwifery.

When the 1939 war came, I was evacuated from London to live with my grandparents in Teignmouth, where she was a regular visitor when off duty. After the worst night of bombing in 1942, I wandered round the Teignmouth garden wondering what had happened to her. The garden was covered with burnt paper blown on the wind from the firebombs overnight. The print stood out against the charred background and I could read legal documents, bank notes and private letters. I found a fragile piece with the Lord's Prayer just readable, carefully I picked it up and put it in a match box. When I finally presented her with my prize, she opened it and there were only ashes inside.

The night before, she had lost everything except the clothes she stood up in. The nurses home at Dix's Field was no more. Thankfully no nurses had been harmed.

I can remember her walking into the house at Teignmouth, a totally weary figure who sat in the first armchair and promptly fell asleep! When she finally woke, she told us how she had felt totally devastated at the bombing of the nurses home. She had walked through the ruined streets of Exeter in the early morning, remembered feeling amused at the sight of a cleaner with mop and bucket going to wash the public toilets as though nothing had happened! Still muddled and shocked, it crossed her mind that, under the circumstances, if a midwife was needed no one would know where to find one. The nearest undamaged building was the library. She went in and told them who she was and where the other nurses could be found. She walked away down the ruined streets and after a while was passed by a small van with a big megaphone on the roof. Above the noise of shovels clearing masonry a voice called where the midwives were to be found if needed.'

'The Exeter Blitz took place on 3rd May 1942. My father was erecting the Morrison shelter, which the council had distributed the day before and which we shared with the lady next door. Mum grumbled about it, as it occupied most of the dining room. My twin sister and I thought it was exciting at ten years of age, as it was another place to play. Dad dragged down an old mattress from the attic to lay on the floor and a couple of blankets to put on top, if necessary.

The air raid siren sounded and Mary and I were dragged out of bed, and put in the Morrison. In came "Aunty" from next door, then Mum. We could hear the noise of the dive bombers, and distant sound of bombs dropping. Dad, who was a railway man, donned his tin helmet and said he would look around. By now, the noise was deafening, planes and bombs, intermingled with frightening moments of silence. Mum, "Aunty", Mary and I were too terrified to speak, with our hands over our ears. When the "big one" came, there was a huge explosion and everything started to fall out – doors, windows, pictures off the wall, china, glass from the sideboard. Dad just managed to fling himself into the shelter, before the ceiling fell in, and cursed and swore at the "Jerries". I prayed and for nearly two hours the Blitz continued, then silence, and the sound of "all clear".

We crawled out of the shelter, avoiding all the broken crockery and Mother made a cup of tea, using a paraffin heater. There was just a dribble of water from the taps. Then there was a shout of, "Get out, everything's on fire." The five houses opposite ours had disappeared and the flames beyond that seemed to touch the sky. We were directed to Heavitree Conservative Club, which was used as a shelter. The place was packed with shocked, dusty people, but there was plenty of tea to drink.

Returning home early next morning, we found the shell of our house, no roof, no windows or doors and everywhere deep in dust. Dad decided it would be best if we went to stay with relatives in Sidmouth, so we found a few tattered clothes and walked to the station. The 30 minute walk turned into a three and a half hour nightmare, trying to find a route into town. I shall always remember coming out of St Martin's Lane, looking up the High Street – huge fires burning, water pumps, clouds of dust. Hundreds of people on the platform, no one bothering about tickets – just wanting to get away. Now 50 years later, Exeter is again a lovely city.'

'Brampford Speke became a dormitory village for Exeter as many people caught the six o'clock train from Exeter, reaching the village some 15 minutes later. They spent the night here to avoid the heavy bombing, returning to the city at 8.20 the next morning.'

'The main effect of the Second World War in Newtown was the blitz damage. Whole blocks of buildings were destroyed. The school's front two buildings were flattened as were the row of shops in front of the school in Clifton Road. The post office opposite the school was hit by an incendiary bomb and the front of the roof had to be replaced. The bomb that hit the school also blew out the post office windows. The rows of houses between Summerland Street and Paris Street which included Russell Street and Spiller's Street, were so badly damaged that the whole was demolished and left as a car park when the city inner bypass was constructed. The lower sections of Little Clifton Street and East John Street were demolished and have since been rerouted and renamed.

There are quite large gaps in many of the streets in Newtown which were either left as green areas or had blocks of flats built to house the people who had lost their homes. In some places the remaining houses were compulsorily purchased to be pulled down and the residents were temporarily housed in other suburbs of Exeter such as Whipton, St Thomas and Burnt House Lane. The scheme to rebuild the houses and flats was a grand plan but in the end only portions were completed because of the expense.

At the end of the war, to celebrate, a street party was held in the longest and least damaged of the Newtown streets, Portland Street. Trestle tables, kitchen tables, work benches were all hauled out into the street and filled with what cakes and goodies rationing could supply. One of the wartime losses the old men around here bemoan is the loss of most of the pubs, either demolished by the bombs or later, but after having 16 pubs, Newtown is now down to four!'

EVACUATION

'If you were going to market, along a quiet road, it was not unusual to be stopped and told to go home again or to be diverted, because the troops were doing exercises. This was when much of the South Hams around Slapton and inland to Blackawton was forced to evacuate, with only six weeks notice. Three thousand people were given notice just before Christmas in 1943. Many animals had to be put down and special markets were held for the farm animals. People had to move in with their relations. Sometimes families had to be split up and their cows would go to someone else to be milked and looked after. This was all necessary so that the troops could train in war-like conditions. Many were killed as they used live ammunition, but all was carried on in secrecy and plans made for the invasion of Normandy which hastened the end of the war.'

DAILY LIFE

Life had to go on, even amidst the air raids, and we struggled to feed our families on the meagre rations and to follow the government's advice to 'Make Do and Mend'. Even the smallest village was affected by the war to some extent, and where the Americans moved in a whole new way of life opened up!

IN EVERY VILLAGE

'Very few villagers at Clayhanger were directly involved in the war, being occupied in farming, but even so, changes came to the village. A searchlight run by a large battery was positioned on the outskirts of the village and the local Home Guard (20 men) would practise defending it against a neighbouring village's force. At night, parties of firewatchers would patrol from one end of the village to the other in pitch dark – great for courting! The blackout was rigorously enforced and there was a special constable in the village who kept an eye out for anyone showing a light. Cars and motorbikes had to have their headlights dimmed by thin strips of black paper stuck across them. This gave such poor light that several villagers ended up in local hedges.

Two bombs thought to have been jettisoned by a German bomber returning from a raid on Cardiff left a 50 ft crater on the outskirts of the village. It is said that "it needed a whole hedgerow to fill it in". The blast bent the leaded church windows, blew out many others and brought down a few bits of ceiling. Beech Court School, from Deal in Kent, was evacuated to the rectory. The headmistress and about 15 of the girls lived in the house with the rector and his family, the remaining girls being boarded out.'

'How the war changed our lives! Stoke Canon's population before the war was about 440, but after September 1939 when evacuees and employees of the Ecclesiastical Commissioners joined us from London, our numbers jumped by 100 in a week! They were all billeted in the village and surrounding area and stayed for six years. The paper mill was used as a naval torpedo store from Plymouth.

After Exeter was bombed many people came out from the town to sleep nightly in nearby Stoke Woods and some filled our village hall. Our Women's Institute was kept busy, most of us looking after our wartime guests, every house being filled with children or adults. All had to be fed using ration books, so our WI members congregated at the village hall in the fruit season and with pots and pans and primus stove, made jam with everyone's surplus fruit.

We had a thriving social life, everyone joining in all activities such as whist drives and, especially, the once a week sixpenny hop. We had our sad times too, waiting to hear about our lads, some missing or taken prisoner. Thank God, all but a handful returned home.'

OVER HERE!

'The war made a big impact on the people of Tavistock. Plaster or Plaister Down Camp on Dartmoor was a military hospital for injured American soldiers and there was large influx of American troops in the town awaiting the D-Day landings. The whole of what is now the golf course just outside the town was covered in tents housing thousands of American servicemen. Black and white were segregated. These were the first coloured people my husband, then aged seven, or indeed the rest of Tavistock, had seen.

The Americans were all very kind to the children, arranging parties and giving them plenty of chewing gum, oranges and tinned fruit. All the large houses in Tavistock, chapels, halls etc were taken over by the troops, and a church hall was the US post office.

This influx of handsome men caused quite a few problems and changed the lives of many country lasses.'

'The war was a special time for Dunkeswell village. At the beginning of the war an airfield was built on the plateau above the village for the Fleet Air Arm, who never used it. Ann's husband's family lost half their land with very little compensation, as did Phyllis's. Eileen remembers hearing the plans being discussed in the pub her parents ran and seeing the plans at a local farm. Wimpey lorries, mud and Irish navvies billeted in the village are an abiding memory. There was never enough ale and stout for the Irish! They were not popular – but Malcolm can remember them buying up all the milk from his father's dairy and sitting along the farmyard wall eating their lunch. The roads were improved and traffic increased. Any objections by the villagers were over-ridden with the claim that "The Germans would treat you worse."

In 1943 the airfield was taken over by the Fleet Air Wing of the US Airforce and the first Liberator landed in August. Some 5,000 men were employed by or served from the base with a loss of 183 lives. They made a considerable impact on the village, and on the pub. "They only had dollars when they arrived," Eileen remembers.

197

"However my mother managed I don't know." There was some bad feeling about the young men who were "having the time of their lives" in a safe billet while residents' menfolk were away fighting. Also the Americans tended to "take over" and go where they liked, blocking the roads with tanks and jeeps, knocking down walls with heavy vehicles and moving into barns. But on the plus side were the candy, tinned fruit and parties they gave to the children, who used to hang about the sentry boxes which marked all entries to the village. Everyone entering had to have a pass and if there was trouble the sentry would fire his gun into the air and the Military Police would arrive.

The children were fascinated and excited by the planes and the activity and had to be warned away from the airfield. Also the Americans were great fun, especially in the snow when Malcolm remembers tobogganing with them through the village on metal sheets. They would make "snow cream" out of clean snow and milk powder, also popcorn. They would drive past the school playground and throw in sweets, at the same time making the teacher blush! The children were invited to parties in the mess and girls were trucked in from surrounding villages for dances. Eileen remembers having passes for the dances, which she still has. At the end of the war Liberators and Fortresses were broken up and buried on the airfield to save transporting them home.

There were anti-aircraft guns around the village but only once were the planes chased back by enemy aircraft. One returning plane overshot the airfield and crashed in Phyllis's father's field. No one was allowed near it but they still managed to get souvenirs.

There were evacuees in the village and Malcolm remembers longing to have some, but with a family of seven children this was not possible. He remembers fights between them and the local children.

There was an air raid shelter beside the school in which Malcolm has since kept pigs. Every house had a Morrison shelter but he only remembers bombs falling once, which brought down one of his ceilings. Phyllis remembered sleeping in the cellar during the bombing of Exeter – with the Clerk of Works in charge of the building of the airfield who lodged with them. A number of Americans came to church and the chapel. Phyllis remembers them coming in straight from sorties, still in flying gear. The following week, some of them would not be there. After services they met in Malcolm's home and Phyllis's. There was quite a lot of fraternising and the village is still paid sentimental visits by Americans who were stationed here. There were a lot of weddings in the village church but they were not usually village girls, of whom there weren't many. The Americans

198

donated a new organ to the church, which was installed in 1947.

After the Americans left there was plenty of local scrounging for what they left behind. When Beryl came in 1952 whenever it rained "you would see the raincoats coming out with US Navy on the back." Phyllis didn't remember missing the Americans. "Life just went on."'

'I lived near Barnstaple during the war and though we were not affected by bombing, there were often American Army units training around the farmyard. My personal memory of them was that they gave us large bars of chocolate, and as sweets were rationed this was a great treat. They also gave us compressed bars of dried fruit which went into my mother's cake mixture. She thought they had better rations than the British troops, and they were very polite to us.'

'We used to have to walk along part of the railway track sometimes to Ventnor chapel and if an American train was passing, the men used to throw out chocolates, sweets, cigarettes etc onto the track and we picked everything up – when the signalman in the box said it was safe, of course!'

'The American soldiers used to drive their tanks through Landkey to wash them in the river by the church after they had been on exercises on the moor. You can still see the scars on the walls through Landkey where the tanks knocked against them.

I had a new bicycle of which I was very proud. One day I saw an American soldier riding it and discovered my younger brother was renting it out in exchange for chocolate bars!'

SEEING STARS

'Film star David Niven came to Saunton to film *A matter of life and death*. I stood for hours in the sea hoping to get a glimpse of him wading out of the waves, only to be disappointed to see a stand-in. I was in tears. A tap on my shoulder made me turn round and David Niven said to me, "You wouldn't want me to catch cold, would you?" Joy!'

'Hollywood stars such as Bob Hope and Carmen Miranda entertained in the nearby army camp, and, stars of a different kind, Generals Eisenhower and Montgomery had a meeting in Bridestowe parish hall. They reviewed the troops at Willsworthy on Dartmoor.'

'Dances used to be held at the parish hall at Braunton. The pianist,

199

a lady, was somewhat temperamental and often slammed down the lid of the piano and went home. On one occasion, a tall handsome RAF pilot took over and played beautifully for the dancers – it was Max Bygraves, before he became famous.'

RATIONS AND MAKE DO AND MEND

'Wartime rations seem now very meagre, with total absence of some foods, but in fact the diet imposed by necessity was very much in line with what some doctors and dieticians advise for today. Radio saw the introduction of health and food tips – who remembers Lord Woolton, Potato Pete and the Radio Doctor? We made Woolton Pie, Victory Sponge, Mock Crab and Mock Banana. Beans were no longer fattening, nor were potatoes, but we should grow and eat as much as we could – so away went the lawns and in came the vegetable gardens. In many town parks the older men and some women toiled on their patches to produce some wonderful fruit and vegetables. On the whole people never complained, appreciated what they could get and adopted the attitude of "They won't get us down".

Clothes were more of a problem and I recall that many women made a coat from an army blanket which they had dyed. They were not bad either. Oh yes, we learned to exploit our hidden talents then. Earrings from coloured buttons, hats from plaited straw.

My personal nightmares included only two ounces of tea a week, whale meat, hard rabbit, Icelandic cod, lack of coupons for the children's clothes (boys seemed to go through a pair of shoes a month) and the small ration of soap. What zealous squirrels we were. This is one of the wartime jingles to encourage us not to waste food –

> "If you have the will to win
> Cook potatoes in their skin,
> Knowing that the sight of peelings
> Deeply hurts Lord Woolton's feelings."'

'When we married in 1940 I needed dockets for furniture. Our quota enabled us to buy a double bed mattress, wardrobe, tall-boy, two dining room chairs and a sideboard.'

'During the 1940s we were living at Colyton, East Devon. Because of the fuel shortages, you could never be sure that there would be enough gas, so my mother used to send me down to the Chantry Bridge to look at the gasometer to see whether it was worth while starting to cook Sunday lunch.'

'As a young girl it was with great delight I found, whilst out walking on the beach, what looked like large tea chests being washed up on the incoming tide. Apparently an American ship had foundered and lost a lot of its precious cargo of scarce commodities whilst bound for Britain. The chests contained mainly tinned soups, peanut butter, chocolate, chewing gum, razor blades, soaps, cigarettes and, best of all, nylon stockings!'

'We were encouraged by "Mrs Sew and Sew" (a puppet figure with cotton-reel body) to "Make Do and Mend". We turned garments inside out; we made two old garments into one new one; we re-knitted woollens; we made rugs from old sacks and rags; we turned worn sheets sides to middle and made pillow covers with the odd bits and we managed without elastic.

Our clothing coupons (60 for a year) covered everything. A coat or suit cost 18 coupons. With no coupons to spare for stockings, we painted our legs with liquid make-up, then drew a line down the back. What a bother it was having to remove this muck before getting into a bath, which had to contain no more than five inches of water.

I remember the MOF asking us to gather rosehips, to provide Vitamin C for the children. These were collected by the WI and WVS. The Ministry paid a penny per lb for them. Ice cream was banned and wedding cakes were elaborate cardboard shells surrounding a plain sponge.

In 1942 some towns got a British Restaurant where a three course meal could be had for elevenpence. Tea, cakes and sandwiches cost less than a penny. Many people stretched their rations by using the British Restaurants.

I remember making a pudding with Ostermilk (for babies) and serving it with parsnips flavoured with banana essence. Result? Not bad! I remember queueing for cream cakes which resembled shaving cream. I remember making scrambled egg for two out of one egg and a spoonful of cornflour and adding rice to mince to eke it out. I remember the joy of getting a couple of ration-free sausages or a bit of offal. I remember eating rabbit till I couldn't bear to pass the rabbit hutch. I remember eating whale meat, which tasted like leather soaked in cod liver oil and snoek which had no taste. I remember National flour, which was heavy, dried egg, which was a blessing and tinned American Spam which was delicious. We saved paper, books, cans, bottles, rags, bones, old clothes, scraps for pig swill, etc. And this economy helped to win the war.'

'On a warm summer day in 1943 there was great excitement in

Torquay. A shoal of mackerel had followed smaller fish into the harbour, and the water seemed to be boiling with the movement of the fish. This was at a time when there was food rationing, we had a small weekly meat ration per head, and although fish was not rationed, it was *very* scarce – so there was a rush to the harbourside to obtain some mackerel.

It was amazing to watch the many ingenious ways of catching the fish people had invented, but one boy aged about nine years, had brought along a large wicker shopping basket and from the sloping ramp into the water – opposite "Bobbys" – he was dipping the basket into the water and bringing it out alive with mackerel. He was then selling them to anyone who wished to buy – he was not short of customers. We all knew that when the tide turned to go out the fish would go with it.

At that time my husband and I were sharing a furnished house in Windsor Road, Babbacombe, with another RAF couple. We, like most other people then, had neither a refrigerator or deep freeze so the mackerel had to be eaten fairly quickly. Our meals for 72 hours after the "mackerel invasion" were very high protein – mackerel grilled, fried and soused!'

'When we had a party at Modbury school hall for VE Day, there was a rush and a long queue for "banana sandwiches". Of course, bananas hadn't been available since the war began. Some enterprising cooks had boiled parsnips, mashed them and flavoured them with banana essence, but they tasted good!'

A CHILD'S WAR

As children we took war almost in our stride, soon accepting as normal the presence of foreigners in our midst and the necessity of sharing our schools and our homes with children from a totally different background. Caring for evacuees cannot have been easy at times for our parents, but in many instances friendships were formed which have lasted decades.

GROWING UP IN PLYMOUTH

'Some of my first memories of growing up in Plymouth were of the Blitz, two ounces of sweets to last a week and a strong tasting American orange jelly, plonked in the centre of a plate of runny semolina at school lunch!

We stretched our feet when measured at school to qualify for extra clothing coupons. But I think the most exciting time, not realizing the dangers, was bed-time. My brother and I donned dark green corduroy siren suits, all in one trousers and jacket, which went over our pyjamas. Then out into the garden and down to the shelter. I can see my bunk now! It seemed so hard and cold and the whole shelter smelt of wet cement. The dog and two tortoises came too. My mother would sit and read until her bedtime, whilst my father, an ARP warden, did his fire watching duty. I presume we slept, but couldn't wait until morning to go and search for shrapnel in the roads around our home.

When at school and the siren went, we grabbed our gas masks and walked in orderly single file down to the basement. There, once settled, we took small knitting needles which had balls of wool stuck onto them, and like old ladies we knitted uneven squares! From time to time, a large sweet jar was passed around from which we took only one. No whole bars of chocolate or packets in those days of rationing. We had great fun when it was gas mask practice . . . who could make the rudest noise by blowing out the rubber sides of the mask!

We were healthy and happy enough and this unusual upbringing did us no harm, but the worry for our parents must have been considerable. I vividly remember catching my mother crying . . . the war took its toll in many ways.'

ALL THE FOREIGNERS

'During the early 1940s the roads around Blackpool were humming with military traffic going to and from Plymouth. Convoys of American soldiers were always looked for because Americans threw sweets and chewing gum to us children as they went by. Like most children I was a collector and I collected cigarette packets. We picked them up on the roadsides. The American ones were Camel, Lucky Strike and another called Chesterfield.

Near to D-Day there were hundreds of American lorries parked along the road to Liverton and the Belle Vue road to Bovey Tracey. All were under camouflage netting and little camp fires were sometimes made in our bottom field. We country children had never seen a person with black skin up until then and almost all these men were black. They were friendly to us and helped to fix bikes and sang us songs. They sometimes had names we'd never heard of, like Tex and Al and Stirling.

Later on we were to meet Americans again. This time they were wounded soldiers who were at the newly built hospital at Stover. "Escapees" were dressed in bright blue hospital clothes and took short cuts through our land to go to The Star in the evenings, keeping a sharp lookout for the Redcaps as they came from the woods opposite and crossed the road.

The next inhabitants of Stover were German prisoners of war and these too we sometimes met in the woods and the grounds of the lake. There were language difficulties here, of course, but we got to know one or two.'

'Growing up in the fishing village (as it was then) of Brixham in the 1930s and 1940s I can remember so many different experiences. Most of the beaches were barricaded during the war to make it difficult for would-be invaders. Therefore, after school our mothers would meet us with picnic basket and off we would trek to the open-air seawater Shoalstone swimming pool at Berry Head. We would spend hours enjoying ourselves at the pool, most of us quite oblivious to the horrors of war although most of our fathers were away in the services. Early one evening in the 1940s we were at the pool as usual when we became aware of the throbbing of engines – they sounded very different somehow, not the usual throb of the old Brixham trawlers. The sound came nearer and then into view around Berry Head sailed a small convoy of funny looking trawlers. As they drew level with us, the engines quite deafening, we children were quite amused to see the decks of these small craft absolutely laden with tables, chairs, beds, mattresses, prams, bicycles and all manner of household equipment. In the bow of one boat sat a grey-haired old lady dressed in black in a huge armchair and on her lap she was clutching a big dog. There were men, women and children of all ages crowded on each and every one of these craft and they were heading for Brixham Fish Quay.

We hastily dressed, our inquisitiveness getting the better of us, and we ran all the way to the quay in time to see them come ashore. Who were these funny people? They were dressed in a weird fashion and spoke a peculiar language. Being mainly country-born children and never having been away from Brixham, we had never before seen "foreign" people. Of course, we soon learned these poor souls were the Ostend fishermen and their families fleeing the Germans as their country became occupied. They had squeezed as much and as many on to their small craft as was safe. The children soon became our friends as we shared desks at school with a Belgian on one side and a Cockney evacuee on the other.'

SOCKS AND SCARVES

'I remember knitting socks for the Navy during the war, in coarse oily wool. Sitting on the school wall at playtimes in the blazing sun, this task could be very trying. We also knitted scarves for the RAF which had to be 56 inches long. I used to put one end of my knitting in a drawer and shut it tight before pulling and stretching the scarf in the hope it would get longer – but it never did.'

FIRST DAY AT SCHOOL

'It was about 1940 when my parents decided it was time for me to join my sister at the convent school in Exmouth. I was four and a half years old, and the convent was divided into two departments; "Sunny Side", the main part, for Roman Catholic children, and "Sunny Corner" for the smaller number of Protestants, up to the age of eleven years.

I was taken to school by my mother, on her bicycle, to join my sister. I remember this apparition dressed in black with her white wimple, taking me screaming from my mother's arms, along the corridor, with the promise that I was going into the same classroom as my sister.

Seated at their double desks were 30 children with their gas masks on, and this sight has stayed with me all my life. No wonder that I never really liked school.'

OVERCROWDED SCHOOLS

'In the 1940s evacuees came to our school at Honiton from the Elephant and Castle area. You can just imagine the difference between we country lads and the ones from the East End of London. This caused an overcrowding problem and for some considerable time we only went to school half a day whilst the evacuees had our classrooms in the afternoon. There was one frightening time when we were playing football in Allhallows playing field and a German plane came over and machine gunned the army camp and the railway station. We moved even faster than when we were playing football!'

'Lessons were taught in the Methodist church hall at High Bickington when I was ten, owing to a large intake of evacuees. We had to sit three to a desk and two classes were taught at the same time, divided only by a curtain, so it was often a case of preferring to listen to the other teacher.

All the windows were covered with strips of tape to prevent flying glass should there be an attack, and every Wednesday we duly presented our gas masks which we then had to put on and see if we could "sniff up" and hold a piece of cardboard for a few seconds. When the air raid siren went we either had to get under our desks and wait until the all clear sounded, or if our mothers so wished, make a dash for home. I was one of the latter and often got home only to have to retrace my steps back to school immediately.

One afternoon a week we were sent out to either collect acorns for pig food or rosehips to be sent away to make rosehip syrup for babies and toddlers.'

'When war started our school in Tiverton doubled in size with evacuees from London. From Stepney to rural Devon was quite a change. The girl billeted next door to us was a talented singer and dancer and had performed in pubs, though she was only twelve. When the sirens went, about 800 children had to be led out to a nearby field. Here we lay down until the all clear sounded! Obviously this was not an ideal situation, so air raid shelters were dug for us, but by the time they were ready for occupation a nearby river had risen and flooded them. So in the end we sat under our desks.'

'Schools from dangerous areas were evacuated to various places in Devon. Clifton College left Bristol because of the bombing and spent the war in Bude, housed in the local hotels. Miss Booker's girls prep school came to a Lydford house, next to Lydford Gorge, from Stoke in Plymouth. A Purley girls school went to Ardoch Lodge on the A30. Two London girls schools shared Sydenham House, Marystowe. There was a boys school at the Two Bridges Hotel on Dartmoor. There must have been dozens of schools sheltering from the bombs.'

WE ALL HAD EVACUEES

'All the farms in the Loddiswell/Aveton Gifford area had to take in evacuees. Many came on private arrangements but the majority were sent from London in trainloads, with their names on a ticket pinned to their coat and with a gas mask (that we all had and had to carry at all times) and very small case or even just a brown paper parcel. They were brought to a school or hall and allocated to various billets. Two small children aged seven and five arrived at Kingsbridge Town Hall and when all the other children had been sent off with their host families, were left forlornly. When my grandmother arrived, the children said afterwards, they thought she looked a kind lady and hoped she would take them, and she did. They spent a long time with her, but later they squabbled so much that she persuaded my mother to have the boy, as he loved the farm. He went to school with us too and stayed for several years, and was very upset when an uncle arrived to take him home. He still says he felt like a brother and keeps in touch with us.

There were children billeted on all farms, so for the first time we had a lot of children to play with. Some girls on the next farm were so impressed with our large barns, with a natural platform at one end, that they got up "impromptu" concerts and taught me all sorts of cockney songs and the grown ups had to come and sit on the straw and clap us.'

'The individual evacuees who came to Mortehoe were mainly from Thornton Heath, near Croydon. They integrated quite well with local children with a few exceptions, town and country ways differing greatly. I remember as a boy getting into trouble with local farmers when we camped and lit fires in the surrounding woods. All of us liked it when the Yanks came to town, as chewing gum and great parties for all the children were in evidence. I can remember clapping and singing with the others at a party given for all the kids at the Bay Hotel in Woolacombe, all to the tune of *Deep in the heart of Texas*.'

'I well remember evacuees coming to Newton St Cyres at the outbreak of war. We found their accents almost incomprehensible – goodness knows what they thought of ours. One other thing they

A happy group of local children and evacuees at Mortehoe in 1941. There was a clash of cultures when city met country, but many friendships made at this time have lasted for years.

brought, and somehow passed around the school, was head lice!

We had two girls billeted with us, for which we were paid an allowance. It must have been quite a culture shock for them as we lived in a fairly rambling farmhouse with no electricity and water that had to be pumped from a well. We got on well together, and their parents and relatives came down to stay. They commented on the darkness – no street lights. It probably broadened our horizons too, learning about life in Walworth.'

'I came to live in Exeter when I married in 1938, and joined the Women's Voluntary Service as war was on the horizon. My first job was at the Guildhall Market in Queen Street. The stalls were cleared away and the huge open space was used to deal with evacuees, who were arriving daily. My job was to take several children round the houses where the owners had offered to have one or two children. On one occasion I ended up with two little sisters who were very dirty and frightened, and no one would take them. As it was getting very late, I took them to my next door neighbour, who already had two children of her own, and she agreed to have them. It was very sad to know that they had never had a meal sitting at a table, and for several weeks would only eat their food seated on the back door steps. By the time I left with my husband to join the RAF, they were quite different children due to my very kind neighbour. I learned later that the rest of the girls' family had all been killed in the London Blitz. Both girls stayed in Devon.'

'Evacuees poured into Exmouth. They were taken to the Pavilion where the Salvation Army, WVS and local councillors with lists of likely billets sorted out the mothers and children. My mother took three sisters, aged twelve, nine and five, from Peckham. They were lovely girls and we had a lot of laughs with them. One day I came home from work and said to my mother that eggs had gone up to threepence each. Five year old Joan looked up and said, "Cor blimey, Auntie, we get threepennyworth of cracks in London." Florrie was very interested in the cooking of the Christmas dinner and every time Mum basted the chicken Florrie was there to watch. In the end she said, "Auntie, what is it going to be like, will it be like rabbit?" "I hope not," said Mum.'

I CAME TO BARNSTAPLE

'Although I have only lived in North Devon for 13 years, moving here from Surrey, I have vivid memories of my mother and myself as a seven year old coming to Barnstaple in 1940, fleeing the devastating bombing of London and south-east England. We weren't on any Government scheme so my mother had to find somewhere for us to live and managed to rent two rooms with a very kind lady in the Yeo Vale area of Barnstaple. My elderly grandparents also came down with us and stayed with a couple living at the bottom of Sticklepath Hill. They stayed the whole of the war – in fact my grandmother died during this time and is buried in the town cemetery. I went to a very crowded primary school on the Strand where the telephone exchange now stands and I remember playing in the cattle market during breaktime on days when there was no market.

My father stayed up in Surrey to look after our house and carry on with his work in London. He came down to visit us every month travelling on the overnight newspaper train from Waterloo. In those days the steam trains used to run from Waterloo right through to Ilfracombe stopping at Barnstaple Junction on the way. I have very clear memories of how unhappy Mum and I were as we walked back over the Long Bridge after seeing my father off on the train back to London and all the dangers there. I can remember one night there was an air raid and a bomb fell – German planes returning from

209

a raid on Cardiff and dropping a left-over bomb. There was great consternation next morning.

I also remember going out into the street with a jug to get milk from a man with a churn on a cart and the milk being ladled into the jug. I had never seen anything like that before. Our milk at home came in bottles and I had never really thought about cows and churns!

We returned home after a year, but continued coming down every year to visit my grandfather. In 1944 when we were down taking a break from the doodlebug raids, the town was full of Americans with the run-up to D-Day, and one GI gave me some chewing gum which I kept for days just nibbling pieces off it.'

AN UNOFFICIAL EVACUEE

'My father worked for a small firm in the City of London, which at the outbreak of war transferred to Devonshire House in North Tawton. The front of this Victorian building was used for offices and in the rear, the staff and their families had their living quarters. Dining rooms, kitchens and bathrooms were shared, as was the vegetable garden, so one could say we grew up in a commune.

My first recollection of North Tawton was standing on the station which seemed to me to be very wide open and windy, waiting to be hugged by my mother who had gone down a few weeks earlier. I was eight at the time.

We went to the local primary school which seemed very dark and I didn't much like the outside lavatories. Every morning Mr Attwell, the baker, parked his van below the playground wall, rang his bell, and then for a halfpenny we were able to buy a dough bun. These were hot and delicious and there was a special way of eating them; you hooked your little finger into the middle and ate the sweet dough, by which time the top and bottom had cooled and become crisp; these were eaten like biscuits.

I recall my curiosity on seeing two elderly ladies in Fore Street, standing at their doors wearing long black skirts and white aprons that reached the ground. Coming from the suburbs of Surrey, this was indeed an unusual sight.

We soon made friends with out contemporaries and embarked on the escapades that most country children seemed to enjoy; scrumping apples and peas, making dens in bushes and picking the first snowdrops and primroses, but the greatest joy of all was the river. It became our playground for what seemed all the summer long. Yeo Lane will always be the gateway to happiness. The little shingle beach under Black Clapper Bridge was where we learnt to swim. At certain times of the day the wool factory released the leat water used for sluicing the fleeces and this filthy water formed a strong current. We children tested our swimming skills by trying to swim against it. What would our mothers have said had they seen us?

The war did not seem to touch us children very much but I do remember being taken out of my bed to the high recreation ground to see a red glow in the sky, and being told it was either Exeter or Plymouth being bombed. The arrival of soldiers to be billeted around the houses caused much talk but the arrival of the Americans caused the biggest upheaval. Their attitudes were so different. For some of us it was the first time we had seen black people.

The method of alerting the people to an air raid was as follows. A policeman would drive his car around the roads with another man standing on the seat with his head out of the roof, blowing a whistle. This practice soon ceased as we had no air raids.

Because the means of travel during the war were restricted, people had to make their own entertainment. There were dances and concerts etc. We children did our bit and one member of our group wrote the script for a pantomime; also we started a children's lending library – all the proceeds went to the Red Cross. As we got older we were allowed to go to Okehampton on the train to the pictures. One never knew when the train would arrive because it might be held up due to bombing up the line miles away. On some occasions it never did arrive!

When we finally returned to our Surrey home after living the greater part of my childhood in a beautiful part of the country, we found the austerity and greyness of post-war Britain very hard indeed. I missed the beauty and freedom of Devon.'

OUR FRIENDSHIP LASTED YEARS

'My family home was bombed twice during the Plymouth Blitz and my parents reluctantly decided that my brother and I should be evacuated to a safer place. And so I found myself at North Road station with many other children from various Plymouth schools. I was separated from my brother and had no idea where I was going. I was sad at leaving my parents. My mother had given me an attache case containing my belongings – two pairs of knickers, two vests, two liberty bodices, two pairs of socks, a jumper, pinafore skirt, slippers and nightwear. And I had my gas mask in a cardboard box which hung around my neck. Inside the box was a stamped addressed envelope for my parents because they had no idea where the children were being sent, and I had to promise that I would write and tell them my address as soon as possible.

The train left the station and most of the children were in tears – I wondered where my brother had gone. We stopped at a place called Sidmouth and were transferred to buses and taken to a "dispersion unit". One by one the children were assigned to waiting adults and horror of horrors! I was the only one left with no one to claim me. After what seemed hours a kind man came and told me that I would be living with him and his wife. I later discovered that his wife was severely asthmatic and the excitement of having a child to live with them had brought on a bad attack of asthma. They were a childless couple but showed me great kindness from the moment I entered their home.

There was a long front garden, full of flowers, a vegetable garden at the back and an allotment not far from the house. I was introduced to gardening and taught the names of flowers and one day I was allowed to cut a bunch of sweet peas – what joy! I always remember the wonder of that time whenever I smell sweet peas. Another revelation came when I had breakfast – I tasted Fry's Chocolate Spread for the first time in my life! I sent off my first letter to my parents and discovered from their reply that my brother had gone on to Lyme Regis. (He only stayed there a few weeks as he was with an unkind family and was terribly unhappy.)

I loved my new family and soon settled well into my new school where amongst other fresh delights I was introduced to country dancing – a love I still enjoy. One day my parents came to Sidmouth and told me that I had passed the scholarship examination to go to high school and as it seemed that the bombing had ceased it was decided that I should return to Plymouth. I had become very fond of these good people who had taken me into their home and had become my substitute family for a few months. Our friendship lasted many years and I made many return visits. Sadly, my foster mother died while still quite young. Some years later her husband remarried and his wife produced a baby daughter. I felt very honoured when they wrote and told me that they had named her after their little evacuee, Pauline. I was one of the lucky children and have never forgotten the generosity of spirit extended to me during those very dark times of the war.'

DOING OUR BIT

Whether it was firefighting or duty in the Home Guard or the ARP, the Women's Land Army or the Ministry, we tried to do our bit to protect our homes and families from the effects of war. Members of the ATS and the Buffs regiment also recall time they spent in Devon during those years.

EVERYONE HELPED

'A searchlight battery was situated in Washfield parish and Mrs E was delegated to decontaminate the soldiers in the event of a gas attack. She was glad there was no gas, but a bit disappointed that she was never able to bath the soldiers.

Everyone was engaged in first aid courses, voluntary fire-watching, nursing in the local hospital, digging for victory or in the Home Guard. A local farm worker was arrested for not attending a Home Guard parade. The Home Guard used to carry their ammunition in a market basket. The Land Army had a hostel nearby and the girls worked hard at unaccustomed jobs. One was told to harrow a field on a tractor but not shown how to stop it, so she had to go round and round the field until it ran out of fuel. She also had trouble with an amorous farmer who tried to lure her into the potato shed!'

THE WOMEN'S LAND ARMY

'When I arrived on the farm as a land girl with one month's training behind me it was in cold February weather. Cutting lengths of kale, loading it up on a cart and drawing it out with a horse into the field for cows to eat was no fun on a frosty damp morning. Nowadays with an electric fence the cows help themselves in the field.

Another cold job was cutting hay from the hayrick with a hayknife – hard work and dangerous too as the hayknife was very large and sharp. Now, hay is stored in bales and is easy to handle – it is probably also stored in a modern barn near the cattle. In 1943 we hadn't seen many baling machines and those that were obtained tied the bales with wire, not cord, which later gave a lot of trouble when cattle ate a piece by mistake and the vet had to be called. The standard cure was to tie the animal in a stall with its front feet raised on concrete blocks – this invariably seemed to solve the

213

problem! Mangel pulling time meant making sure your braces were in a good state as continual bending and straightening could find the weak spot – same applied to your back too!

On the farm where I worked there were six carthorses, besides ponies and the cob which the Boss used to ride around the stock every day – this would now be a Land Rover or similar. There was one brood mare who had a foal regularly – the stallion used to "visit" her and she also worked her passage. The chief horseman often used to walk up to the farm in the evenings to check on his charges. He did most of the ploughing, after grooming and feeding, others worked the ground and the "lad" was the turnip boy, in charge of a horse and cart, spending all day pulling up turnips, loading up and tipping them in the various tip holes in the barns to be fed to the cattle and sheep. The horse knew exactly how to back up to the tip hole and I much enjoyed this job when I was "promoted" to it. I was treated very kindly by the workers, being extremely ignorant of nearly everything! One old boy didn't approve of us "maidens" working on the farm and we spent many days working in silence. He referred to me as "that there landmaid" but we got quite friendly in the end.

Loving the outdoors, each day was a holiday for me even when doing such boring jobs as picking up stones, digging up "daishels" or thistles and worst of all, picking up the tiny apples used for cider making. These always seemed to fall amongst stinging nettles and I longed for milking time to come around in this job.

Corn harvest in those days was a long drawn out time if the weather was unseasonable and wet just when the corn was being cut and stooked. It was cut by binder, driven by an old Fordson tractor, tied and thrown out. Someone would go around and poke the sheaves into rows and then it would be stooked, in different ways according to the sort of corn – for instance, wheat would be stooked something like a wigwam. When dry the sheaves had to be carted and ricked and I remember one year when it poured day after day and we stooked and restooked the corn, pulled it apart to dry and got soaked many times before we ricked it in a poor condition. Now the combine harvester does the whole job in a few hours. Time marches on, sometimes even for the better.'

'At first I was in a hostel in South Wales, then I moved to Honiton St Clyst and finally ended up at Barnstaple in a little hotel called The Waverley, which was used as a Land Army hostel. The beds were very hard and there were bare boards on the floor.

We went out to farms all over North Devon, doing the milking, weeding, planting and picking potatoes, haymaking and helping to

Land Army girls were a familiar sight on farms across Devon during the war, filling the places left by men called up for the Services.

build up the ricks, as well as various market garden projects. We had to be up early, about six o'clock, to be ready by 6.45 to go out to the farms. We travelled by Land Army lorries and got back to the hostel at about five o'clock in the afternoon.

Some farms we liked going to because we always had a hot meal in the middle of the day but at others we didn't even get a cup of tea and we had to eat our packed lunches instead.

Eventually the hostel closed and I went to a farm at Hache Barton, near to South Molton. I stayed in the Land Army after the war until I got married.'

THE ARP AND THE HOME GUARD

'During the war the Galmpton Institute (now the village hall) was the Air Raid Precautions post, with the Red Cross in the billiard side. The gentleman in charge of the ARP was a German by birth and the lady who ran the Red Cross was also German by birth! We had a siren on the hall roof, and we got our orders from Torquay when to sound it. Next door was the Auxiliary Fire Service station.

The village was full of troops. The Americans had their HQ at Greenway House, where they had a lot of landing craft on the river Dart, and Galmpton Warbro was an American ammunition dump, while further on towards Brixham they had a field hospital at Lupton. The Royal Navy had landing craft and other ships from Galmpton Creek towards Totnes, while just above Waddington was an Italian POW camp. The shipyard at Galmpton was in full swing, building RN motor launches and motor torpedo boats, their crews billeted locally.'

With all this going on, a Fifth Columnist was discovered in the farmhouse across the road from our hall, who used to signal to enemy planes at night through a fanlight in the roof. This went on for quite a while until one of our planes spotted a bright light and reported it to the troops stationed within the boundaries of the village. He was soon discovered by the police and arrested.

There were two anti-aircraft guns on the common between the packing cases and tented accommodation for the crews, and they caused some excitement one day when they shot down an ME 109. The plane flew on over the village when the pilot baled out. He came down in the apple orchards behind Treebys milk yard. The pilot gave himself up to the ARP officer. It turned out he was only 17 years old and was pleased to be out of the war. The Home Guard were disgusted to find that we, the ARP, had got him and that the Red Cross ladies had provided him with tea and biscuits.'

'I worked with the WVS in the local canteen for the troops stationed in Dawlish – I cooked so many chips and ersatz eggs that by the end of the war I was beginning to look like them. I also did three nights a week ARP telephone duty, whenever the siren sounded cycling (complete with tin hat and gas mask) to the local council offices until such time as the Powers That Be decided it would be better if we slept on site from 8 pm to 8 am. Many a tin of baked beans was consumed during those nights.'

'A German plane crashed near Kenton during the war and the young pilot, somewhat bemused and frightened when confronted by a detachment of the local Home Guard, promptly gave himself up to a local man dressed in his fireman's uniform. The local Home Guard was very active and it is suspected that all kinds of privately owned armouries were put to good use.'

FIRE FIGHTING

'In 1940 I was called for War Service. I joined the NFS and was stationed at Crossmeads Fire Station, Exeter, doing 24 hours on duty and 24 hours off, travelling from East Budleigh station by train at 7.30 am to report at nine. I was on duty during the Exeter Blitz in May 1942 and my shifts coincided with the worst two days of bombardment. The Germans dropped many incendiaries and high explosive bombs on the city causing extensive damage and many fires. Touring the city later in the morning with the canteen with drinks and sandwiches, it was very frightening.'

THE ATS

'From the summer of 1940, my ATS unit was stationed in Ilfracombe, serving with No 36 detachment Royal Army Pay Corps. Many hotels were requisitioned for offices and living accommodation. Our work entailed dealing with regimental accounts and correspondence. Civilian clerks were taken on, and we received a steady intake of newly recruited ATS and Pay Corps soldiers to help with the ever-increasing workload.

In addition to coping with these duties, our Pay Office contingent was expected to provide defence for a section of the coastline. A certain amount of weapon training and drill was obligatory, and official parades became a normality. One such event for the ATS was a Royal Parade on the occasion of a visit by HRH Princess Mary, the Princess Royal, who was Commandant of the ATS.

As our daily working life settled into a routine, we were able to give some thought to "off-duty" time. The Pay Corps formed an orchestra and a male voice choir, and a hall, known as the Garrison Theatre, was put at our disposal for concerts and dances. A section of the Auxiliary Military Pioneer Corps arrived in Ilfracombe, and they also formed an orchestra. Exploring the Devon countryside gave us added pleasure. Walking over the Torrs to Lee, with a stop en route for refreshment at the Blue Mushroom Cafe was a firm favourite.

Ilfracombe had no air raids, but German planes regularly flew over in the hours of darkness to drop bombs on northerly industrial targets. Looking across the Bristol Channel we could see the burning towns on the South Wales coast.

News from home was often upsetting, but we shared each other's joys and sorrows. Many of us had relatives and friends in the Services who were never to return. A number of ATS girls married Pay Corps soldiers, myself included. These were some of the happier occasions.

I recall a dear lady from Mortehoe who "unofficially" adopted us girls. I think she was a retired nurse, and every morning she would cycle to ATS headquarters at the Grosvenor Hotel to assist the Medical Officer with the "Sick Parade". She was always there when we needed her, with a comforting shoulder for any homesick girl to cry on.

My husband and I have returned to live in Devon in our retirement. The Ilfracombe of the war years will always have a special place in our hearts, and we often think of the many fine people we met, and with whom we shared those years of our youth.'

'At 18 I went into the ATS and trained for six weeks at Guildford before transferring to the Royal Citadel Plymouth – an eerie place with long dark passages. Then on to Wembury Coastguard with RA (now known as HM Cambridge). I was on duty one night plotting ships when a German submarine entered Plymouth harbour. They got him and it was quite a sight to see it blown up, flames everywhere.'

THE 'BUFFS'

'The "Buffs" regiment was in the South Hams for almost a year during the war. I was in A Company and as most of its members were aged 20 years and from north London, you can imagine the overflow of our natural youthful exuberance. Our regiment HQ was at The Albion in Kingsbridge; at the other end of the scale the common soldier was in the workhouse.

The whole of the area we looked after was classified as restricted. Cameras etc were right out, so there were no photos. One of the platoons was stationed at Wonwell beach, some in a Nissen hut and the balance in the cottage on the right of the bay looking across to Mothecombe. To the left of the cottage up to the pillbox there was a mixed minefield at high water mark, about 20 paces in depth, fenced on the land side.

Troops were eventually withdrawn from Wonwell for this beach was well covered from Mothecombe private beach, the then summerhouse being a machine gun emplacement, also surrounded by a minefield. With the explosion of mines on Wonwell beach for no apparent reason I was sent out from Bigbury to sort things out. The local policeman was there when I arrived and in a few minutes we were treated to another explosion. Young Tom May arrived to say his dog was missing and now we knew what had started things off. Of the dog there was just the odd bit of fur. This first set had disturbed all the rest of the mines and whereas they had been set to 40 lbs weight they were now so unstable that as little as one ounce could set them off. My job was to keep a log of those that had gone off and their position. It took a week before the explosions stopped and I rejoined the lads in Bigbury.'

FOR THE MINISTRY

'On leaving school in 1940 I started an apprenticeship at J C Tozer's which was then situated in Fore Street, Devonport. The shop was on the corner of Marlborough Street and Fore Street. I was training to become a cashier. I sat in a wooden enclosure with a slot in one side for the assistants to pass through their bills and money for items they had sold. All around the inside of the booth were long "strikes" with numbers on. Each assistant had a number, and the copy of the bill was put on the spike. At the end of the day, all the duplicate copy bills were totalled and balanced with the money taken. If our work didn't balance we were made to sit with the Head Cashier until it did.

I moved on to a job with the Co-op Butchery Department at Frankfurt Gate, but didn't stay there long as one morning I went in to find the place had been bombed!

From there I moved on to what was then known as the Food Office, Milk Department, these days known as the Ministry of Food. We were housed in what is now the big Mencap Building at Peverell and we also had another office in Mutley, where I used to go fire watching with another of the girls. In those days I went everywhere on my bike, including visits I had to make in the course of my job.

I remember having to go to a woman who lived in Exeter Street because she hadn't completed her milk form properly. When I reached the house I found she lived right at the top. As I arrived at the door her husband came rushing out. "Stay with her, I'm going to phone for the doctor," were the welcoming words he threw at me as he receded at a galloping pace down the several flights of stairs! I hesitantly went in; there was an awful screaming and groaning coming from one of the rooms. I was petrified. I walked over to where the noise was coming from and stood there with my eyes popping out of my head. The woman was in labour, although being "as green as grass" I didn't know that at the time. Her husband eventually came back and I was gone, without of course getting my form filled in.

I left the Milk Office (not surprisingly) and went into the Food Enforcement Office, dealing with licences etc. I used to visit different vegetable shops checking on their prices and the condition of goods on sale.

At one time myself and two other women employees had to count the number of people going into a particular cafe. We spent the day in an old bombed building in a side road opposite the old Palace Theatre; the men employees took over at five o'clock in the afternoon and stayed until the cafe closed. We carried out this surveillance for a week and it resulted in the cafe owner being prosecuted for false returns.'

THE WAR ENDS

Victory in Europe was greeted with joy and celebration all over the county, with street parties hurriedly arranged in towns and villages alike. But there was sadness too, as the full toll of the war became apparent. And, once the euphoria had died down, there were new problems to be faced as couples desperately sought a place of their own in which to start a new life.

VE DAY

'On VE Day we stood to attention in the school playground to sing the National Anthem, *Land of hope and glory* and *Jerusalem*. There seemed to be hundreds of Union Jacks and streamers fluttering in the breeze. There were street parties, the return of the Navy and the land troops – and family life and devastated Plymouth started to be rebuilt.'

THE LAST POST

'During the war military church parades were held in Exeter cathedral on Sunday mornings at nine o'clock, when a small contingent of soldiers or other servicemen who happened to be stationed in the area would march to the cathedral for a short service. This was taken by the Rev George Bidgood, the garrison chaplain in the city. He was a wonderful man and very brave – he had been the last British chaplain to leave Dunkirk, choosing

Towns and villages pulled out all the stops to celebrate VE Day in 1945, whether with highly organised affairs or simple street parties like this one at Churston.

to stay on the beach with the men until he was ordered to leave for his own safety. My father and I used to walk to the cathedral and would be the only civilians there (my father was a friend of the organist, Mr Willey Cole). It was wonderful to hear the all male congregation singing the hymns and their voices echoing round the beautiful cathedral, part of which was in ruins at that time due to the bombing in the blitz.

Several times during the war, national days of prayer were called for and churches everywhere were packed. The cathedral was no exception. Another time when the cathedral was full was when the Thanksgiving service was held to mark the end of the war in Europe. The singing was wonderful with such a large congregation. The quire of the cathedral was not used due to bomb damage, but I remember the trumpeters of the Salvation Army went up through the gates and stood among the ruins to sound the Last Post and Reveille, in memory of those who had fallen. It was a very moving moment.'

HE CAME HOME

'They went out together for the first time on Wednesday 24th August 1938, the day that Len Hutton scored 364 runs for England in a test match at the Oval; he will tell you. They did not always see eye to eye at first and when war came they went their separate ways, he to the RAF and she to the ATS. But they kept in touch and met a few times when she came home on leave from Catterick and he could wangle a pass and hitch-hike home for a few hours. In 1943 he popped the question and she said, "Yes".

Back at the squadron he hurried to the nearest jeweller's to buy the ring. He did not have enough cash but paid a deposit, "till next pay parade". By then, though, he was being interrogated in a German prisoner of war camp and it was many months before the postcard to his next of kin could convey the message to send her £7 and to find a jeweller named Verity. She would know the town; he could not mention it by name because of security. Verity's still had the ring waiting for her. They said it was not an unusual occurrence.

He came home in 1945 and they married two months later; the following year she presented him with a daughter and two years later a son. Much later they were blessed with five grandchildren. They are still married and see eye to eye perhaps a bit better than at the start.'

ALL WE COULD GET

'Life after marriage in 1945 was no joke! Houses were at a premium, no council houses, no building, so in desperation I resorted to bribery when I knew a terraced house was to become vacant.

Imprinted on my memory is my first visit to No 5. There was a huge jar of pickled onions on the table and the walls everywhere were painted dark green halfway up from the floor and the rest bright yellow distemper – but I didn't have any choice.

Gaslight in the kitchen, stone floor, a six inch stone sink, wooden draining board, gas boiler and only cold water. Indoor cupboard to store the coal; every time the coal was delivered there was a shower of coal dust.

The previous tenants, I was told, were gipsies – who I imagine had not heard of indoor sanitation. Imagine the state of the downstair ceilings!

Furniture dockets provided the basics – the rest was secondhand. The springs in the Utility bed creaked every time we moved. The put-u-up chair was a put-u-down chair – it broke the first time it was used. Dockets also provided the curtains and linoleum.

My son arrived in 1946 and my new baby clothes brought to me in the nursing home were full of moth holes! This rated a full scale investigation on my return, to find in the attic an old mattress, a feather bed, two stuffed animals – a paradise for moth breeding!

Soap was rationed but some kind soul at the Food Office forgot my extra soap ration for baby – we were washing with shaving soap to save the ration for washing nappies.

The place was overrun with mice. I even found one under the eiderdown where I kept a spare nappy for early morning baby cries. You could have sailed the QE2 in the puddles in the backyard where previous tenants had successfully broken the asphalt. The bathroom had a copper geyser which, when lit, went off with such a bang it shook the house!

My house was the first privately-owned one in the road and my rent was £1 a week (my income £3); the others were twelve shillings and sixpence for a bay window and ten shillings for the others.

We bought the house in 1960 for £750 and we are still here!'

THERE IS HOPE

'On Christmas morning 1946 my Christmas present was a second-hand Humber bike with front basket. A new bike would have been a miracle just after the war. In the basket of my wonderful bike was a large bag of toffees. Off I went for a ride and as I went down Saunton hill a group of German prisoners of war were marching up to Saunton Golf Club, which had been turned into a home for POWs. They were guarded by two British soldiers. I stopped, passed my bag of toffees around, and wished them "Merry Christmas" and rode off.

Twelve years later, by now mother of two girls, I went to my mother-in-law's farm for Sunday tea. I was glancing through her copy of *Woman's Weekly*, when I read one of the letters on the front page. A lady wrote in to say her German husband had been a prisoner of war in a Devon village and one Christmas morning as they were marching along a road feeling so far away from their own families, a young girl with blonde hair had stopped and given them each a sweet. As she went away she said "Merry Christmas". Her husband said that one of the other prisoners remarked to him in German, "There is hope". I am so glad I stopped.'

HIGHDAYS & HOLIDAYS

MAKING OUR OWN
ENTERTAINMENT

In the days before television, there seemed to be so much going on. Village socials, dances, plays, the circus – all sorts of entertainment and much of which relied on local talent to augment the professionals. Then there was the radio to listen to, from the earliest cat's whisker, or the cinema to visit for a few pence.

NEWTOWN ENTERTAINMENT

'There were two notable entertainments in Newtown, Exeter, that directly involved the residents, and one visiting entertainer.

The visiting entertainer was an accordian player, Hubble Bubble. He would walk up and down the Newtown streets playing the same tune over and over again. Nobody seemed to mind hearing the same tune although some children would rag him and often follow him up and down the roads.

Between the wars the children of Newtown would be the entertainers. They would collect in the cellar of one of the houses in Summerland Street. They would set candles in jamjars and practise singing and dancing and a bit of acting. They would then put on a show charging either one halfpenny or some pins for entry (pin money!).

Election time was the other great entertainment. The candidates would visit the pubs and buy the old men drinks. The reaction of the men was that if the candidate had money to buy pints for all, he didn't need their votes. The candidates were generally Liberals and Independents. They would pay the children three pennies each to carry banners for them singing their praises. Unfortunately the children had figured out that they could get three pennies from both candidates so first they would carry the banners of one and sing his praises and then abandon him and go to the other. Another good thing about elections was a day off school because the school was used as the voting station.

Newtown was not very far from the London Square where the Theatre Royal stood, just at the top of Paris Street. Leading lights in the theatre were Leonard and Edith Crump. Surviving members of the family still live in Newtown and often trips were made to the theatre to see Edith and Leonard.

And of course Exeter City football team's ground is within walking distance and several of the older men have lifetime membership so that they can go and see the team playing. Football was also played in Belmont Pleasure Ground and festivals and fetes were often held there. Even the Fire Department had competitions in the park.'

THE VILLAGE SOCIAL

'We would often have a social in the village hall at Sidford. There would be entertainment such as conjuring, jokes, stories, a sing song, dancing and games, all for about a shilling.'

'Entertainment was unsophisticated. The village concert at Otterton took the same shape each year, local men singing the popular songs such as *I'm shy, Mary Ellen, I'm shy* or *If ever I marry again*, as well as reciting a few well remembered monologues. There was always a hard worked, very popular pianist. A whist drive followed by a dance was also often held. The schoolchildren would put on a concert occasionally. I remember being dressed as a mushroom – swathed in white muslin and holding a white umbrella lined in pink which I gradually opened while one of the other girls sang *Grow little mushroom, grow*.

Our WI was founded in 1924. Other than the Mothers' Union, there was nothing for village women to do for recreation so the Institute became very popular. My mother was a founder member but our neighbouring farmer would not allow his wife to join. "Us shall be ruled by women," he told my Dad.'

TREADING THE BOARDS

'Travelling players came to the villages between the wars. Children were used as extras in such plays as *Uncle Tom's Cabin* – and it took a couple of days to get all the black make up off.'

'The local theatre group would arrive in Bere Ferrers and stay a week or two. They were professional actors and the villagers paid to see them evening after evening. At other times, pantomimes would be put on by local people in the parish hall.'

'My love of theatre came through visits to the Birmingham Repertory Theatre and Gilbert and Sullivan productions at the Alexandra, so to be invited to attend the WI production of Longfellow's *Hiawatha*

227

in Okehampton in 1948 was a must. Picture, if you can, the old Victorian church room in North Street which the enthusiastic members had turned into a "Canadian" scene; the chorus of 40 to 50 ladies dressed in sacking fringed at the hem, belted round the waist with handpainted cardboard belts, their heads adorned with plaited wool hair – and feathers.

The tall, the short, the plump, the thin, the one with the twitch and the one with the nodding head – the squaws sang with gusto. At first I found it all most amusing, stifling my laughter with a handkerchief. But the welcome, the enthusiasm and the friendliness of the squaws, giving of their best, eventually had me joining their ranks.'

'The Flutterbyes was a concert party based, I presume, in Exeter. It was in the spring they paid us a visit. Not in Lent though. Nothing whatsoever took place in Lent.

This party included two young ladies, "Blondie" and "Coppertop", who sang obviously "risque" songs and wore few clothes, to the consternation of the staid villagers and our dear bachelor rector (who I am sure said an extra lot of prayers when he got home). "Why," as a villager said to my grandmother, "does he go each time?"

The audience at the back of the hall was another class altogether, all the young men of the village complete with nailed boots, whistling and stamping. I can hear it now, although at the time I did not realise what all the noise was for. They, like the rector, probably did not sleep too well that night.

There was also a conjuror who got children onto the stage, and got flour and eggs and milk from our clothing. He stirred it all in a top hat, set it alight with a match and out of the hat popped a Rhode Island Red hen. Having been told in Sunday school of the Devil and all his works, this was surely it!

The Congregational church was the place for the Magic Lantern. *Bells across the Meadow* and *Orphan of the Storm* were but two of the titles. The smell of the lantern defies description. Heart rendering was the plight of the orphans, and such was the sadness that we were really carried away until Whoosh up would go the flames from the equipment. The ladies would gasp and scream, and we thought it exciting.'

LISTENING TO THE RADIO

'I remember the earphones. My grandparents only had two pairs and they used to listen and nod and nod. We children got so annoyed because we couldn't hear a thing.'

'My father made our first radio – he used to twiddle a couple of little wires (the cat's whisker) across a crystal. You can imagine the surprise when we could hear music and talking coming out of the earphones. We would sit around and wonder at the magic of it all, how a man's voice could come through that little piece of wire. Things got a bit more modern after that – our wireless had a loudspeaker with an accumulator, a glass battery which had to be charged every week. A man called and brought us a fresh one, taking away the flat battery.'

'Dad and I used to listen to the radio a lot. Mother and Grandmother were always in the kitchen doing something and when they did listen, they were either mending or writing letters. We listened to a lot of comedy shows – there seemed to be an awful lot. One of our favourites was *ITMA*, standing for It's That Man Again, starring Tommy Handley. It's funny how the catchphrases then seemed to stick. In this particular show, there was a cleaning lady called Mrs Mop played by Molly Weir and she used to say, "Can I do you now, Sir?" Another programme was *Much Binding in the Marsh* and each week they did a topical theme singing a poem/sonnet type of thing. One of the up and coming programmes for us youngsters was *Dick Barton, Special Agent*. It was an evening, 15 minute, programme at 6.45 pm – I'm not sure how many evenings it was on, but I know the Parson said he could not visit at that time! There was always a play on a Saturday late, I expect at least 9.30 pm, with Valentine Dyall who had such a spooky voice. There was a detective serial I used to like – Paul Temple.

You weren't allowed to sit and listen, you had to be doing something – "idle hands etc". Mother taught me how to knit and do embroidery but I hated the actual sewing. Mother used to "make do and mend", darning socks with a "mushroom". You put the sock on a thing which looked like a mushroom, made of wood with a long handle, and the sock went over the top piece – the holes were very large because there weren't any synthetic materials in those days. Men's shirt collars were turned and if there was ever a button missing, my mother had a huge box with every conceivable coloured and size of button imaginable.'

GOING TO THE CINEMA

'One of my earliest memories is of the silent films my father showed in a local hall. I can remember the packed audience sitting on wooden benches – I think the admission charge was threepence. The hall was heated by a huge coke stove, and the gas lighting had to

229

be re-lit by hand at every interval between reels. There was only one projector, which had to be hand operated. A very steady hand was required to do this but sometimes if the show was running late my father used to speed up the reels, particularly in the exciting bits!

I can remember seeing Charlie Chaplin, and Pearl White, who often featured in serials which left her tied to a railway line with the train steaming around the corner and "Continued next week" flashing onto the screen. Even as a small child I was struck by how pretty Mary Pickford was with her hair in ringlets and her 1920s clothes. My favourite was Felix the Cat, a cartoon. The pianist used to sit me on the piano and teach me the song *Felix keeps on walking*. I had a Felix cuddly toy, quite a large black and white cat standing on his hind legs and he was quite my favourite. The pianist was a very important person and could play anything to suit the mood of the film, with no music of course, and constantly changing from "Hearts and Flowers" for the sentimental bits to stirring patriotic tunes where suitable and "chase" music for the cops and robbers.

After the show all the reels had to be rewound by hand, but I had been taken home and put to bed long before then. I remember more than once being carried out protesting that I wanted to stay to the "real end".

My father used to take all the equipment in a Model T Ford around the villages to show the films and I understand that they gave a lot of pleasure in days when there was no television, and not many people had the wireless, which was in its infancy. It was at about this time that my father built a wireless which had headphones and I remember climbing on my mother's lap and listening to the sounds which came from those strange contraptions which people wore on their heads, but of course everyone thought that it was absolutely wonderful in those far off days.'

'Entertainment at Iddesleigh consisted of social evenings and dances in the village hall. A cycle ride to Dolton, three miles away, meant you could watch a film (worked by hand and constantly breaking down, though no one minded) for sixpence – threepence extra for a cushion!'

'We used to have silent films in the Town Hall at Colyton on Saturday afternoons. At half time his wife used to play tunes on glasses of water.'

'Buses ran from Frithelstock for the very essential Saturday evening excursion to Bideford for the cinema. Known as the "picture bus", three were often needed to bring back all the rural dwellers at about eleven o'clock, going as far as Shebbear every week. I suspect that more than one wedding was as a result of a meeting on the picture bus.'

'In 1944 we used to go to the "bug house" at Paignton on Saturday afternoons. We could watch two films and a serial for ninepence.'

DANCING THE NIGHT AWAY

'My mother, born in 1882 at Ashburton, used to tell me of her happy memories of the Staverton Ball (invitation only) held in the Court Room at Staverton. Gentlemen wore gloves and signed the lady's programme indicating which dances they wished to have with her. Discontinued during the Second World War, it was later revived and held in the Seymour Hotel, Totnes, for some years, minus the programme and gloves, but often on a New Year's Eve with balloons and paper hats. It was a wonderful experience to wear an evening dress for the very first time.'

'When Dad didn't have much money and he was wanting sixpence to go to the local dance, he was given one cartridge to go and shoot a rabbit – hopefully – which he could sell and raise the money.'

'In the early 1930s we cycled to dances, carrying our ankle-length dresses in a case on the carrier if wet, but if fine tying a piece of elastic around our waists to enable us to loop the dress up to a safe height to cycle. The dances finished at two o'clock, after which we safely cycled home.'

'As we grew older we were allowed to cycle to dances. There would be about 150 to 200 bikes left outside, so if you were early yours would be on the bottom of the pile!'

SPORTING LIFE

'After the First World War a room was built as a sports centre for the men returning from the Front. Later on a football team was started and two MPs gave a cup each to be played for, so of a Saturday afternoon the village was dead. Everybody who could get away went in coaches or by bike or motorbike to the football match wherever it was held.'

'In 1913 a golf course was started on De Bathe Moor near North Tawton. It had nine holes. Leonard used to caddy for May Tavener,

231

the local flour miller's daughter. He had to collect her golf clubs from her home in the middle of the town, take them to the club, caddy round the course, carry them back to her home and then he got threepence. On one occasion she was late, so Leonard teed up, sliced his drive and lost the ball. He had to do the caddying that day for nothing. There were those who would stand on a lost ball, "find" it afterwards and get sixpence for it.'

THE CIRCUS COMES TO TOWN

'One year the circus came to North Tawton. The big top was erected in the Square, around the town clock and completely covering it. It took up all the space in the Square and the clock became the centre of the circus ring. The wild animals were caged inside the tent, whilst children were given elephant rides around the ring. Alfie had his cap snatched by a caged gorilla.'

HOLIDAYS AND OUTINGS

Visitors have long made a beeline for Devon's glorious beaches and countryside, and Devonians themselves are not slow to take advantage of days off. It was really only with the coming of motorised transport, though, that we were able to travel very far, and local days out remained eagerly anticipated, and treasured for many years.

AUGUST BANK HOLIDAY

'August Bank Holiday Monday was the chosen day when workmen had a day's holiday. Whole families travelled to Bigbury on Sea in two horse-drawn waggonettes hired from the local publican and the village carrier. Adults wore second best clothes as seawater would ruin good material. Men wore bowler hats or caps with their suits. Men and women had to alight and walk up the steep hills. From St Ann's Chapel we looked for the sea, Burgh Island and the rocks. Soon someone shouted "The sea, the sea, I can see the sea!" We trotted down Folly Hill, up a short steep rise, across the Warren (now

A Sunday school outing to Teignmouth in 1935 – hats for the girls, caps for the boys, and second best clothes for playing in the sand.

the car park), potted with rabbit holes and burrows, and down to the stables and cart shed (now Tom Crocker's Inn).

Food and drink were unloaded and carried up the steep steps to three fishermen's cottages (now the seaside shop) where trestle tables were hired and erected outside where the fishermen dried and mended their nets. The older ladies remained behind to get the lunch; the men made for the Pilchard Inn, the women and children to the warren or beach according to the tide. One o'clock everyone returned for a meal. Snowy white tablecloths had been laid, sliced chine of pork, ham and thick slices of bread set out; the cider and ginger beer jars uncorked. Then came the traditional Devonshire apple pasty and cream. A must for August time. All afternoon we paddled, made sand castles, or the fisherman rowed us around between the Island and the coast according to the tide. It cost one shilling per boatload. Five o'clock we returned to the cottages for tea. The fisherman's wife provided the boiling water in two enormous kettles. Time then to prepare the horses for home. Chattels were stored and passengers loaded, except the men who had to walk up Folly Hill. The children's buckets were filled with pebbles and shells, bunches of sea pinks and, most precious, a strip of seaweed, crinkled and brown, our weather-glass to use on dry land.'

233

THE DAY OUT

'When I lived near Muddiford, which is near Barnstaple, Fridays during the war were a real red-letter day, especially during the school holidays. The one bus a week would go to Barnstaple and we would spend the day there. We would go straight to Pearces Restaurant, in the High Street, for coffee, with cream served in little jugs, and lovely plates of gooey cream cakes. We would then buy our ration of sweets – always "rats tails" as we got a lot for our ration and money. They would be meticulously counted and shared between my sister and I on returning home, and if there was an odd one my mother would eat it to save an argument. My grandfather lived with us and getting him ready for the bus was a real palaver. We'd clean his boots and they would have to shine like a mirror, for which he would give us sixpence. He wore flannel shirts without a collar and would wear what he called a "shaker" (a white false front and collar) which was starched as stiff as cardboard. My mother would have to insert a stud in the collar, which wasn't easy as he had a long beard, and put on his tie and lace up his boots. He looked quite smart in his striped trousers and black jacket.'

The Whitchurch church choir outing by charabanc in 1924. An outing to the seaside was an eagerly awaited treat in days when holidays were few and far between.

234

HOLIDAYS IN EXMOUTH

'I used to come from Kent every year in the late 1940s to holiday in Exmouth. Trunks were sent on a week ahead so that they were at the boarding house before we arrived. It then cost two shillings and sixpence for a bedroom. The landlady would cook us breakfast and dinner, providing we bought the food. We used to go to the dairy on Sunday mornings for a dish of cream. The holiday was spent on the beach in a hired beach hut, where we cooked snacks on a small oil stove. We always looked forward to our night at Exmouth Pavilion.'

CATERING FOR THE VISITORS

'Up until about 1914 in Mortehoe, apartments would be let by families who provided their visitors with four good meals a day for two guineas a week. The gentry used to come to the village and leave their carriages at the top of the hill and walk down to Barricane Beach, famous for the large variety of shells to be found there. Tea tents were put there during the season. The season was shorter then – a saying was, "Volks won't come till the kidney beans come."'

'As more people wanted a holiday in the country by the 1930s, a new venture for farmers was taking in paying guests. Many arrived by train and needed to be met at Loddiswell station. My mother advertised in a railway magazine called *Holiday Haunts*. Most people just wanted to walk in the countryside and expected full board – breakfast, dinner, a cream tea and supper. Later on, when visitors arrived by car, they went to the sea during the day and often invited me to go with them. They liked to have a packed lunch, which meant having to cook a meal for them in the evening, an unheard of thing in the country then.

Farmers' wives who took in guests were able to attain some financial independence, and many began to think for the first time of improving their homes.'

'My parents kept a hotel at Torquay before the war, which my sister and I helped to run. The best rooms were three guineas with full board. Other rooms were two or two and a half guineas. I had to take hot water round in the mornings and also take a slop bucket round before hot water was put in.'

MEMORABLE OCCASIONS

Royal occasions were celebrated with enthusiasm, whether it was a chance sighting of a Royal visitor or the more formal junketings for jubilees and coronations.

EDWARD, PRINCE OF WALES

'During the depression years – in 1924 – the then Prince of Wales (later to be, briefly, Edward VIII) visited Devon and on his tour passed through Talaton village. A crowd of people gathered at the Beacon to see him pass and when the Prince saw them he made an unscheduled stop. Some of the mothers held up small children for him to touch.'

Bonfires were lit across Devon to celebrate George V's Silver Jubilee in 1935. This huge fire was erected on Gibbet Hill at Mary Tavy.

JUBILEE AND CORONATION IN THE 1930s

'George V's Silver Jubilee in 1935 was marked in Starcross by the Sea Scouts and Girl Guides going to church for a special service. In the afternoon sports were held in a field where Parkers Road is now. A tea was provided and each child was presented with a mug. In the evening the adults celebrated by having a meal in the Reading Room. Two years later, the Coronation of George VI was celebrated in a similar way.'

'At Peters Marland the Silver Jubilee in 1935 was celebrated by every child being given a commemorative mug, made from clay from the Claymoor works.'

'Bonfires were lit in the evenings – ours at Cheriton Fitzpaine was on the local hill known as Cadbury Castle.'

MARRED BY TRAGEDY

'We celebrated the Silver Jubilee with a bonfire on the field which is now the park at Weare Giffard, with food, sports etc. All the village was gathered there in the afternoon. At five o'clock Mr Powell the farmer at Weare Barton was coming to light the bonfire. He did not arrive so two local men went to see what was the matter. They found a bull running up and down the farm lane by the church. Mr Powell's body was lying on the ground; he had been gored right through the body three times.

The bull would not let them get near the body, so they let out the cows to distract him and this made matters worse! By this time it was dark. Police and firemen arrived and eventually hosed the bull into a field and the body was taken up. Next day the bull was shot.'

CORONATION OF ELIZABETH II 1953

'A committee was formed at Kingston to raise funds for the celebrations. Whist drives were well patronised at that time, and an occasional euchre drive, while country dancing was popular and a dance known as the Kingston Cross Hands was always included. So we had these entertainments to help boost the funds. A subscription list went round and we collected quite a lot of money, enough to pay for the expenses incurred. Much was given in kind, such as a sheep, pieces of beef, poultry, barrels of beer and cider. For weeks the school staff and children were busy making the decorations for the rooms. Union Jacks were painted round portraits of the Queen and Prince Philip and long banners hung from the walls. In fact you couldn't see the walls for the decorations.

First there was a fancy dress walk through the village as far as the church where they were judged. The field opposite Well Park was used for all the outside activities – children's races of all kinds. We stayed on until all the men on the farms who were working could join in and have their share, later on we had the sports for the older people, the greasy pole, tug of war, toss the sheaf etc. As it got darker everyone drifted into the Reading Room where there was more entertainment, singing and dancing. It was quite late when we closed down but everyone had a happy day. Mr and Mrs Cattley provided the children in the school with Coronation mugs.'

THROUGH THE YEAR

Every year brought its own delights with each new season, from Lent Crocking to Punky Lanterns. Some customs were local, some days were national holidays, while others, such as Empire Day, have disappeared entirely from our calendars. There were more solemn moments, too, such as Armistice Day, which were an important part of our lives.

THE NEW YEAR

'The church bells would be rung on New Year's Eve, when they would celebrate with some bottles or a small barrel of cider. I have been told by my father, who was captain of the bellringers for some 25 years, that a Langtree ringer returning home across the valley after ringing out the old year and the new in, could still hear the Peters Marland ringers ringing, well after the New Year was in.'

'In the early 1950s the highlight of our year was the party held at Gidleigh village hall on 1st January. The fun in the seasonally decorated hall started about 8 pm, with the hall full of families, from the tiniest baby to great-grandparents. The older men congregated in the "cosy room" warmed by a glowing log fire to play sixpenny nap while the ladies gathered in the kitchen, bringing their contributions for the supper.

The party got under way with the Paul Jones, ladies in the centre ring circling clockwise and the men on the outside going the opposite way. When the music stopped we took the person opposite as partner for the first waltz. This resulted in some odd matches but it didn't matter as we were all known to each other. The process continued with a change of partners for the quickstep and the slow foxtrot. We were all given an elaborate paper hat made from crepe paper and gold card.

By now everyone was in party mood so the MC, Bill Hill from Ensworthy, organised party games, old favourites like musical chairs and pass the parcel, with hilarious forfeits. Bill always came up with some energetic new games in which no one minded making fools of themselves. Participants and onlookers alike laughed until their sides ached.

The local musicians, Percy Wadman on accordian and Will Hannaford and Jim Cooper on squeeze boxes and others struck up the Grand March Lancers. Six sets of eight, squeezed on the floor for the intricate movements. One involved two couples linking arms and whirling round while the men lifted we girls so our feet swung out horizontally. How we shrieked!

After this, we were all glad to sit down for supper, ham and cheese sandwiches made with white bread, sausage rolls, splits spread with cream and jam, cream on mince pies, trifles, sponges and fancy cakes. No one thought of slimming in those days. Tea and rough cider were the only drinks. While supper went down we were entertained by David Alford playing the bones, accompanied by his mother on the piano. Percy Wadman sang his comic songs full of innuendoes at which he laughed as heartily as his audience. A lady sang some Victorian parlour ballads, which caused a lot of unseemly suppressed mirth.

More games and dances – the Valeta, St Bernard Waltz, progressive Barn Dance, Military Two Step and the Hokey-Kokey and yet another set of Lancers.

By 3 am we could dance no more, so after Auld Lang Syne we made our way home following another jolly, happy evening at which all ages and classes thoroughly enjoyed themselves.'

LENT CROCKING

'Early in the 1930s I was an assistant teacher in a small village school a few miles west of Okehampton – Bridestowe. It was during my stay here that I became familiar with an old custom known as "Lent Crocking" or "Lent Sharding" (crocks or shards are Devon words for pieces of broken crockery), which took place on Shrove Tuesday.

239

We know Shrove Tuesday as Pancake Day but a hundred or so years ago people called it Lenshard Day. The Monday before Lenshard Day was known as Collop, or meat, day (a collop being a slice of meat). This meat meal, with pancakes, was traditional prior to the Lenten fast. I remember my grandmother mentioning Collop Monday, although I don't think it was connected with any special custom. Several Devon villages kept up the Lent Crocking custom, certainly up to the 1930s.

In olden times the children of very poor families went around the villages begging for food, so that their mothers could make a big meal on Shrove Tuesday even if there wasn't much to eat during Lent. So maybe this was how the custom of Lent Crocking started. In fact a couple of centuries ago children, armed with broken crockery, would pelt a householder with the sharp pieces if that householder refused to co-operate.

However, back to Bridestowe c 1932. Excitement mounted and by noon there was an exodus of pupils to the village (no school dinners, then of course). The headmaster had retired to his own cottage, obviously having witnessed all this in previous years. Groups of children went up to the various houses, knocked on doors and began to chant the Bridestowe version of the Lent Crocking rhymes (other villages had different versions). Generally the kind householders gave money or sweets to the youngsters. I suspect that the village shop did very well out of Lent Crocking – certainly there were some very sticky mouths and fingers that afternoon!

This version of the rhyme was told me by my husband, who is Bridestowe born and who remembers, as a lad, being given a whole half a crown at one of the big houses:

"Lent crock, a pancake
A fritter for your labour
A dish of flour, a piece of bread –
What you please to give me.
Pray give me something
An apple or a dumpling
Or a piece of crumple cheese
Of your own making,
Or a piece of patty cake
Of your own baking.
I see by the latch there's something to catch
I see by the string, there's a good dame within
Trippy, trappy, trow,
Give me my mumps and I'll to go!"

(Mumps = dues; crumple cheese = dried, hard cheese; patty = a little pie, cake or pasty.)

This custom has presumably died out – in Bridestowe anyway, as at a recent hundred years exhibition only one or two "oldies" vaguely knew the words. Some 1930 scholars remembered the occasion I have described, but not the words.'

LADY DAY

'On 25th March farm hands were traditionally hired or fired. Their jobs included living in tied cottages, together with fringe benefits of fresh milk and a firkin of cider daily. Some farm hands lived-in, being fed by the farmer's wife but receiving a low wage. Farmers always feared any rent review on Lady Day, since an increase in their rents made survival very difficult during the 1930s.'

GOOD FRIDAY

'Good Friday was always a day off for the workmen around Thurlestone, which if the tide was right could be a day to go to Bantham to pick cockles up the river and in the afternoon to plant seed potatoes.'

CLUB DAY

'The Club Walk was always held on the Wednesday after Whitsunday at Kentisbeare. We had a band which led the way. The men belonged to the Friendly Club and would walk around the village visiting each farm for a drink of cider. When they returned they went to the Club Room where there was always a meal of roast beef, spring cabbage and potatoes prepared by the ladies and the publican. In the afternoon the children went up in the field behind the pub for sports. All the girls had to wear white dresses because it was Whitsuntide. I remember that Mr and Mrs Radford would make a banner of flowers and put it up across the road. It was beautiful, and was put up in Silver Street for several years. Outside the church wall were stalls with gingerbread, cockles and mussels for sale. The stallholders came in from outside the village. We all looked forward to Club Day.'

'The Talaton Friendly Society, "An Institution to Promote Union and Charity among Agriculturalists and Tradesmen", had been established in 1855. The dues were three shillings a year with a penny ha'penny to the clerk, and the funds were kept in a strongbox which had five different locks and keys. Three were kept by the stewards, one by a landlord and one by the clerk. Sickness benefit was paid to members unable to work for six days – one shilling and eightpence per day if confined to bed, one shilling if able to walk. No pay on Sundays. There were many rules and regulations which if broken resulted in fines. Every seventh year each member left ten shillings in the fund and the remainder was divided out in proportion to the amount paid in.

The highlight of the year was Club Day on Whit Tuesday, when the weather always seemed good. Ottery St Mary Silver Band arrived and the churchwarden would go to the rectory and collect the rector. A procession would form up behind the rector, the churchwarden, the banner bearer and the club members with their staves, to march through the village to the church first and then to the Talaton Inn for the dinner.

There would be stalls selling gingerbread, jelly babies, liquorice and sherbet, and in the early 1930s the first ice cream, kept in containers of solid ice. The afternoon was given to a football match and sports for the children. There was also a trotting derby, mainly for carthorses, and a gymkhana in the Church Mead which attracted horses and their riders from miles around. Afterwards, a tea marquee was in operation with various sideshows. The day would end with a dance.'

Maypole dancing on May Day at Kentisbeare school in the early 1920s; it was practised for weeks beforehand.

MAY DAY

'After much practice at school, we would dance round the maypole at Sidbury, with gaily coloured ribbons. Everyone was always determined not to put a step wrong, watched by doting parents.'

'As children about 1915 at Braunton, we always had a piece of glass six inches square on May Day. We pressed wild flowers against the glass and covered the whole thing with brown paper. A flap was then cut in front which could be lifted up to see the pretty pressed flowers. We used to ask for a pin to see the peep show.'

EMPIRE DAY

'Each year we made quite a thing of Empire Day on 24th May. For a week before the day we used to practise marching round the playground in rows of four. On the day itself we marched through the streets of Okehampton to Fore Street. Here a platform had been erected with the Union Jack floating above it. The Mayor in his red robes used to stand by the flag and with the town band playing we marched past, saluting the flag as we went by. This was always in the morning, as in the afternoon we had a holiday.'

FETES, FAIRS AND CARNIVALS

'There was a village fete in the rectory garden at Stoodleigh each year, with a dance in the evening. This was illuminated by night lights in coloured jars hung by string around the garden, as the dancing took place on the lawn. My mother used to buy linen in the London sales and sell it at a profit for the fete funds, while my father obtained job lots of crockery and lingerie for the same purpose. Luxury goods were hard to come by in the 1920s and were a welcome addition to the fete.'

'Carnival time at Okehampton in the 1920s was a great occasion. The fire engine came round the streets clanging its bell to wake everyone up, and there were sports in Fore Street before breakfast. I remember the wheelbarrow race and a row of buns, each tied with string to an overhead rail. Men would try and eat one with their hands tied behind their backs. Sometimes the buns were covered with treacle and Dad tied a big white handkerchief around his neck to protect his suit. Everyone wore fancy dress that day.'

'At Kingsteignton we had the Ram Fair. It started long ago and has

243

Entries for the Decorated Pram competition at a village fete in the 1920s. Fetes were great social occasions and brought the whole village together in friendly rivalry.

been kept up. It is said that the brook water was once used for baptising babies and one year it dried up and there was no water; a ram was sacrificed on the dried up bed and the water began to flow again. The people thought it was a miracle and every year since then we have had a Ram Fair. A ram is roasted and later the meat is made into sandwiches and there is a May Queen with attendants, a procession and lots of games.'

'Every year the fair came to Honiton, and the Mayoress gave all the children free rides for one hour. Another custom, which still goes on today, is Throwing Hot Pennies. Pennies are heated up and thrown from the upstairs window of a public house in the middle of Honiton High Street – the children catch as many as they can, but the pennies really are "too hot to handle".'

'A highlight of my life in the 1930s was the ride to Widecombe Fair, in an old car with a roof that rolled back and leather seats. We left at half past seven in the morning with a farmer and we had to do all the farm work before we left, and get back again in time for milking.'

'My earliest recollections of Dawlish go back to the 1920s and the annual fair held along Station Road and Marine Parade with the helter-skelter, coconut shy and the confetti that people threw at each

244

other. Then there was the hand-pushed fish and chip van with the ha'penny bags of chipples – small pieces of tasty batter.'

'One of the highlights of the year for children (and indeed adults) living in and around Crediton in the early years of the century was the annual fair. It took place at the end of August and was generally known as Kirton Fair (Kirton being the local name for Crediton).

In those days almost everyone came to the fair, not just young people. People from the villages and countryside around about came, usually on foot, particularly on the Saturday night, to meet friends and family whom they had probably not seen since the fair twelve months previously.

The fair was held either in the Exhibition Field or in a field in Mill Street (opposite the Crediton Inn), sometimes in both fields. The rides were not as fast and frightening as today. Indeed they were quite splendid, such as Messrs Whitelegg's Galloping Horses, or Anderton & Roland's Golden Dragons, or Gondolas. There were also small rides for the children. Later, chair-o-planes were introduced and the Noah's Ark took the place of the Galloping Horses and as the motor car became more plentiful, dodgem cars became popular.

There would also be hooplas, coconut shies, shooting galleries and Try Your Strength machines, and confectionery stalls selling nougat and "fairing" – an assortment of, among other things, sugared almonds and cinnamon sticks only sold at fair time.

There was a variety of apple grown locally known as Kirton Fair. It was small, sweet and yellow, ready for eating at about fair time.'

'Bampton is a small town in North Devon on the main London road to Ilfracombe until the motorways were built.

On the last Thursday in October, a Pony Fair has been held for the last few hundred years. The main attraction was the ponies that were driven into the town after being rounded up on Exmoor by the farmers. They were driven all the way by "foot" and "hoof". After the war, because of the RSPCA regulations, they had to be transported by lorries.

Not only was there a special market for the ponies, which incidentally were sold for pit ponies, with just a few to the gentry for their children to ride, but there was a cattle market. On the one day in the year it was so large that the overflow of animals were put in the side streets for selling. We had to push our way through cattle and sheep to get from one place to another. If, as so often happened, it was raining, we had to pick our way amongst all kinds of slush.

The long main street was full of "Cheap Jacks" and the fair stalls (such as Roll-a-Penny). Now it is mostly fast food stalls and clothes.

There was a large pleasure fair and all the amusements were driven by wonderful traction engines – these were all highly polished. The music was supplied by Wurlitzer organs. The fair families lived in the most luxurious caravans and travelled from town to town.

On one Sunday at the beginning of October, the pleasure fair would travel from Bridgwater to Barnstaple, through Bampton. The streets were narrow with nasty bends. It took hours for the caravans and trailers to negotiate the corners (sometimes taking the odd brick from the houses). We called this Sunday, "Fair Sunday", and the vicar always kept his morning service short as people would stay for hours watching the procession of caravans.'

'For the Sandford Revel a greasy pole was erected outside the Lamb Inn, with a leg of mutton suspended from the top. This was won by the man who climbed to the top. Traditional "pig's ears" biscuits were baked for the Revel, for sale and to be given to the children.'

'On a date near to All Saints Day, 1st November, children at East Budleigh village school attended church and were given a bun. This custom was started and endowed in Victorian times by a local benefactress as a thanksgiving for the arrival in Devon of William of Orange in 1688 to ensure the Protestant Succession. Rumour says these buns were originally thrown from the church steps, but in my time in the 1930s they were handed to us as we left church. Today they are thrown, wrapped, from the church tower, much to the delight of the children.'

'There was, and still is, a festival at Sidbury, starting with putting out the white glove at The Royal Oak and throwing out hot coins from the windows of that pub and then The Red Lion. The children were allowed out of school, in rotation according to class, to grab as many of these as possible, burning holes in the youngsters' pockets and all too soon being used to buy sweets and cakes from the local bakery and stores.

The next day was Sidbury Fair Day, the High Street lined with stalls selling gingerbread men, sugared almonds and other fairings. Cattle, pigs, sheep, chickens, geese and ducks were auctioned, and all kinds of farm produce sold. Naphtha flares tied with twine to the sides of the stalls provided the light at night, with many in a merry mood by the end of the day.'

NANNY KNIGHT'S REVELS

'This was a very important annual event at one time at North Tawton and it is said that the Revels were started under this name in 1910 by a Mr Knight, whose wife, presumably "Nan" or "Nanny", had left him but returned. He celebrated originally with races in the street but this grew and finally moved down into two fields at the Barkyard. It is said to have been a continuation of the old St Peter's Patronal Day, which had ceased some time before.

Nanny Knight's Revels used to start with a band in the Square which marched down to the bottom of the town to the two fields. There were various home-grown entertainments in one field, such as Aunt Sally by Jack Steer. In the singing contest Charlie Setter would sing *Carve a little bit off the top*. There were treacle buns hanging on strings for the children to try and bite and a bran dip with coins mixed in it. The children all dived at once to see what they could find and came out covered with bran. There were skittles for a pig, an old bath filled with water with coins at the bottom for children to try and retrieve with their teeth. There were sports and races. In the other field would be a visiting fair, including a menagerie. Ice cream was made by Annie Vanstone who kept the sweet shop. This she used to make with the aid of ice delivered by train. There were halfpenny cones and penny wafers. The Revels finished off in the evening with a sixpenny hop with everyone in their best clothes. These delights all ended in about 1930.'

THE FLYING CIRCUS

'Open land at Salcombe Hill provided a reasonably level airstrip and we had visits from a plane which gave trips during the day, one person at a time, and in the evening gave a display with fun events like the "bombing" of a clown with flour. The great event was when Alan Cobham's Flying Circus came with an assortment of aircraft including autogyros and a larger passenger plane.'

'I was taken to Totnes races, held on the marsh, in about 1920 and saw my first aeroplane. I was always of a nervous disposition and when I saw it take off and land I was so upset and frightened I had to be taken home early and put to bed!'

'There was a small airfield on Haldon and one year Sir Alan Cobham came to give an air display and we went along to have a family picnic and watch. There were ten-shilling trips over Dawlish, and my brother and I remember so well the dreadful argument my mother and father had as we sat on the picnic rug – he wanted to take us on this flight and she thought it was the most dreadful and foolhardy thing she had ever heard of, risking our lives. But

Father got his way, bought our tickets and that was my first flight – in a little bi-plane, looking over the sides.'

DITTISHAM REGATTA

'We used to have a regatta at Dittisham every August. It was a day we looked forward to eagerly. During the morning sailors came up from the Britannia, an old wooden wall used as a training ship for naval cadets before the Naval College was built. They brought rows of flags, which they put up on scaffold poles, erected in barrels along the front of the quay. Then at two o'clock the races started. The first event was a pair-oared race for schoolboys and Sammy and I won that one year. We each received half a crown as a prize. At the end of August we had the regatta at Dartmouth to look forward to, and whatever money we could save we kept to spend at the fair, so you see the prize meant a lot to us. We used to gain more money by minding the boats of people who rowed up from Dartmouth during the summer to land and have tea. Some were a bit mean and paid you only a penny when you had looked after their boat for two hours, but others would give you sixpence and that was wealth indeed.'

Bampton Fair was held in October, when the town filled with people attending the pony and cattle sales or enjoying the fairground attractions.

HARVEST HOME

'The Harvest Home cream tea and sports was a highlight of the village year at Sidbury. The Sports took place at David's Close, part of Ridgeway Farm, with Ridgeway Farm Dairy being used to prepare the food for the cream teas, consisting of loads of sandwiches, chudleighs and cream, doughnuts, currant bread and other goodies, prepared by a band of farmers' wives, who made and gave the clotted cream. Coppers in the washhouse were used to boil the water for the tea urns. The Sidmouth Town Silver Band was in attendance. A huge marquee was erected in which the teas were served on trestle tables, all the children receiving a free tea, some coming back for a second sitting.

The kitchen at Ridgeway Farm was set aside for the use of mothers breastfeeding their babies, and was a wonderful showcase for presenting with pride their new offspring.

The Sports included races for children and adults on an oval sloping course, with prizes. A marathon race took place around the village. Also included was Putting the Weight, and skittling for a live pig, given by a farmer. Most cottagers kept a pig in the back garden, feeding it on kitchen waste and collecting acorns and beech nuts.

The Sports culminated with a tug-of-war between Sidbury and Sidford.

For the Harvest Festival the church was beautifully decorated with flowers, fruit and vegetables, and tidy sheaves of wheat, oats and barley. The village baker baked special loaves of bread in traditional shapes. There was great rivalry amongst the village gardeners to produce the biggest and best specimens, such as vegetable marrows and harvest cabbage, and the rosiest of apples. The fruit and vegetables were afterwards given to the Sidmouth cottage hospital. The church bells were rung, prior to a service in the early evening.'

'I well remember the Harvest Home teas held in the schoolroom at Alverdiscott and my mother was one of the ladies helping. Each had their own table with their own silver tea service and best china; starched linen tablecloths and the thinnest of thin bread and butter and, of course, clotted cream and home-made jam.'

'Harvest Festival services in church were very full, as all farmers and everyone in the countryside wanted to thank God for the harvest, but my mother always refused to sing the line "All is safely gathered in" if we were late and hadn't finished getting the corn in!'

PUNKY LANTERNS

'On 31st October the children gather in front of The Tuckers Arms in fancy dress, all carrying their lanterns (a hollowed out mangel with a candle inside). They walk over the bridge and back again singing appropriate songs! They then go to the village hall where their costumes are judged, after which they go to the hall to enjoy refreshments and a social evening.'

BONFIRE NIGHT

'A torchlight procession on Bonfire Night left the village hall at Denbury and made its way to the village green. Once a mock-up Houses of Parliament was erected on the green, Guy Fawkes (Sam Beer, an old villager) set it alight and was chased to the Union Inn where he was caught and marched to the village hall, where a "court" had been set up with judge and jury. He was tried, found guilty and marched off to "prison". Everyone taking part wore appropriate dress.'

'Kenton apparently had a notorious reputation on Bonfire Night and the local police were kept very busy. Opportunity was taken by some of the young lads to settle old scores.'

'Bonfire Night was a great night at Plymtree. At the bottom of Ridgeway was a triangular grassy area known as the "green spot". A huge bonfire was made there. A local family who had a paper delivery round saved all unsold papers during the year, which were mixed in with other combustible material. The older boys would have golden syrup tins, put a little carbide inside, ignite it and off the lid would come with a very loud bang. Louder still if put in a drainpipe under the road!

We had fireworks too. Not the great pieces of today, but squibs, Roman candles, Golden Rain, Rip-raps and, of course, rockets and Catherine wheels. I never knew of anyone being hurt even in the slightest way, even when there were no grown ups with us. Next day we had to clean up all the mess and ashes in our school dinner hour and after school, which we did without question.'

'At Dittisham earlier this century, the greatest event of the winter was Guy Fawkes Night. For days we gathered material for the bonfire which was made down by the river. The guy was made to represent someone who had become unpopular or notorious during the previous months. Once I remember it was the local policeman and another year a man who had been convicted and fined for stealing apples from someone else's orchard. When it was dark we gathered at the far end of the village dressed up in some fashion and wearing a mask which cost a penny. We had a supply of fireworks which were cheap and not nearly so dangerous as those of the present day. I usually wore an old blouse and skirt belonging to one of my sisters. We processed through the village, the adults carrying the guy and torches made of material coated with tar. Arriving at the bonfire the guy was placed on top and the fire lighted. We then danced round and let off our fireworks. I can remember the evening ending with a good scrubbing to remove the grime caused by the smoke.'

ARMISTICE DAY

'I can just remember the end of the First World War. To me it meant that my Daddy came home, but there were children in Beer whose fathers did not return. Half the adult males were fishermen and members of the RN Reserve, called to the colours on 3rd August 1914. During the Second World War I lived elsewhere, but when I came home to retire and attended a Remembrance Service in November, the Chairman of the British Legion stood and said, "Let us remember our dead" and read a list of names. *Every* name brought a face to my mind as I knew them all and I knew where they had died. It was then I understood what it was to be a Village Boy.'

'Everyone in Littleham wore a poppy. The Silence was kept on 11th November, with schools having marched to the war memorial. A hooter from the lozenge factory signalled the beginning and end of the Silence. Boys from the grammar school cadet corps then sounded the Last Post.'

CHRISTMAS

'The burning of the Ashen Faggot took place on Christmas Eve on most farms at Rackenford. My father and grandfather would cut down some green ash wood from the hedge, then straighten it out and tie it up with three or four bands around. After tea it was brought out into our large living room and put on red coals in the open fireplace. After just a short time it would burn through, then it would crack and pop away to a beautiful fire. We asked our friends and neighbours round, all sitting by the fire – there were big flames by this time – eating mince pies and drinking farmhouse cider. Every time the bands burnt through everyone would have a drink. Carol singers from Rackenford would arrive later in the evening.'

'My father's family, who had for generations farmed near Oke-hampton, employed perhaps six to eight men and my father told me how on Christmas Eve the workmen made what was known as an Ashen Faggot. A large log was chosen – the length of the open fire – and around it in ever diminishing size other logs were bound tightly with wire bands, until only small sticks were used. This would be carried into the kitchen in the evening and would be burnt in the huge open fireplace. Everyone connected with the farm would be there, all the women and children as well. Barrels of cider were waiting at the back of the kitchen! Every time a band burst each man would be given a mug of cider. The bigger the faggot the more bands and the more cider. This ended as a custom in 1918. When I was a child in the 1920s we continued it in a smaller way with a faggot to fit a conventional grate – and we also drank only home-made raspberry wine!'

'My father was the village postman and in those days people used to give him a drink on his Christmas Day round. Of course by the time he got home he was a bit tipsy, and he would lie on the sofa and drop off to sleep. Then Mum would get really annoyed because she could never wake him up when we were all ready to go to Gran's for Christmas dinner. She would have to leave him and we would walk about two miles to Gran's cottage. But my Dad always arrived in time for tea – Christmas cake, jellies, mince pies, crackers and presents for each of us and oodles of cream that Gran had made herself.'

'On Boxing Day the men at Huntsham went out rabbiting, catching them with ferrets and either nets or shotguns. In the evening at our farmhouse the furniture was pushed back, and one of the men got out his melodeon and everyone danced until midnight.'

Index

254

256